THE HUMAN SITUATION

INTEGRATE

EDUCATION

As we all know, a little learning is a dangerous thing. But a great deal of highly specialized learning is also a dangerous thing and may be sometimes even more dangerous than a little learning. One of the major problems of higher education now is how to reconcile the claims of much learning, which is essentially specialized learning, with the claims of little learning, which is the wider but shallower approach to human problems in general.

This is, of course, by no means a new problem. My grandfather, T. H. Huxley, a man who was never happy unless he was doing three or four whole-time jobs at once, counted among his whole-time jobs in the 1870s the creation of modern English education. He worked a great deal on elementary and secondary education in London and he also did a lot to turn London University into a modern university, that is to say into a university with a high degree of specialization in various fields. The interesting thing is that by the early 1890s he was already deeply preoccupied with the problem of excessive specialization. About three years before he died he actually worked out a plan to co-ordinate the various specialized departments in the University of London so as to create some kind of integrated education.

Delivered on February 9, 1959

I need hardly add that my grandfather's plans were never put into effect and that the problem of integrated education remains exactly as it was—despite the fact that it is a problem which concerns everybody in the field, and despite a number of attempts that have been made to solve it. These attempts have included simply adding pieces of humanistic information to the specialized scientific information; co-ordinating science and the humanities by means of a historical approach, which has certain merits; and the rather closely related Hundred Great Books programs. I don't think any of these is altogether satisfactory. My own feeling is that an ideal integrated education calls for an approach to the subject in terms of fundamental human problems. Who are we? What is the nature of human nature? How should we be related to the planet on which we live? How are we to live together satisfactorily? How are we to develop our individual potentialities? What is the relationship between nature and nurture? If we start with these problems and make them central, we can obviously bring together information from a great number of at present completely isolated disciplines. I think it is probably only in this way that we can create a thoroughly integrated form of education.

Meanwhile, however, this integrated education doesn't exist. Here I think may be found the reason why a person like myself, who has what may be called a kind of encyclopædic ignorance in many fields, may be of use in an institution of higher specialized learning like this one. A man of letters can perform a valuable function in the world at present by bringing together a great many subjects and by showing relationships between them. It is a question of building bridges.

We have an interesting word, *pontifex,* or bridge builder. It is the Latin name for a member of the college of priests in Rome, the head of which was called *pontifex maximus.* (Actually, the accepted etymology of *pontifex* is probably a false etymology. I am almost certain that the original word was not *pontifex* but *puntifex,* which in an old pre-Latin language, the

Oscan language, means the maker of propitiatory sacrifices. The Romans translated this into their own language as *pontifex*, the maker of bridges.) In a religious context *pontifex* means builder of a bridge between Earth and Heaven, between the material and the spiritual, the human and the divine. The whole idea of the *pontifex*, the bridge builder, is a very profitable one, and we can meditate upon and make use of it in a very productive way.

The function of the literary man in the present context, then, is precisely to build bridges between art and science, between objectively observed facts and immediate experience, between morals and scientific appraisals. There are all kinds of bridges to be built, and this is what I shall try to do in the course of these lectures.

But there is a great problem facing the man of letters who tries to build bridges. It is interesting to go back into the history of literature and to see that this problem was considered quite carefully by Wordsworth, at the end of the eighteenth century, in the preface to *Lyrical Ballads*. He says that the remotest discoveries of the chemist, the botanist, the mineralogist will become for the poet a subject matter no less suitable than any other on the condition that these subjects become interesting to human beings at large and can be considered in the context of what they do for men as 'enjoying and suffering beings.'[1] This is profoundly true. If the effects of science are to be incorporated into art they must in some way become something more than mere facts, and scientific theories must become something more than mere abstractions and generalizations: they must become facts of direct experience, facts which mean something, facts which have an emotional content. But here we are up against a vicious circle, for while it is quite clear that the facts of science cannot become suitable material for poetry and literary art in general until they become emotionally tinged and

1. William Wordsworth, Preface to the second edition of *Lyrical Ballads*.

involve us as persons, it is also clear that they are unlikely to become so emotionally tinged, and involved in the general feeling tone of humanity, until they have already been expressed in artistic form—for it is the function of the artist to make available for the rest of the community large areas of value and meaning. You can say that in a sense the emotion and value patterns of people's lives are largely created by the artist, who finds expression and form of words suitable for making known and interesting what was previously either unknown or uninteresting. Thus we are on the horns of this dilemma: we need to have the facts of science tinged with emotion before they can become fully valuable for us in emotional terms. I suppose the way out of this vicious circle will be through the providential arrival at some time or other of some vast genius who will break through and somehow create for us the necessary verbal apparatus through which the facts and theories of science can become the fitting material of art. Naturally we cannot foresee how and when such a genius will arise, but the wind bloweth where it listeth and possibly this mysterious bridge builder, this *pontifex maximus,* will someday come into existence.

Now I am certainly not a *pontifex maximus,* but even a *pontifex minimus* can do something for the time being. The question is one of finding a suitable vocabulary in which to deal with these problems. At present we have a large variety of vocabularies: we have the vocabulary of ordinary speech, we have the vocabulary of prose literature, we have the heightened vocabulary of poetry, and we have the abstract vocabulary of scientific theory. (We also have the absolutely catastrophic vocabulary of textbooks, which I find extremely painful to read. It is no wonder that, given such vocabulary, scientific facts and theories are not felt to be relevant to us as 'suffering and enjoying beings' —or perhaps they are felt to be relevant as suffering beings, but certainly not as enjoying beings.) What we do not have at the moment is the form of words with which to express the coming together of scientific fact and scientific theory with our direct experience.

One cannot overstress this necessity for words. There is a very interesting and instructive story which concerns the great French painter, Degas, and the equally great French poet Mallarmé. Degas in his spare time used to write verses. One day he met Mallarmé and said to him, 'It is a terrible thing, Mallarmé. I don't know what happens. I have such wonderful ideas, but when I write them down, the verse is very bad, and it isn't poetry.' Mallarmé answered, 'My dear Degas, poetry is not made out of ideas, it is made with words.' It is precisely this genius for putting ideas into words which somehow have an X-ray power of penetration that marks the great men of letters.

We can say that the whole program which we need to accomplish if we are to have an integrated viewpoint is, in a sense, summed up in an extraordinary phrase in Shakespeare, where Hotspur says:

> But thought's the slave of life, and life time's fool;
> And time, that takes survey of all the world,
> Must have a stop.[2]

It is one of those fantastic things one finds in Shakespeare; in a line and a half he throws out an entire philosophy and then passes on to something else. 'Thought's the slave of life', we cannot think abstractly without being involved as physiological beings, as members of this living community on the planet; and 'life time's fool', the passing of time tends to undermine everything and produce constant change; and yet 'time, that takes survey of all the world, must have a stop', there is a religious, spiritual side to life—time must have a stop in the timeless and eternal world. It is these three worlds—the world of abstractions and concepts, the world of immediate experience and objective observation, and the world of spiritual insight—which must, in any integrated point of view, be brought together.

Needless to say, this is a pretty difficult proposition. How can we describe, for example, a mystical experience? What we need is a language that will permit us to speak of such a profoundly

2. William Shakespeare, *King Henry IV, Part I*, V. iv. 81–83.

personal experience in terms of philosophical concepts, in terms of biochemistry, and in terms of theology. At present these are three totally separate and unconnected vocabularies; our problem is somehow to discover a literary, artistic vocabulary which will make it possible for us to pass without any serious jolt from one point of view to the other, from one universe of discourse to another. When the problem is posed in a specific form such as this, one can see very well that it is excessively difficult. We really do need a poet like Shakespeare—a *pontifex maximus*—to solve it for us. Meanwhile I shall do my best to go ahead with my limited resources and see what I can do in the way of building bridges.

Let us now change our metaphor from one of engineering to a very expressive metaphor of domesticity and speak about what has been called the 'celibacy of the intellect.' The trouble with all specialized knowledge is that it is an organized series of celibacies. The different subjects live in their monastic cells, apart from one another, and simply do not intermarry and produce the children that they ought to produce. The problem is to try to arrange marriages between these various subjects, in the hope of producing a valuable progeny. And the celibacy is not only among different aspects of the intellect; it is also a celibacy of the passions, a celibacy of instinct. This theme of the isolation of the passions is a very characteristic feature of contemporary literature. If you go to see certain plays—for example, by Tennessee Williams, a dramatist of enormous talent, which I greatly admire—one sees an almost complete celibacy of the passions. They exist in a chemically pure state without any connection with the intellect whatsoever. They are living a life entirely of their own. If you were to take these plays as a serious picture of contemporary life, you would certainly be very much deceived, as I was thinking the other day when I saw one of them very well staged in the theatre. The mere fact of putting it on required such a passionate combination of people using their intellect and keeping their will firmly fixed on the subject that it was itself a complete denial of the reality of the view of life in which the passions are divorced from the intellectual and voluntary activities of human beings.

At any rate, what we need to do is to arrange marriages, or rather to bring back into their originally married state, the different departments of knowledge and feeling which have been arbitrarily separated and made to live in their own monastic cells, in isolation. We can parody the Bible and say, 'That which nature has brought together let no man put asunder'; let not the arbitrary academic division into subjects tear apart the closely knit web of reality and turn it into nonsense.

Yet, here we are up against a very serious problem: any form of higher knowledge requires specialization. We have to specialize in order to penetrate more deeply into certain separate aspects of reality. But if specialization is absolutely necessary, it can be, if carried too far, absolutely fatal. Therefore, we must discover some way of making the best of both worlds—of the highly specialized world of objective observation and intellectual abstraction, and of what may be called the married world of immediate experience, in which nothing can be separated. We are both intellect and passion, our minds have both objective knowledge of the outer world and subjective experience. To discover methods of bringing these separate worlds together, to show the relationship between them, is, I feel, the most important task of modern education.

I would like to quote a very beautiful sentence from a letter written by T. H. Huxley to Charles Kingsley on the occasion of the death of Huxley's small son, aged four. Kingsley had written a letter of sympathy, and my grandfather wrote back at great length on the whole problem of immortality and the position of the scientist in the modern world. He said,

> Science seems to me to teach in the highest and strongest manner the great truth, which is embodied in the Christian conception of entire surrender to the will of God. Sit down before fact like a

little child, and be prepared to give up every preconceived notion, follow humbly wherever and to whatever abysses nature
leads, or you shall learn nothing.[3]

One sees here that the scientific process is intrinsically an ethical process, a side to science which is insufficiently stressed at
present. The humility of the scientist in the face of fact and
observation is a thing of tremendous importance from an ethical point of view. This was seen very clearly as long ago as the
time of Francis Bacon, who, though not himself a serious man
of science, did lay down a number of general ideas of great
significance for the development of science in the seventeenth
and eighteenth centuries. Bacon was hostile to scholastic
philosophers, and even to Greek philosophers, who presumed
to make statements about the universe without taking the trouble to find out what the facts really were. There are a number
of remarkable passages in Bacon where he talks about the wickedness of these philosophers. He speaks of Plato and Aristotle
as guilty men. (Bacon's hostility to Plato and Aristotle was rather
unjust. Aristotle, after all, was a very important scientific observer.) There is a famous passage in *The Advancement of
Learning,* for example, where he says the scholastics were like
spiders, weaving webs out of their own heads without any consideration of what was going on in the world, and the webs were
admirable for the fineness of the thread and the workmanship,
but without any substance and without any fruit.[4] In the same
way, in the preface to one of his minor books, *The History of the
Winds,* he speaks in a very eloquent and powerful way about
the ethical quality of science. He says,

Therefore, if we have any Humility towards the Creator; if we
have any Reverence and Esteem of His works; if we have any
Charity towards Men or any Desire of relieving their Miseries and

3. Thomas H. Huxley to Charles Kingsley, 23 September 1860, quoted in
Leonard Huxley, *Life and Letters of Thomas Henry Huxley* (New York: Apple-
ton, 1900), vol. 1, p. 235.
4. Francis Bacon, *Advancement of Learning,* I, iv., 5.

Necessities; if we have any Love for natural Truths; any Aversion to Darkness; and any Desire of purifying the Understanding; Mankind are to be most affectionately interested and beseeched to lay aside, at least for a while, their preposterous, *fantastick* and *hypothetical Philosophies* (which have *led Experience* captive, and childishly triumphed over the Works of *God;*) and now at length condescend, with due Submission and Veneration, to approach and peruse the *Volume of the Creation;* dwell some time upon it; and, bringing to the work a Mind well purged of Opinions, Idols and false Notions, converse familiarly therein.[5]

This is a splendid passage, and one which should be meditated on, because it is precisely the reluctance to accept preconceived notions and to turn one's opinion into a thesis rather than a working hypothesis which is the hallmark of a genuine scientist and which constitutes the essential ethical nature of scientific activity.

Bacon felt very strongly that one of the values of science was in its fruits, that it could do a great deal to lessen human want and human suffering. As we know, it certainly can do this. But it can also do other things of which we are painfully aware at the present time. As Bacon was never tired of saying, knowledge without love can be profoundly corrupt and even evil. He blamed philosophers like Plato and Aristotle not only because they lacked the humility to study objective facts and base their reasoning upon those facts, but because they had pursued knowledge purely for the sake of intellectual satisfaction, not with the motive of love or in order to help human beings.

Now the shoe is rather on the other foot: the overweening philosophers of today are members of the scientific school who have forgotten scientific humility. We are all familiar, for example, with the extreme bumptiousness of the early behaviourists. When one reads some of the early writings of J. B. Watson, one is absolutely flabbergasted that anybody who professed to be

5. Francis Bacon, *Silva Silvarum: the Phaenomena of the Universe,* trans. Peter Shaw (London: Knapton, 1735), vol. 3, p. 5.

scientific could have made statements so sweeping and dismissed so cavalierly such enormous areas of human experience.
To 'scientists' such as these certainly Bacon would have brought
the reproach that they were (a) over-weening and (b) lacking in
the love which alone can make knowledge precious and valuable.

Our problem, then, is somehow to reunite the different aspects of the world as we know it, to recreate the married state
with which direct experience makes us familiar. For we *are* all
the time familiar with the fact that the world of concepts and
abstractions is balanced by the world of immediate experience,
and that the inner experience is there at the same time as the
objective description of nature built upon inferences. But what
is the philosophical relationship between these two sides of our
knowledge, the inner and the outer? I am inclined to think that
philosophically minded scientists like Max Planck are right in
conceiving that the two worlds, the abstract and the immediate,
are simply aspects of the same reality, that the basic Reality is
a neutral monism which is seen from one point of view as
atomic physics (for example) and from another point of view as
immediate experience of value, love, and emotion. We can't go
into this view at the moment, but I wanted to mention it and
to point out that the building of this fundamental bridge is an
urgent, urgent problem in our world.

I deliberately kept the title of this course as vague and as
general as I could, so as not to commit myself too far in advance
or to pretend that I know too much. Our business will be to take
various aspects of the human situation to see how bridges can
be built between facts and values. I shall start with a consideration of man in relation to the planet, for we live on this particular planet and, whether we like it or not, we have to get on with
it indefinitely. Unfortunately, I am sorry to say, all the stuff
about going to Mars and so on seems to be pretty good nonsense. It is very much more important to see what we can do
with Earth, and unfortunately what we are doing with Earth is

disastrously bad. I shall try first of all to set forth the facts of what we are doing with our planetary environment and consider what the ethical corollaries of these facts are and what *Weltanschauung* would help us to remedy them. Then I shall talk about the relationship between the sources that are available now and those that will be available in the future. I will build a slight, hypothetical bridge into the future.

After that I think we shall turn to the strictly biological problems of the human individual and discuss man from the point of view of heredity and from the point of view of environment, and try to establish some kind of balance between these two factors which so profoundly influence our existence. The problem of man in society will follow, and there I shall spend a good deal of time in discussing what seems to me the most profoundly important sociological factor of modern times: the growth of technology and what may be called the technicization of every aspect of human life. Then I will move on to other aspects of the social life, and in due course I hope to get down to the problem of the individual, the problem of human potentialities and what can be done to realize those that at present remain to a large extent latent in a large portion of the people. Needless to say, in this connection there will have to be discussions of art and of the problems of creation and insight.

We shall wander very far afield in this search for bridges. By the time we are at the end we shall have covered a great deal of ground, and we will also be extremely bored with what I have to say, but fortunately I shall then quietly disappear.

MAN AND

HIS PLANET

W<small>HAT</small> is our relationship with
the planet? What are we doing with the world on which we are
living and how are we treating it? How is it likely to treat us if
we go on treating it as we are now?

I shall begin to answer these questions with two quotations
from the Bible. The first comes from the Psalms: 'The trees of
the Lord are full of sap: the cedars of Lebanon, which he hath
planted' (Psalms 104:16). The second comes from the Song of
Solomon, where the face of the beloved is compared to the
cedars: 'His countenance is as Lebanon, excellent as the cedars'
(Song of Solomon 5:15). These great trees have a kind of mythical quality. We have all heard of them from our earliest years;
hospitals are named after them, and they have become a sort
of household word. I remember when for the first time I went
to the Middle East, one of the things I was most interested in
seeing was precisely the cedars of Lebanon.

Lebanon is a very small country which consists of a coastal
strip not more than a few miles wide at the foot of towering
mountains which go up to about ten thousand feet. The mountain range is a hundred to a hundred and fifty miles long,
twenty-five or thirty miles wide, and I expected, when I drove
up into it, to find the cedars of Lebanon in profusion, as un-

Delivered on February 16, 1959

doubtedly they once were. We drove and drove for hours up enormous hills and finally, after mile upon mile of absolutely barren country, came upon an enclosed space in which there were approximately four hundred cedars. Flying over the range later on, I saw two or three other such groves, and I believe there are in all perhaps fifteen hundred or two thousand cedars left. This is all that remains of the gigantic forest that supplied King Solomon with the timbers for his temple—if you remember, Solomon made a treaty with Heiram, King of Tyre, in which Heiram agreed that the timbers should be brought down to the coast, towed in floats to whatever port was appointed by Solomon, and then dragged to Jerusalem—and that for centuries supplied Egypt, which grows no trees of its own except palm trees, with all the timber it required.

This illustrates in a very striking way what man has been doing to his planet over the course of the centuries. He has found profusion in· nature and in all too many cases he has completely devastated what he has found. Here we had a magnificent forest: these trees are very fine. You must have seen them in botanical gardens—the specimens grow all over Europe now, where they have been imported, and do very well in temperate climates. But, as Chateaubriand pointed out, *'les forêts précèdent les peuples, et les déserts les suivent'* (forests precede civilizations and deserts follow them). During the time he has been on earth—which is anything from a half million to perhaps a million years—man has been increasingly a profound geological force. He has changed the face of the planet upon which he lives, sometimes for the better, but in all too many cases for the worse.

In the nineteenth century, the environmentalist school spoke of environment as conditioning and creating cultures but left out of account altogether the fact that cultures condition the environment—that man has certainly done almost as much to change the environment as the environment has done to mould the course of history.

In general, we may say that the realization that man is a

changer of nature did not begin until the late eighteenth century. The first great classical work on the subject was written in
1865 by George Perkins Marsh, who was the first American
Ambassador to the new Kingdom of Italy. In this book Marsh
collected all of the European material to date on the subject of
man and nature and set it forth in a kind of philosophical context. One of the precursors in the field, it remains an extremely
valuable book.[1]

Let us begin by talking about the positive contributions
which man has made to changing the planet. For example, most
ecologists will now agree that the tropical grasslands, and quite
possibly the grasslands of the temperate zone, were actually
created by man and have been maintained by him in their open
grassy state for hundreds of thousands of years. I suppose the
most important of man's contributions are those he has made
in bringing valuable plants or animals from one part of the
world to another. In classical times such trees as the peach, the
plum, the walnut, and the almond were brought from the Near
East, the Middle East, and even the Far East to the Mediterranean; such valuable fodder plants as alfalfa and certain types of
clover were brought from the Mediterranean and domesticated
throughout Europe and later on in the New World; and such
plants as peas and vines were carried from the West to China.
The introduction of potatoes into the Old World from the New
was revolutionary, as was the importation into Africa, Asia, and
Southern Europe of Indian corn, from South and Central America.

What is true of plants is also true of animals. The most obvious
case is the importation of the horse into the New World. The
American Indians did all their hunting on foot before the Spaniards and the first English settlers introduced the horse. The
North American Indians then rapidly took to this new quad-
ruped, and you will see the same thing in South America. The

1. *Man and Nature*, rewritten and republished as *The Earth as Modified by
Human Action*. Reprint of 1878 edition (St. Clair, Mich.: Scholarly Press).

only domesticated animal which the Incas, for example, possessed was the llama—the alpaca and the vicuna—which, in a pinch, can carry about twenty or thirty pounds on its back. But this was all they had, except for human beasts of burden, for transporting goods up and down those extraordinary mountain trails in the Andes. They have also adopted the sheep, which has entered into the Indian folklore of the Andes, and has become a kind of native animal there.

An interesting importation, from the East to Europe, was that of the cat. It came from Egypt (the local wild cat of Western Europe was never tamed) and didn't make itself much at home in Western Europe until the early Middle Ages. We can see, in the old fairy story of Dick Whittington, for example, how extremely valuable cats were and how remarkable they seemed. In the Saxon law preceding the Conquest of England a cat was so valuable that anybody who killed someone else's cat was expected to pay for it by pouring enough wheat to make a pile high enough to cover the cat suspended by its tail.

Another animal import from the East to Europe was the invaluable domestic chicken. It was brought from India into the classical world and has been with us ever since, laying eggs. It is a strange thing to realize that in the early classical period people had no eggs.

These are some of the immensely important changes for the good that man has brought to his planet. Now we have to consider the reverse of the medal. Man has lived only too frequently on his planet almost like a parasite living upon the host it infests. And whereas many parasites are sensible enough not to destroy their host, because after all if they destroy their host they destroy themselves, man is *not* one of the sensible parasites. Instead he has very often lived upon his host in such a way as absolutely to ruin it.

What are some of the ways in which man has proved most destructive? We will begin with the animals—a very depressing story, for we are wiping out creatures of extraordinary beauty and interest at rapidly increasing rates. If one looks at the statistics compiled by the International Society for the Protection of Nature, one learns that fifty species of mammals only were wiped out during the nineteenth century, forty more have been lost since 1900, and six hundred species are probably doomed to extinction at the present time. There is the case of the traveller pigeon, which existed at one time in such fantastic numbers that its flights used to darken the sun. In the colonial and early post-Independence days one of the amusements of the inhabitants was to drive out to the woods where the pigeons nested, knock down the nests with the young squabs in them, fill entire wagons with these creatures, and drive home. Obviously, they couldn't eat most of them, and many were just thrown away to rot by the roadside. The same thing happened with the bison, which once counted fifty to sixty million head on the plains. Now the traveller pigeon is completely extinct and there are only a few thousand bison left.

Another very odd case is that of the Indian rhinoceros, which is now practically extinct owing to the fact of human—above all, Chinese—superstition: the rhinoceros horn was regarded as a kind of love philtre or amulet, and enormous prices used to be paid for it. I remember years ago going to visit the great warehouse in the docks of London where ivory, horn, and tortoise and pearl shell were brought in and auctioned off. I was very surprised to find that rhinoceros horn was selling at a considerably higher price than ivory, entirely because of the huge Chinese market for what was supposed to be an aphrodisiac; which clearly it was not. To satisfy a human superstition these interesting creatures now have been butchered off, and the kindred species is rapidly disappearing in Africa.

In many parts of the world the crocodile is disappearing. We shall miss this highly unsympathetic animal because he performs a very valuable function, as is now being discovered: crocodiles kill off the enemies of fish as well as the weak and diseased in the fish population. Where they have disappeared the fishing is much worse.

The great wild species of Africa survive at all solely because there are national parks in various parts of Africa where these animals are carefully protected. Presumably they will continue to survive, for the benefit of science and for the delight of people who wish to go outside the all too human world and see what the rest of the creation looks like.

Let us now consider the plant world. We will begin with the forests. I have already talked about the cedars of Lebanon, an immense forest of magnificent trees which have virtually disappeared, leaving the mountains to be eroded. In many places all the topsoil has been washed away and nothing remains except the naked rock; such places, it is quite clear, can never be reforested, and this same situation occurs again and again in every part of the world.

Man has been deliberately destroying forests since the hunting period: to clear forests—to increase visibility—the hunting tribes tended to burn off the underbrush, permitting the game to be hunted much more easily than it could be in a very dense forest. And, since agriculture began, probably about 8000 B.C., men have been cutting (and burning) forests in order to create new places where they could plant food crops. The whole process was greatly speeded up after the beginning of the iron age, when it became possible, with the use of iron ploughshares, to break soils much too heavy for the wooden ones which had been used in the past. Another invention important to the greater spread of agriculture came towards the eighth century, when what appears to be an extraordinarily simple device, namely the horse collar, permitted horses to pull a much greater weight and to put much more strength into their pulling than they had been able to do with the previous forms of harness. Such technological advances, plus a slow but steady increase of population, have naturally led to the clearing of enormous forests.

Equally important in more recent times, especially in the destruction of forests which surround urban centres, has been the use of timber as a fuel. If you read Diderot's *Encyclopaedia*,

you will find a very, very interesting account of the provisioning
of Paris with wood for space heating. All the forests around Paris
had been largely exhausted and the wood came in from hundreds of miles away, being floated on great rafts down the Seine
and its tributaries. The rafts were then moored off the quays of
Paris and the wood distributed. Diderot, one of the few intellectuals of the eighteenth century who was deeply interested in
the technological progress of his time, stated that this could not
go on and that the only hope was to use coal for space heating;
in fact, at about this time coal did begin to be used on a considerable scale, which helped to save the forests from total destruction.

Besides space heating, wood was used in industry. All ores
were smelted with charcoal until steel was made with coke for
the first time at the beginning of the eighteenth century, so that
there was a prodigious destruction of forests wherever there
was a metallurgical industry. The same happened wherever
there was a glass industry. Although glass was a very early
invention—it goes back to about 3000 B.C.—it was very expen-
sive and difficult to make until the art of blowing glass was
perfected in the first century A.D. This invention very rapidly
led to the formation of glass industries all around the Mediterranean and as far north as Cologne and England, with the consequence of an enormous massacre of the forests.

Another very important reason for the destruction of forests
was the building of houses and, even more significant, of ships.
It is interesting to find how early the timbers suitable for building ships were exhausted in Western Europe. The French navy
couldn't find suitable timber in its own territory from about the
end of the seventeenth century and had to be supplied largely
by timber coming from as far afield as Albania. The Spaniards,
at the time of their great naval expansion during the sixteenth
century, were depending not upon wood from Spain, but upon
wood coming from the Baltic. You will find a reference in
Pepys' *Diary* saying, 'God knows where our oak is to come

from.' And in fact the oak was running out. By the eighteenth century, the period of Britian's naval supremacy, the oak for its ships was coming predominantly from the New World—from New England and the Eastern seaboard of this country. As for the rest, it was teak from the Indian Empire. Fortunately, perhaps, the Battle of Hampton Roads in 1862 proved that the iron ship was definitely superior to the wooden, and consequently shipbuilding ceased to be a reason for massacring forests of slow-growing trees.

The area where one sees the deforestation most clearly is in the Old World, most visibly in the ancient civilized world around the Mediterranean. You see it also terribly clearly in the Northwest here and around the Great Lakes. There are, of course, great forests remaining in the United States, but the annual cutting of timber exceeds annual growth by about 50 per cent. It is quite obvious that you can't go on with this kind of thing for very long and hope to have many forests.

The forests in Europe used to come right down from the northern part to the Mediterranean coast. Today there are very few areas on the Mediterranean coast where you can still see traces of the ancient forests. In the south of France, east of Hyères, there is about a hundred square miles of forest called the *Forêt des Morts;* it is all that remains of the great primeval forest, which had already largely disappeared even in classical times, and which just vanished during the Middle Ages, largely because of the glass and soap industries of Marseilles and the shipbuilding industry of Toulon and Marseilles.

For those who are interested in landscape painting, it is a curious thing to realize that what we consider the typical landscape of Provence, such as we see in the paintings of Cézanne, is a relatively modern landscape. It represents hills which have now been weathered down, practically to their bare bones. Probably many of them are hopeless cases and can never be reforested. They are extremely picturesque, but we must remember that they are thoroughly a product of degeneration and destruction. The same thing is true of other parts of the Mediterranean. If you go to Tunisia and drive inland from Sousse, you will see a gigantic Roman amphitheatre, El Djem, which is second in size only to the Coliseum, standing in the middle of the desert. El Jem was situated in a province which in Roman times was called *Frugifera,* the fruit-bearing province. Today it is almost completely deserted, with a few Arab huts scattered about at the foot of the great buildings. This same picture occurs again and again. Homer speaks about the tall oaks and pines of Sicily. Now you can cross Sicily from one side to the other and hardly see a single tree. There are a few places where attempts at reforestation have been made, but this once extremely well-forested, well-wooded country is now almost completely naked. The same is true of Greece, of Palestine and Syria, of Spain, and of Southern Italy.

Now we have to pass to another area of destruction at least as important as the destruction of forests—and resulting in some measure from it: the destruction of the soil.

The soil is a living organism. It owes its fertility to the existence within itself of great numbers of ecological communities of microscopic and macroscopic organisms of every kind. The topsoil, however, which contains almost all the soil's fertility, is not deep. The 2.8 billion people who are now inhabitants of the planet depend upon a layer of soil rarely more than about ten inches thick—and it takes three hundred to one thousand years to create an inch of it, so one sees the extreme danger of any process causing soil destruction.

Soil erosion, of course, happens all the time; it is one of the regular processes of geological change. But there is an immense difference between the slow erosion of nature left to itself and the rapid and destructive erosion which takes place when man wantonly strips the land of its vegetable cover, cuts down the forests, tears up the grass, or uses bad agricultural methods which leave the land vulnerable to the wind and the rain. Unfortunately, as we have seen, man has been committing such crimes against nature for a very long time.

One of the best descriptions of erosion was written, curiously enough, by Plato in his dialogue, the *Critias,* where he speaks of his own native country of Attica. It is worth reading because it is remarkable how accurate the description is. He says:

> In comparison of what then was, there are remaining only the bones of the wasted body, as they may be called, as in the case of small islands, all the richer and softer parts of the soil having fallen away, and the mere skeleton of the land being left. But in the primitive state of the country, its mountains were high hills covered with soil, and the plains, as they were termed by us, of Phelleus, were full of rich earth, and there was abundance of wood in the mountains. Of this last the traces still remain, for although some of the mountains now only afford sustenance to bees, not so very long ago there were still to be seen roofs of timber cut from trees growing there, which were of a size sufficient to cover the largest houses; and there were many other high trees, cultivated by man and bearing abundance of food for cattle. Moreover, the land reaped the benefit of the annual rainfall, not as now losing the water which flows off the bare earth into the sea, but, having an abundant supply in all places, and receiving it into herself and treasuring it up in the close clay soil, it let off into the hollows the streams which it absorbed from the heights, providing everywhere abundant fountains and rivers, of which there may still be observed sacred memorials in places where fountains once existed; and this proves the truth of what I am saying.
>
> Such was the natural state of the country, which was cultivated, as we may well believe, by true husbandmen, who made husbandry their business, and were lovers of honour.[2]

Plato gives this description of the frightful erosion already taking place in the fifth century B.C.—but he ascribes almost divine qualities to the husbandmen who obviously caused it. Rather as Ellsworth Huntington[3] did forty years ago, Plato attributed all the trouble not to man but to a change in climate.

2. Plato, *Critias,* 111.
3. American geographer, 1876–1947.

He thought that what had happened to Attica had been caused by a series of deluges. But I think that if he hadn't been so interested in platonic ideas and had been a little more concerned with what the husbandmen were actually doing, he probably would have seen that it was precisely these divine husbandmen who had done things to the soil which had left it in the ruined and impoverished state in which the Greeks of his own time found it—and Heaven knows it was relatively fertile then compared to what it is now. One may say that perhaps Plato would have done better to devote more attention to these dreadfully practical problems of nature than to the rather abstract metaphysical problems which engaged him.

And one can say something of the same kind about Socrates, who said that he saw no object in going outside the city walls because everything of interest was within them, and that his business was solely with men. But men do have to live on the soil and live in community with nature, and one wonders whether Socrates wouldn't have done more good to his fellows if he had paid a little more attention to what went on outside the city walls.

Those of you who are acquainted with the literature of the conservationists will know what an immense amount of land has been destroyed here in an extraordinarily short space of time by wantonness. The same thing is true in many other areas of the world; there are vast areas of erosion in China, in Africa, in South America, and in Southern Europe. And the dreadful process goes on and on, becoming progressively more and more dangerous as more and more people are born into the world and have to be supported and the increasing pressure drives peasants and farmers to attempt to get more and more out of the soil.

The combination of human destructiveness and population increase is an enormous and frightening fact. It is clearly one of the major problems confronting human beings at the present time. But it mustn't be thought that all people have been destructive all the time and everywhere. On the contrary, in many parts of the world, quite primitive people have shown remarkable understanding of preserving and conserving the soil. I had the opportunity of visiting the Inca regions of the Andes this summer. To see the Inca terraces rising from the floor of the Urubamba River two or three thousand feet up the side of a mountain is an exceptional sight. Some of this wonderfully cared-for terracing is made with dressed stone, and some of the terraces are used to this day—they permit quite intensive agriculture on incredibly steep slopes (often thirty-five degrees). You go to a place like Machu Picchu, a fantastic city built on a sugarloaf hill, and you discover that its population, which was quite small—probably not more than two or three thousand—was able to survive for two or three centuries at least on its elaborate system of terracing. You will also find extraordinary examples of terracing in Indonesia and the Philippines: among the Igorots in the Philippines there is a wonderful rice cultivation. You will see the same thing in Java, and there is good reason to suppose that many of these rice-growing terraces have been used for a thousand, perhaps even two thousand years.

These are remarkable achievements, but one of the saddest things is to realize that the good examples which some people have set in some parts of the world have certainly not been followed in others. You will find the remains of the ancient pre-Spanish Inca terraces within thirty miles of Cusco, where the worst kind of farming practices have been used in barley cultivation and where the most fearful gullying and erosion is seen. One wonders why on earth modern farmers couldn't have taken the hint; evidently, as someone said, the greatest lesson of history is that nobody ever learns the lessons of history.[4] Similarly, it is extraordinary that the methods of contour

4. Hegel, *Philosophy of History*. Introduction: 'What experience and history teach is this—that people and governments never have learned anything from history, or acted on principles deduced by it.'

ploughing which are now being applied more and more to agriculture in this country were really not developed until thirty years ago, although a hundred and fifty years ago the process was already apparent to Thomas Jefferson, who talked about soil erosion and soil exhaustion. These facts are all the more disturbing when one realizes that, owing to the increasing pressure of population upon resources, there is extraordinarily little time.

There are several most powerful instruments of soil destruction which man has employed during the ages, but the most disastrous has probably been over-grazing, which has been going on at least since the domestication of sheep and goats—probably seven or eight thousand years. There is a very ironical point here: We generally feel a great sympathy for Abel and a great dislike for Cain, but let us never forget that Abel was the man who had sheep and goats and Cain was the agriculturist. Actually, if there was ever a justified homicide, it was probably Cain's destruction of Abel, because the followers of Abel in fact have performed incredible feats of destruction all over the world. Both the goat and the sheep are highly destructive; they are thin-lipped animals which pull up the grass by the roots and leave nothing. The sheep has accomplished frightful destruction in Spain. One of the oddest chapters of Spanish history is the history of Mesta, the great co-operative of the shepherds, who were in perpetual conflict with the agriculturists and who, in the course of about three hundred years, succeeded in turning Spain almost into a desert.

Here it is worth mentioning something which has only been discovered within the last few years. It had been supposed that Southern Italy assumed its present barren aspect towards the end of the Roman Empire, the breakdown of agriculture at that time having led to deforestation and loss of fertility. But a recent discovery has shown that this is not true. During the war the Royal Air Force made an almost complete air map of Italy, photographing it very carefully with slanting light, which permits one to see the archaeological traces. It was found, to every-one's surprise, that what had previously been supposed to be barren since the time of the Roman Empire was in fact quite fertile at that time and even during the Dark Ages. You can see the traces of the fields and of the terracing and of the founda-tions of peasant houses. It is now realized that the destruction of this fertile and forested area in Southern Italy was a conse-quence of the introduction during the twelfth and thirteenth centuries of the Spanish methods of shepherding, which were completely ruinous to the country, and which left it in its pre-sent desolate state.

The goat is much more active than the sheep and can even climb trees to eat its food. It is quite fantastic what the goat has succeeded in destroying; it includes the whole Mediterranean basin. One of the worst things goats do is to prevent forests from reproducing themselves: they attack the young shoots as they come up and bite them down to the ground.

One of the few really good things that can be said for the British and their occupation of Cyprus is that they did persuade the inhabitants of the forested west end of the island to give up their goats in favour of forests. It was all done quite democrati-cally. The administrators went from village to village and talked about the relative advantages of goats and forests: goats have considerable advantages here and now, but the advantages of forests later on are very much greater. A great many villagers were persuaded to tether their goats and to give up a certain proportion of them, with the result that there has been a re-markable revival of forests on the mountains of western Cyprus. Similarly, in Lebanon there is absolutely no prospect of refor-estation (where it is still possible) until the goats are kept under control. Lebanon is divided politically along religious lines—the Moslems, the Druses, the Maronites, the Armenians, the Greek Orthodox. I was told the story of the Maronite bishop who came into the ministry of agriculture and said, 'You will be glad to hear, Your Excellency, that we are doing very well with our goats in the mountains, but I regret to say the Orthodox goats are still creating an immense havoc.'

Goats go on creating awful havocs in spite of all legal restraints. Great efforts have been made in Algeria and Tunisia to control the goats by law, but it is almost impossible to enforce the law, and the destruction goes on. And in Madagascar the government, which should have known better, introduced a valuable kind of goat which produces some useful hair, with the result that now, after some twenty-five years, only 20 per cent of the forest remains.

If over-grazing is of enormous importance in the creation of conditions for erosion, equally important, and possibly more important because it has been going on longer, is fire. We have already seen that man has used fire deliberately since earliest times to clear land for hunting and agriculture. The forests of Western Europe were largely cleared by fire—one sees traces of this even in the place names in England: 'Brentwood' means just burnt wood; 'Brindly' means burned lee or burned clearing. But far more destructive than man's deliberate efforts have been the accidental fires resulting from his carelessness.

Geologists find a notable increase in fossil ashes from the beginning of Pleistocene time, about a million years ago, which would seem to indicate that even at that very remote period man or his near human ancestors had discovered fire. We know in any case that Peking man, who dates undoubtedly from 250,000 years ago (and possibly from half a million), had fire, and accidental fires have been occurring ever since.

One of the great tragedies in this country has been the fabulous amount of forest destroyed by accidental fires. The record is incredible: on this coast, in Washington, there were fires in 1865 and in 1868, one of which destroyed a million acres, the other six hundred thousand. There were very few fires in the area before the settlers arrived in 1847; after this date, they were absolutely incessant. There was the great Idaho and Montana fire of 1910, which destroyed eight and a half billion feet of lumber, and, one of the worst, the Tillamook fire of 1933, which destroyed twelve and a half billion feet. This is what the United States would have consumed in one year, and it was wiped out in a single fire in a week. It has been calculated that in Oregon, from the first settlements to about 1908, when fire protection was installed, about thirty-two billion feet of lumber had been cut and used while about forty billion feet had been destroyed accidentally by fire. Now elaborate firefighting organizations have been created, but anyone who sees the difficulty of controlling even a brush fire in California—we have had them recently—can realize that it is still profoundly difficult to control this engine of destruction. When one reflects that in countries like Chile forest fires are completely without control and rage for weeks, blackening immense areas, one sees the enormous importance of this human geological force.

What man is doing to his world unfortunately makes a gloomy picture. There is very little way to make it non-gloomy. In one of the next lectures I shall try to make a bridge from these facts to the problem of morality, the problem of what our philosophical views of nature should be. For we should think of these brute facts not only in a purely practical way, but also in a kind of metaphysical and ethical and aesthetic way. It is terribly important, I feel, that we should be able to think of these things with our whole nature, not merely as technologists, not merely as people who want to eat and to have timber products, but as total human beings with a moral nature, with an aesthetic nature, with a philosophical trend in our mind.

MORE NATURE

IN ART

I N my last lecture I presented
the factual side of the situation in which man finds himself in
relation to his planet, the rather dismal story of the way in
which he has ravaged and greatly destroyed the world—the
home in which he travels through the Universe. In this lecture
I propose to speak about the events on the other end of the
bridge. I want to talk about the human or psychological end,
because I feel that we must always try to bring together these
two generally separate aspects of life, the purely factual and
scientific, and the purely human-value end.

Let us begin with the practical problems involved. We now
know enough to repair a good deal of the damage which has
already been done to our planet and to prevent further damage
from occurring. The necessary information and knowledge
exist. But as usual there is a great gap between the ability to do
a thing and the likelihood of its being done. It is very easy to
describe the conservation methods which should be put into
effect at once, but it is extraordinarily difficult to carry out what
we know we can do.

First of all, in order to implement a satisfactory conservation
program, we have to communicate with immense numbers of

Delivered on March 2, 1959

human beings. After all, there are in the world several hundreds of millions of peasant farmers and workers who, if conservation is to be carried out effectively, must in some way be influenced to work along the lines which we know they should work along. Simply to establish relations with these people is obviously one of the major problems. And once relations have been established, there is the problem of persuading them to give up old traditional methods in favour of better modern methods. Furthermore, these vast numbers which are already here are increasing at a tremendously rapid rate. And the heavier the pressure of population upon resources, the more urgent becomes the need of man to produce food and the greater the temptation to use exploitative methods. Man simply has no choice but to live for the next year, and he must do his best to extract his living from soil which has often been already damaged and is in a precarious condition. The Germans have a good term for this kind of exploitative economy; they call it *Raubwirtschaft* (robber economy).

Now we have to consider a simple psychological fact. It is extremely difficult for human beings to follow a course which, though it may be manifestly helpful in the long run, in the short run imposes hardships upon them. This is a most serious problem, one which we shall come up against in several other contexts. How, by democratic means, are you going to persuade people to adopt measures which are excellent in the long run, but which may cause some discomfort in the short run? How are you going to persuade people not to exploit the soil when they desperately need food, and when this need is increasing year by year? This is not merely a question of organization and capital; it is a question of getting people to accept certain ideas. The trouble is that it looks as though it is going to be exceedingly difficult to reach the countless millions of people who must be indoctrinated and to get them to act upon what we know is the scientifically best method of doing things, without considerable totalitarian control and coercion.

The only alternative to coercion is persuasion and education. Unfortunately these democratic methods take time, and because of the rapidity of the increase in population there is exceedingly little time. Nevertheless, since we are committed to the democratic idea, we have to think in terms of education and persuasion, and for this reason we have to think about the mental climate in which a proper approach to the planet on which we live can be made. And this involves a reconsideration of the problem of ethics, the problem of the general philosophy of life, and problems of artistic expression and artistic sensibility.

Let us begin with the ethical problem: What ought to be the relation of the human race with the world upon which it lives? I would say that the most obvious consideration emerging from the facts which were brought out in the last lecture is that the golden rule holds good not only for man's dealings with other men, but also for his dealings with lower animals and even with the inanimate world. The rule—do unto others as you would they would do unto you—applies not merely to man but to nature in general. There is a perfectly clear utilitarian basis for this ethical point of view. If we want to be treated well by nature, we have to treat nature well; as a matter of plain fact, if we harm or destroy nature, nature will do us harm and will destroy us.

It is worth pointing out that this ethical point of view, in which nature is regarded as having rights and we are regarded as having duties toward nature, is not found within our Western tradition, nor within the theological-scholastic tradition of the Middle Ages, which still remains orthodox in the more conservative churches. Instead, we have what seems to me to be a very shocking formulation, which is that animals possess no souls. Therefore they have no rights and we have no duties towards them, and consequently they may be treated as things. I feel that this is a most undesirable doctrine and also a most unrealistic one, because not only have we no right to treat animals as things, we can go further and say that we have no right to treat

things as things. When we treat even inanimate objects as
things which we can exploit to our heart's content, the consequences are disastrous. We have to treat the planet as though
it were a living organism, with all the love and care and understanding which any living organism deserves. If we do not treat
it in this way, then we shall destroy the world on which we live,
and this destroyed world will in turn destroy us.

A very helpful idea in this context is the Greek idea of hubris.
Hubris means wanton violence inspired by bumptiousness, arrogance, and the pride of power. The Greeks insisted that the
gods would never put up with an arrogant man who committed
hubris. And the interesting fact is that, in Greek thought, one
could commit hubris not only towards other human beings, but
towards nature. In Aeschylus's tragedy of *The Persians,* one of
the crimes of Xerxes is that he has committed hubris not only
against the Greek people—by invading them—but also against
nature. To us, the particular crime against nature that he committed would seem rather forgivable—he built a bridge of boats
across the Hellespont—but the principle seems to be profoundly true and right: We are capable of committing crimes of
violence against nature, and they are as bad in their way as
crimes of wanton violence committed against men. It is unfortunate that this idea did not go on into the Judæo-Christian
tradition, where the fundamental notion is that man is the lord
of creation and is in some way apart from nature and free to do
what he wants with it.

The idea of man's being apart from nature is actually a fairly
recent one. Primitive man never had this idea; he has always
regarded himself as a part of nature, as intimately and fundamentally concerned with and imbedded in it. This idea has
been expressed by primitive peoples in such notions as totemism, which defines man's relationship to animals and even his
identity with them; fertility rites, which insist on the fact that
human sexual processes are identical with those of nature, and
that there is a deep-rooted connection between the two; and in

notions of polytheism and the divineness of natural objects. This was the primitive pattern of the world, and remnants of it went on for many centuries after the acceptance of Christianity, in the so-called witch cults in Western Europe, for example, which were essentially old fertility cults that had survived from very ancient times. In general, however, the conception which primitive man had of his oneness with nature was abandoned throughout the civilized world during a period which began about the eighth or seventh century B.C.; the whole conception then changed to the idea that man is in some sense apart from nature and that deity is transcendent and also apart from nature. The process is seen in India with the rise of Jainism and Buddhism; it is seen in the Near East with the rise of the Hebrew prophets; it is seen in Greece with the rise of Pythagoras and the Orphic religion.

Now there has been, so to speak, a counter-revolution. In a curious way we can say that the revolution accomplished by Darwin a hundred years ago—this is the centenary of the *Origin of Species*—was a revolution away from the traditional Judæo-Christian notion of man's relationship to nature and back towards the primitive idea of man's union with nature. We seem to have passed on a kind of spiral course through the totemistic stage—a very early stage of cultural evolution—into a more self-conscious stage in which a sharp line was drawn between man and nature, and around to a point immediately above the totemistic stage which is an analogue to it on the scientific level. We see the old intuitive feeling for nature transformed into the ideas of ecology. We see totemism transformed into the science of animal behaviour. We see polytheism transformed into the new biological philosophy of organicism—the idea of organisms within a greater organism.

It is perfectly clear, when we come to think of it, that we are indissolubly one with nature and depend completely on the natural environment. Anybody can do a simple experiment to find out how much he depends on the natural environment even though he lives in a world of television and automobiles. He merely has to put a clothespin on his nose and tape up his mouth to find out that he can't do without his natural environment for more than about sixty seconds.

Not only are we physically dependent on the outward environment, but we are also psychologically dependent on it in a very interesting way. This has been shown by the experiments conducted in recent years by D. O. Hebb at McGill University in Canada and John C. Lilly at the National Institute of Health in Washington on the effects of what is called 'limited environment'. If individuals are completely cut off from external stimuli, the most extraordinary things begin happening—mostly very unpleasant. Curiously horrifying visions and nightmare thoughts invade the mind, so that we discover that stimuli from the external world are required just to keep us sane. It is not only that we need the external world to keep us alive, we need the external world to keep us from going mad. When we go into the matter more thoroughly we find that this direct psychological and physiological dependence is not merely upon our immediate environment, it is upon environments very remote, both in space and time. It is obvious, for example, that our entire life depends upon physical events taking place in the sun. It is also quite clear that our continued existence depends upon events taking place in distant mountain ranges and in the tropical and polar regions where our weather is made. Over-populated countries such as England and most of the Western European countries depend for their very existence on events taking place far away and completely outside their political jurisdiction. What is going to happen to Western Europe when the New World has no more exportable surpluses? (Professor Paul Sears of Yale foresees that this will probably happen by 1980.) Nobody knows, but clearly the problem is of extreme importance in our political thinking.

We are also dependent on events which took place in very remote periods of time. Most of the world is still immensely dependent upon coal and oil, both of which are the products of events which took place in the distant past; thus we find ourselves bound up with the world in the closest possible way. The details of this binding up of ourselves with the world, and of all parts of the world, in a single quasi-organic whole are studied in the science of ecology, which is an extremely recent science —the word was invented by Ernst Haeckel less than a hundred years ago—and has unveiled the basic facts that living organisms exist in exquisitely balanced communities and that this balance can be very easily upset.

What has become abundantly clear from the study of ecology is that man has rushed in where angels feared to tread and in ignorance and stupidity and arrogance has everywhere upset these balances in a very alarming way. In the previous lecture I talked about deforestation and erosion, which are the more conspicuous examples, but similar examples on a smaller scale abound. The interesting thing is that we discover after the balance has been upset how delicate it was; and we also realize that it is incredibly difficult for us to foresee what the results of our actions are going to be when we upset the balances of systems where the disturbance of any one element will throw the whole system out of gear. Take a simple example of a few years ago, when the Forest Service attempted to do something on behalf of a special variety of deer which lived in the Kaibab Forest on the north rim of the Grand Canyon. There were only a few thousand of the deer left. The Service thought that the poor things were being persecuted by too many mountain lions, and men were sent out to slaughter a great number of the mountain lions. The result was that, in a few years, the deer population went from four thousand to nearly a hundred thousand. The deer ate up the entire range in the Kaibab Forest; then there were frightful epidemics and they began dying like flies. Only when mountain lions were reintroduced and had killed off the more sickly deer was a stable balance re-established. Gradually the forest recovered from its over-grazing, and the deer flourished fairly well.

This kind of thing has happened again and again. In Scandinavia, hawks were killed off because they killed game birds. The game birds multiplied, they got diseases, they almost became extinct, and the hawks had to be reintroduced. Much odder still is the result of the elimination of hippopotami from large areas in Africa. The fish population in the lakes and rivers where they lived depended to a large extent for nourishment on the minute animals which came from the excrement of the hippopotami. Since the hippopotami have been destroyed the whole fish population has gone too, and the natives have much less protein to eat. So we realize that in dealing with these extremely delicate ecological balances, we come in in the clumsiest way, without really knowing what we are doing.

Not only do we upset the balance by destroying elements, we also upset it by introducing new elements. The introduction of the Chinese crab into Hawaii and the West Indies was a disaster, and a still greater disaster was the introduction of the rabbit into Australia, Patagonia, and other parts of the world. The only place where the introduction of the rabbit didn't result in a disaster was Ceylon, where fortunately they were kept down by poisonous snakes—animals which may be extremely useful to us and do us much more good than harm in spite of the fact that we don't happen to like them.

All this shows how immensely careful we must be in relation to the world. It is only by a combination of love and knowledge that we can get on in the world, and it is only on condition that we act with love and knowledge that we can dominate nature. We must remember that man is a paradoxical creature: he is one with nature, but he is a completely unique animal inasmuch as he can become conscious of his position and inasmuch as he can influence nature in an enormous and sometimes terrifying way. Whether we like it or not, it is quite clear that henceforward we have to take responsibility for what is happening on our planet, because if we don't take responsibility and if we don't act according to our knowledge of and affection for nature, we shall destroy the ground on which we are living and finish off our species.

I have said that with Darwinism we have returned to the primitive position, but on a higher level: we now recognize our oneness with nature and try to act upon it in a rational way. I think it is worth making a digression here to point out that the modern conception of nature has a great deal in common with the traditional views of the Chinese, that in a non-scientific, intuitive way, the Chinese anticipated modern scientific thought in many respects. The Chinese way of thinking about nature has always been very different from that of Western man. In the first place, unlike European philosophers, the Chinese have never thought in terms of substance. European philosophers have always asked, What is so-and-so? The Chinese have never asked this question; they've always asked, What are the relations between so-and-so and so-and-so? Now thinking about relationships rather than substance is quite characteristic of modern science. Not only did they think in terms of relation, the Chinese thought in terms of pre-established harmonies, of mutual action and reaction within fields of force.

These notions go back in China to the foundation of Taoist philosophy, probably in the sixth century B.C.; already in Chuang Tzu, in the fourth century B.C., we see the very clear formulation of a philosophy which is extremely close to modern organicism. The Chinese idea was that things are what they are and act upon one another in the way they do act by virtue of their position within a system of patterns. The Chinese spoke about individual patterns being subsumed in the Great Pattern, the Tao. They haven't been bothered with the idea of mechanical causation (which is extremely difficult to apply to biological entities) and have been able to think in organic terms from very early times. Strangely enough, this organic, organismic conception of life was carried over to Europe in the eighteenth century and had a profound influence on the European philosopher

Leibnitz, who became interested in the translations of Chinese philosophy which the Jesuit fathers brought back from China, especially in the philosophy of Chu Hsi, a twelfth-century neo-Confucian who had combined the notion of Taoism with those of Confucianism. Leibnitz's philosophy in turn has had a profound influence on such modern organicist philosophers as Whitehead, Needham, Bertalanffy, Smuts, and Lloyd Morgan. The fundamental Chinese idea of the Tao has been likened to a kind of cosmic field of force, which is a field of force not only in the physical world but in the spiritual world: things are what they are and act as they act simply because of their position in the cosmic pattern.

An ethic and a philosophy are very important in creating a suitable mental atmosphere in which we can act in the right way towards our natural surroundings, but we need more than an ethic and more than a philosophy. We need an aesthetic, an organized sensibility which will polarize our feelings and thoughts in an artistic way towards the world. I am an old and unregenerate Wordsworthian; I regard Wordsworth as among the four or five greatest English poets and as a man who contributed insights of enormous importance in regard to what our relationship towards the world should be. Wordsworth's whole idea was that man and nature are closely interlinked, that morality goes right back into our relations with the world, and that our sense of the divine can be most powerfully mediated through our relations with the world of nature. He says, for example:

> One impulse from a vernal wood
> May teach you more of man,
> Of moral evil and of good,
> Than all the sages can.[1]

And he speaks in *The Excursion* of being

1. William Wordsworth, 'The Tables Turned', 21–24.

> Rapt into still communication that transcends
> The imperfect offices of prayer and praise[2]

He felt very strongly this spiritual relationship of man with nature, and he felt its importance. He felt also that in nature man could discover his own deepest mind, that in his relationship with nature he could discover his spontaneity and an immediate, unsophisticated experience of life.

The quite recent development in European poetry and art which Wordsworth represents has a close relationship with the literature and art of the Far East. In Chinese and Japanese poetry and landscape painting we find images that are curiously prophetic of the Wordsworthian attitude towards nature; in that strange art form of Japan called the haiku, a tiny poem in seventeen syllables, we find it again and again expressed in an abbreviated and elusive way. Consider for example a poem by Basho, which goes like this:

> The hanging bridge
> Creeping vines
> Entwine our life[3]

A bridge of living substance links man with the material world, as Wordsworth says in his memorable words in the 'Tintern Abbey':

> . . . a sense sublime
> Of something far more deeply interfused,
> Whose dwelling is the light of setting suns,
> And the round ocean and the living air,
> And the blue sky, and in the mind of man.[4]

This idea, which is characteristic of the nineteenth century in the West, was commonplace in the Far East many centuries before. We see it not only in poetry, but in the rise of landscape

2. William Wordsworth, *The Excursion*, I. 215–216.
3. R. H. Blyth, *Haiku* (Hokuseido: 1952), vol. 4, p. 13.
4. William Wordsworth, 'Lines composed a few miles above Tintern Abbey', 95–99.

painting. Landscapes virtually without figures were painted in China at least one thousand years before they appeared in Europe. There is something profoundly religious in landscape painting inasmuch as it seems to explore and to express that layer of the unconscious which is beyond the personal unconscious and which, it seems to me, is just as much given, impersonal, and not immediately connected with me as the external world. So the value of landscape paintings is not merely that they present us with images of the external world, but that they present us in the most powerful way with images of this deep, fundamental essence of Mind at large, from which the individual mind takes its source. This 'nature mysticism', as it has been called—it's a rather unfortunate term, but I don't think we can invent any other—was in the nineteenth century a thing of extraordinary importance, and I think it represented a very wholesome reaction to the ravages of the industrial revolution, which covered the whole world with an incredible hideousness and led to the enormous expansion of cities and the foisting upon man of a technological environment.

The Wordsworthian reaction followed, imitated and continued by many other poets, in this country in Whitman, above all in certain of the short essays in *Specimen Days*, which have a kind of quietness about them which much of his poetry does not have. One feels so much with Whitman's poetry that he was addressing a very large audience, but in the little essays of *Specimen Days* describing his life in the country after his stroke, we have the impression that he was talking to himself. There are descriptions of sitting by a pond and watching kingfishers, or deriving a sense of life by holding onto the sapling of an ash, or sitting under an oak tree, which are wonderfully beautiful, and one can see the religious value the Wordsworthian attitude towards nature had in the bustling, spreading world of modern technology.

In the present world, and this is a fact which disquiets me, the prevailing nature mysticism of nineteenth century landscape painting and poetry seems to a great extent to have evaporated. It is as though contemporary artists have resigned themselves to the new technological environment and are not paying much attention to the given environment of nature. We have seen in painting a retreat from landscape painting into non-representational painting, into the use of abstract forms which are supposed to be symbolic and expressive of events in the mind, but which to me are a good deal less expressive than the landscapes in which, say, the Sung painters, Constable, Turner, or the Impressionists expressed the states of their mind. And we see in poetry something of the same kind. I personally find a great deal of contemporary poetry too abstract for my taste. There is a great tendency to use abstract phraseology to escape from the concrete, factual description of natural things into descriptions of some aspect of our technological civilization. For my own part, I am old-fashioned enough to feel that I would like another reaction towards nature poetry, nature mysticism, and nature landscape painting of an earlier day. It could not be the same thing, of course; we can never repeat what happened in the past. But its general tendency would be towards health and genuine religious feeling which we could very well do with more of at the present time.

What we see then is that we are in a position to patch up the damage we have done to the planet and prevent more damage being done. But it is going to be exceedingly difficult because there are many factors which militate against it. And we need the right kind of mental atmosphere, one in which it will seem natural to people to do what we ought to do in relation to our planet. We need an extension of our present system of ethics; we need a philosophy, some form of what I would call realistic idealism, which will harmonize man with nature and which will take account of all the facts. And we need, finally, not only a good ethic and a good philosophy, but also a good art, which will give us the terms in which we can feel as well as think about this problem—an art which, I regret to say, I don't think exists today because of the reaction against the previous manifestation of it in the 19th Century, but which I do feel very strongly deserves to come back and to receive all the attention of a young talent.

THE POPULATION

EXPLOSION

Today I want to pass on to what is happening to the human species and to think a little about what our philosophy and our ethical outlook on the subject should be. This lecture is essentially about human numbers and their relation to human well-being and human values in general.

Needless to say, any accurate estimation of human numbers is very recent, but we can extrapolate into the past and come to what seem to be fairly good conclusions. Although there are some fairly wide margins of difference among the experts, the numbers they come to are roughly in agreement. They agree that in pre-agricultural days, for example in the lower Palæolithic times, when man was a food-gathering creature, there were probably not more than twenty million humans on this whole planet. In later Palæolithic times, after organized hunting had been invented, the number probably doubled. We can make a rough estimate of what an organized hunting people could do because we know how many Indians were present in North America when the white man arrived—not more than one million in the entire North American continent east of the Rockies—and this gives one an indication of the extremely low

Delivered on March 9, 1959

density of population possible in a hunting economy. The Great Revolution came about 6000 B.C. with the invention of agriculture, and the creation of cities in the next millennia. By about 1000 B.C., after five thousand years of agriculture, there were probably about one hundred million people in the world. By the beginning of the Christian era, this figure had a little more than doubled: it was somewhere between two hundred million and two hundred and fifty million—less than half the present population of China. The population increased very gradually in the following years; sometimes there were long periods of standstill and sometimes there were even periods of decrease, as in the years immediately following 1348, when the Black Death killed off 30 per cent of the population of Europe and nobody knows how much of the population of Asia.

By the time the Pilgrim fathers arrived in this country, it is estimated that the population of the world was about twice what it had been on the first Christmas Day—that is to say, it had doubled in sixteen hundred years, an extremely slow rate of increase. But from that time on, from the middle of the seventeenth century, with the beginnings of the industrial revolution and the first importation of food from the newly developed lands of the New World, population began rising far more rapidly than it had ever risen before. By the time the Declaration of Independence was signed, the figure for the human population of the world was probably around seven hundred million; it must have passed the billion mark fairly early in the nineteenth century and stood at about fourteen hundred million around the time when I was born in the 1890s. The striking fact is that since that time the population of the planet has doubled again. It has gone from fourteen hundred million, which is already twice what it was at the signing of the Declaration of Independence, to twenty-eight hundred million. And the rate of increase now is such that it will probably double again in rather less than fifty years.

Thus the *rates* of increase have been increasing along with the absolute increase in numbers. The net rate of increase did not reach 1 per cent per annum until the beginning of this century. It has now risen to an average of 1.6 per cent per annum for the world at large, and there are considerable areas of the world where it exceeds 2 per cent and even reaches 3 per cent or more. Now, a 3 per cent increase when compounded annually (population increases as money increases, by compound interest) doubles the population in about twenty-five years, and a 1.5 per cent increase doubles the population in about fifty years; thus a 1.6 per cent increase will double the population in somewhat less than fifty years. The fact that the rate of increase never reached 1 per cent until the twentieth century, and that in the short time since about 1905, when this point was reached, it has already reached the figure of 1.6 per cent, is extraordinary. It indicates very clearly that we are living in a world for which there are no historical precedents whatsoever and that we have to resign ourselves to thinking in entirely new ways about a problem which our fathers never had any occasion to think about so intensively.

I indicated that, at the present time, there are large differences in the rate of increase in different parts of the world. Western Europe had its great increase during the eighteenth and nineteenth centuries. Although the rate never came up to even 1 per cent per annum, the increase was very rapid and startling at the time. The population in Europe has now reached about four hundred million and is increasing at less than 1 per cent per annum; it is thought that it will take about a hundred years at the present rate for Europe's population to double again. Meanwhile, in other parts of the world that were not increasing rapidly in the nineteenth century, populations have begun to increase at a great rate. We are now seeing the kind of thing that happened in Europe a hundred or a hundred and fifty years ago happening on an enormous scale in Asia, in Africa, in South America, in the Caribbean Islands. So we see that the increase is considerably less over the greater part of the

Western world than it is in the Asiatic and the African worlds.

Let us now consider the reasons for the steps in the increments of population in the past. Primitive man was limited by his methods of collecting food. Food collecting—wandering about picking up acorns and snails and frogs and things—obviously can support an extremely small population. When hunting becomes organized—when you have flint arrows, when you have invented the bow, and when you have fire hunts and organize whole tribes to chase the game—then considerably more people can be supported. So the experts think that the population doubled at that time. With the invention of agriculture, there is immediately a very great population increase, as it becomes possible to go on to a much higher level of production and to found cities, to create the division of labor, and to create what we call civilization. The proto-agricultural era lasted with very few changes until the later seventeenth century, when we got the beginning of the industrial revolution coupled with the first results of the exploitation of virgin lands in the New World. Without the supply of cheap food from the New World it probably would have been impossible for Europe to industrialize as it did; but the historical accident by which vast lands were suddenly opened up made it possible to take a great many peasants off the land in Europe and put them into factories and keep them fed while they were building up the new industrial society. It was this extra supply of food which initiated the modern advance in population; all species live up to their supply of food and then are wiped out as the numbers outrun the supply.

A new factor based upon discoveries in physiology and medicine has entered the picture in recent years: the factor of public health. What is happening now is not that the birth rate is increasing—in fact in many cases it has decreased slightly—but that the death rate has been lowered to a startling extent, mainly by public health measures. The change began in the nineteenth century, with people realizing, for example, that they had to have clean water. Even before Pasteur's discovery of bacteria, it had begun to dawn on people that it was a good thing to be clean.

It is interesting in this context to read about the early efforts of the disciples of Jeremy Bentham, the utilitarian philosopher, to clean up London. The rich, who lived in their own part of the town, had been entirely indifferent to the appalling conditions which prevailed in the eastern part of the City. But when cholera and other diseases like typhus, which raged in the East End, began to invade the smarter sections of the West End, they decided that something had better be done. Men like Sir James Kay-Shuttleworth succeeded in about forty years in transforming London from a pest-hole of the most revolting character into a relatively clean city. The result was a dramatic rise in the expectation of life: the average expectation of life in ancient Rome was about thirty years, as in modern Asia; the average expectation of life in the United States and Great Britain is now about seventy years.

Today, with the newest weapons in the public health armoury, the most amazing revolutionary changes can be brought about in an extraordinarily short time. The two most powerful weapons are the antibiotics and the insecticides— coupled with the discovery that malaria and yellow fever, for example, are insect-carried diseases and that other tropical diseases are also carried by small animals. Consider the case of Ceylon, where the population was held almost stationary by endemic malaria. After the end of the Second World War public health teams were sent into Ceylon with DDT, and malaria was completely stamped out in less than five years. In Europe, on the other hand, malaria had been endemic for centuries (you will find it referred to constantly in the plays of Shakespeare as 'ague'). In London it took at least three hundred years of draining soil and drying up the area all along the Thames estuary to get rid of the mosquito and thus get rid of malaria.

While it took about three centuries of hard work in Britain to get rid of malaria, it took only five years with modern methods in Ceylon! And what have been the results? We have saved people from the miseries of malaria, a large proportion of whom would have died in early life or in middle age from the disease. But while the death rate has fallen very nearly to European levels, the birth rate has remained what it was when three or four out of every five children regularly died and it was necessary to produce large families in order to preserve the race at the existing levels. The result is that the population of Ceylon is now increasing at the rate of 3 per cent per annum, which means that it will double in twenty-four years. The land, however, is not elastic. Although some new land will come into production owing to the fact that it can now be ploughed under because of the destruction of the malaria mosquito, it will not be enough; and meanwhile, incredible problems have already arisen. It is more and more difficult to feed the population on local resources and the exportable crops such as tea and rubber do not suffice to buy sufficient foods. Capital is extremely difficult to come by because there simply isn't enough money circulating for people to save. And nobody quite knows what on earth is going to happen when the population doubles.

This same situation is particularly striking on many islands, where there is no possibility of expansion. It is very striking in Mauritius; it is very striking on some of the Mediterranean islands such as Sardinia and Sicily; it is a fearful problem throughout the Caribbean. I was talking last year with the Prime Minister of the New Commonwealth of the Caribbean, Sir Grantley Adams (who previously was the Prime Minister of Barbados), and he was telling me about the state of his home island. Barbados now has a population of 1400 to the square mile with only one industry—sugar—and no other resources at all, and nobody has the faintest idea of how they are going to get on in the future; and Barbados is in only slightly worse condition than many other islands. One has to confront the painful fact that this newly independent community is probably

non-viable from an economic point of view, and the situation
will probably become worse as time goes on owing to the increasing pressure of population upon resources. The same situation can be seen in Egypt, where at the present time something
like 25 million people are trying to make a living off 5.25 million
acres of arable land. Here one can put in, parenthetically, the
fundamental reason why Egyptian policy has been so trouble-
some to the West in recent years: It is a biological reason; these
people cannot live on their resources and they must throw their
weight around so as somehow to get people who have capital
to invest in their country. It is completely pointless to envisage
the politics of such a country as Egypt, and indeed of many
other countries of the world, from a purely political point of
view. You have to think in terms of biology to gain any understanding and to formulate any sensible policy.

Let us now ask ourselves what the practical alternatives are
as we confront this problem of population growth. One alternative is to do nothing in particular about it and just let things go
on as they are, but the consequences of that course are quite
clear: the problem will be solved by nature in the way that
nature always solves problems of over-population. When any
animal population exceeds the resources available to it, the
population tends (a) to starve and (b) to suffer from severe epi-
demic and epizootic diseases. In the human population, we can
envisage that the natural check on the unlimited growth of
population will be precisely this: there will be pestilence, fam-
ine, and, since we are human beings and not animals, there will
be organized warfare, which will bring the numbers down to
what the earth can carry. What nature teaches us is that it is
extraordinarily dangerous to upset any of its fundamental balances, and we are in the process of upsetting a fundamental
balance in the most alarming and drastic manner. The question
is: Are we going to restore the balance in the natural way, which
is a brutal and entirely anti-human way, or are we going to
restore it in some intelligent, rational, and humane way? If we

leave matters as they are, nature will certainly solve the problem in her way and not in ours.

Another alternative is to increase industrial and agricultural production so that they can catch up with the increase in population. This solution, however, would be extremely like what happens to Alice in *Through the Looking Glass*. You remember that Alice and the Red Queen are running a tremendous race. To Alice's astonishment, when they have run until they are completely out of breath they are in exactly the same place, and Alice says, 'Well, in *our* country . . . you'd generally get to somewhere else—if you ran very fast for a long time as we've been doing.'

'A slow sort of country!' says the Queen. 'Now *here*, you see, it takes all the running *you* can do, to keep in the same place. If you want to get somewhere else, you must run at least twice as fast as that!'[1]

This is a comic parable of the extremely tragic situation in which we now find ourselves. We have to work, to put forth an enormous effort, just to stand where we are; and where we are is in a most undesirable position because, as the most recent figures issued by the United Nations indicate, something like two-thirds of the human race now lives on a diet of two thousand calories or less per day, which—the ideal being in the neighbourhood of three thousand—is definitely a diet of undernourishment.

Furthermore, all observers in the food and agricultural organizations and other international organizations busy with this problem agree that the situation now is a little worse than it was thirty or forty years ago; the average individual has less to eat and fewer goods than he had in the past. Whereas thirty years ago something like 50 per cent of the world's population was definitely undernourished, almost 65 per cent is undernourished today. The reason for the steady worsening of the situa-

1. Lewis Carroll, *Through the Looking Glass,* Chapter 2.

tion is clear: in a country such as Mexico or Guatemala or Ceylon, where the population is increasing by 3 per cent per annum, all production, both agricultural and industrial, must also increase 3 per cent per annum in order to preserve even the present low and unsatisfactory standard of living. If there is to be any improvement, the increase in production must certainly be 4 per cent and preferably 5 per cent per annum. But it is most difficult to keep up an increase in agricultural production of 2 or 3 per cent per annum, much less 4 per cent. This was done in Japan for forty or fifty years by the most extraordinary effort and amazing industry of the Japanese, but it is extremely unlikely that it can be done in many other parts of the world, especially in underdeveloped countries where there is a prodigious lack of capital. Capital, after all, is the margin that remains when the fundamental needs of the population have been satisfied, but in most of the underdeveloped countries the fundamental needs of the population are never satisfied.

It is incredible how little capital a country like India can raise. The last figures I saw from the United Nations were that most Western countries have at their disposal about seventy times as much capital as the underdeveloped countries, while at the present time the underdeveloped countries *need* about seventy times as much capital as do the developed countries. The situation illustrates the terribly significant and painfully true statement in the Gospels, 'to those who have shall be given, and from those who have not, shall be taken away even that which they have' (Matthew 25:29).

Along with the shortage of capital in underdeveloped countries there are great shortages of trained manpower, which is just as necessary to increasing production as adequate supplies of capital, so that it seems extremely difficult to envisage the possibility of increasing production sufficiently merely to keep up with the increase in population, much less to outrun it. So much for our second alternative.

The third alternative is to try to increase production as much as possible and at the same time to try to re-establish the balance between the birth rate and the death rate by means less gruesome than those which are used in nature—by intelligent and humane methods. In this connection it is interesting to note that the idea of limiting the growth of populations is by no means new. In a great many primitive societies, and even in many of the highly civilized societies of antiquity, where local over-population was a menace, methods of limiting population were employed. The methods included some which we would certainly find extremely undesirable, although less fearful than the natural means. The most common was infanticide—killing or exposing by leaving out on the mountain unwanted children, or children of the wrong sex, or children who happened to be born with some slight deficiency or other. Abortion was also very common. And there were many societies in which strict religious injunctions imposed long periods of sexual continence between the birth of each child. But in the nineteenth and twentieth centuries various methods of birth control less fearful in nature have been devised, and it is in fact theoretically conceivable that such methods might be applied throughout the whole world.

What is theoretically possible, however, is often practically almost impossible. There are colossal difficulties in the way of implementing any large-scale policy of limitation of population; whereas death control is extremely easy under modern circumstances, birth control is extremely difficult. The reason is very simple: death control—the control, for example, of infectious diseases—can be accomplished by a handful of experts and quite a small labour force of unskilled persons and requires a very small capital expenditure. In the case of Ceylon, malaria was stamped out simply by spraying swamps and pools with DDT and spraying the interiors of houses. Similarly, digging wells for clean water is quite a cheap procedure. But when we come to increasing production, or to decreasing the birth rate, we find ourselves confronted with problems which can only be solved by the co-operation of the entire population. Increasing agricultural production requires an immense amount of educational work among millions of smallholders and peasants and farmers, and any policy of birth control requires the co-operation of the entire adult population. So the current state of imbalance is likely to continue for a long time.

The problem of control of the birth rate is infinitely complex. It is not merely a problem in medicine, in chemistry, in biochemistry, in physiology; it is also a problem in sociology, in psychology, in theology, and in education. It has to be attacked on about ten different fronts simultaneously if there is to be any hope of solving it. First of all, there has to be a great deal of fundamental research into biology and the whole problem of reproduction, in the hope of producing some satisfactory oral contraceptive which can be distributed easily and cheaply to masses of people. I was talking last year with researchers in the Rockefeller Institute who told me that they think there is still a great deal of fundamental research to be done. We just don't know enough yet to be able to produce an entirely satisfactory oral contraceptive. And unfortunately very little money is going into this research; in general, far more goes into physical and chemical research than into biological research, and far more goes into other areas of biological research than into this particular area. Nevertheless, assuming that enough money and ability are put into this problem, it can probably be solved within ten years and something completely satisfactory produced and manufactured in bulk. But within ten years the population of the earth will have increased by five hundred million.

Then we have to consider the time it will take to get the new oral contraceptive accepted by countless millions of men and women all over the world. Some interesting research into this kind of problem was undertaken years ago by the English Fabians, Beatrice and Sidney Webb. They made an historical study of the average time it took for an idea which at its first enunciation seemed revolutionary and revolting to be taken for granted and to be acted upon by the whole population. They concluded that the average time is twenty-eight years—roughly the length of a generation. It is very difficult to persuade adults to change their points of view; they have to die off before a new generation can accept new ideas. If it takes ten years to produce chemically, by basic research, what we want, and then another twenty-eight years to get the product accepted, by this time the population of the earth will have increased by about a billion and a half. Again, we are up against the awful Alice-Through-the-Looking-Glass parable, rushing on in order to stand in the same place.

Merely from a technical and temporal point of view, we are obviously in a very tight spot. But we have also to consider the political point of view. There would undoubtedly have to be either world-wide agreement or regional agreements on a general population policy in order to have any satisfactory control of the situation at all. But there is absolutely no prospect at the present time of our getting any such political agreement.

The trouble is that political leaders just don't think in biological terms. Here is a rather interesting speculation: What might have happened if the only man who had had considerable experience in practical biology, and who was in politics, had become President of the United States? I am referring to Henry Wallace. Henry Wallace was undoubtedly a very bad politician, but he did think in biological terms, and by helping to develop hybrid corn he had done something which was unquestionably and unmitigatedly good for the entire human race—which is probably more than can be said for any other man in public life that I can think of. Maybe if we had had such a man for President the whole thinking about these problems would have been pushed away from the field of politics, where they are completely insolvable, towards the field of biology, where they are possibly solvable. We might have seen a policy which would have made a great deal more sense in the long run than the one which is now being pursued by all parties—from the long-range point of view, a kind of monstrously frivolous and irresponsible fiddling while Rome burns. We fiddle with the awful business of nationalistic power politics when our basic problem is whether the human race, expanding as rapidly as it is doing now, can survive in any decent condition—and what we are to do to preserve the world in any tolerable state for our great-grandchildren or even for our grandchildren. Unfortunately we missed our chance, and there has never been, at the head of a great State, a man who has habitually thought in biological terms.

Another problem which I think we must just briefly mention in regard to the increase in human numbers is the educational problem. The enormously rapid increase makes it almost impossible to realize the idea of providing a basic education for everybody. Immense efforts have been made, above all since the end of the Second World War, to provide elementary education throughout the world. But the fact remains—these figures were published just two months ago by UNESCO—that the absolute number of illiterates is greater today than it has ever been, in spite of all efforts. We have now eight hundred million children to educate, but we also have seven hundred million illiterate adults. In the underdeveloped countries (a) there is no capital for building schools, (b) there is no tax money to pay teachers, and (c) there are not nearly enough trained teachers. Even in this country, the richest country in the world, grave complaints are heard that schoolrooms are overcrowded, that we don't have enough school buildings, and so on. Imagine what the problem is in countries like Mexico or Brazil or Ceylon where there is a much higher rate of population increase and far fewer resources, both in money and in trained manpower. We are then confronted with the awful probability that we are just going to go on having more and more illiterate adults than we ever had before. And we have to remember that these adults will be illiterate, not within the framework of a traditional civilization—where it didn't matter very much whether or not they were illiterate—but within the framework of a traditional civilization which has broken down completely and which is being replaced by the worse features of our own Western civilization.

Now we have to ask ourselves what our attitude should be towards these problems. We come to the other end of the bridge. We pass from the world of facts to the world of values. What we think about all this depends entirely on what we regard as the end and purpose of human life. If we believe the end and purpose of human life is to foster power politics and nationalism, then we shall probably need a great deal of cannon fodder, although even this proposition becomes rather dubious in the light of nuclear warfare. But if, as I think most of us would agree, the end of human life is to realize individual potentialities to their limits and in the best way possible, and to create a society which makes possible such a realization, then we find ourselves equipped to think in a rational and philosophical way about the population problem. We see that in very many cases the effort to raise human quality is being thwarted by the mere increase of human quantity, that quality is very often incompatible with quantity. We have seen that mere quantity makes the educational potentialities of the world unrealizable. We have seen that the pressure of enormous numbers upon resources makes it almost impossible to improve the material standards of life, which after all have to be raised to a minimum if any of the higher possibilities are to be realized: although it is quite true that man cannot live by bread alone, still less can he live without bread, and if we simply cannot provide adequate bread, we cannot provide anything else. Only when he has bread, only when his belly is full, is there some hope of something else emerging from the human situation.

Then there is the political problem. It is quite clear that as population presses more and more heavily upon resources, the economic situation tends to become more and more precarious.

As there is a tendency in precarious situations for centralized government to assume more and more control, there is therefore now a tendency towards totalitarian forms of government, which certainly we in the West find very undesirable. But when you ask whether democracy is possible in a population where two-thirds of the people are living on two thousand calories a day, and one-third is living on over three thousand, the answer is no, because the people living on less than two thousand calories will simply not have enough energy to participate in the political life of the country, and so they will be governed by the well-fed and energetic. Again, quantity militates against quality.

Another (to me) very disturbing and painful result of quantity which affects the quality of human life is the fact that more and more of the increasing mass of people is being confined to gigantic cities, that more and more people are therefore living completely out of touch with the natural environment and are instead surrounded by an environment of unutterable dreariness and squalor. When one comes to think of it, there probably never has been a beautiful city of more than, say, two or three hundred thousand inhabitants, because a beautiful city is beautiful in relation to its natural surroundings. You can have cities with magnificent central areas such as Washington, D.C.; but if you walk out of the central areas Washington cannot be said to be very beautiful, for you go through square miles of extraordinarily dreary slums and second-rate middle-class residential areas. The same thing is true of other, much larger, cities such as New York and London and Tokyo. There are mile upon mile of fearful dreariness, where the children never see any natural object at all and see only ugly human objects. This situation is a blight upon the world at the present time, and as far as I can see it is destined to get worse and worse. I cannot help feeling that this is a very deleterious state of affairs for the human spirit.

Finally, the unlimited increase in human numbers practically guarantees that our planetary resources will be destroyed and that within a hundred or two hundred years an immensely hypertrophied human species will have become a kind of cancer on this planet and will ruin the quasi-organism on which it lives. It is a most depressing forecast and possibility.

I think one can say from this last point that the problem of quality and quantity is really a religious problem. For, after all, what is religion but a preoccupation with the destiny of the individual and with the destiny of society and the race at large? This is summed up very clearly in the Gospel when we are told that the Kingdom of God is within us but at the same time it is our business to contribute to the founding of the Kingdom of God upon earth. We cannot neglect either of these two aspects of human destiny. For if we neglect the general, quantitative, population aspect of destiny, we condemn ourselves, or certainly our children and grandchildren, as individuals. We condemn them to the kind of life which we should find intolerable and which presumably they will find intolerable too.

There are no certain theological objections to population limitation. Most religious organizations in the world today, both within and outside the Christian pale, accept it. But the Roman Catholic church does not accept any method of population control except that which was promulgated and made permissible in 1932—the so-called rhythm method. Unfortunately, where the rhythm method has been tried on a considerable scale in an undeveloped country such as India, it has not been found to be very effective. The fact that the Church recognizes this problem was brought home very clearly in 1954 at the time of the first United Nations Population Congress, which took place in Rome, when the late Pope, in an allocution to the delegates, made it quite clear that the problem of population was a very grave one which he recommended to the consideration of the faithful.

Whether the present attitude towards the methods of birth control will be changed, I don't know. It is a matter of some interest that one of the main arguments against current and possibly future methods is their 'unnaturalness'. Precisely the same argument was used in the Middle Ages, and right up until 1515, against the taking of interest on money. It was an argument based on statements in Aristotle that money is barren and has no right to breed. A hint of this is found in the first act of *The Merchant of Venice*, where Antonio, talking to Shylock, speaks about 'barren metal' breeding and asks, 'Or is your gold and silver ewes and rams?'[2] It was all right for living creatures to breed, but it was quite wrong for money to do so. This position was gradually modified, the last modification taking place at one of the Lateran Councils in 1515. I don't know whether a similar change may take place in the attitude toward 'unnatural' methods of birth control. Be that as it may, the fact remains that everybody agrees in principle that over-population is a great danger, and the differences are now mainly questions of means.

We can conclude, then, by saying that over-population is quite clearly one of the gravest problems which confront us, and the choice before us is either to let the problem be solved by nature in the most horrifying possible way or else to find some intelligent and humane method of solving it, simultaneously increasing production and balancing the birth rate and the death rate, and in some way or other forming an agreed international policy on the subject. To my mind, the most important prerequisites to such a solution are first of all an awareness of the problem, and then a realization that it is a profoundly religious problem, a problem of human destiny. Our hope, as always, is to be realistically idealistic.

2. William Shakespeare, *The Merchant of Venice*, I. iii. 135, 95.

HOW ORIGINAL

IS ORIGINAL SIN?

UNTIL now I have talked
about the human situation in relation to the planetary scale,
which is the largest possible one. In this lecture I want to bring
it down to the much smaller scale of the individual and to
discuss genetics and environment and their relations with our
general philosophy of life and political ideals.

I shall begin with a question, and the question is this: How
original is original sin? This is a question which has preoccupied
men in all countries for a very long time. How original is what
seems to be the fundamental badness of man, so strongly
stressed in orthodox Christianity? And how original is what may
be called 'original virtue', which is stressed more strongly in the
Taoist and Hindu traditions (where the basic nature of man is
called the 'Atman', and is identical with the basic nature of the
Godhead), but which is also within the Christian tradition—
what Quakers called the 'inner light' and the medieval mystics
used to call the 'scintilla animae' (spark of the soul) or the 'synderesis'.

This question of original sin and original virtue has been
asked ever since man started philosophizing about himself, and
it has been answered in a great variety of ways. Within the

Delivered on March 16, 1959

Indian tradition it has been answered in terms of the theory of karma: each of us comes into the world with the end product of innumerable past lives, which somehow have to be worked out life after life. This is an idea of heredity; our original destiny is pre-ordained for us by previous existences, which we inherit. In the Greek tradition the problem is discussed in terms of the relationship between man and the gods on the one side and necessity on the other, a necessity which nothing can change and which dominates even the gods. Finally we come to the Judæo-Christian tradition, where in the past the question was discussed in terms of grace and free will, of nature and grace, of predestination and salvation by works.

The problem of predestination is summed up in four curious lines from a poem by Matthew Prior—a most surprising poem, because Prior generally wrote rather frivolous and charming lyrics while this is a long reflective poem about religious problems.

> Cou'd destin'd Judas long before he fell
> Avoid the terrors of a future Hell?
> Cou'd Paul deny, resist or not embrace
> Obtruded Heav'n, and efficacious Grace?[1]

In the history of Christian theology the whole problem was thrashed out in the beginning of the fifth century in the great controversy between Pelagius and St. Augustine. It is worth going into this in some detail because it seems to summarize in the context of an earlier tradition a problem which still vexes us: the problem of nature and nurture.

Pelagius was apparently a Briton, either from Scotland or, possibly, from Ireland. He was brought up in the tradition of the British Church of that period, which was profoundly affected by the Eastern Church rather than the Roman Church, and he made his way to Rome as a middle-aged man in about 400. He found Rome then, as it generally was for many centuries there-

1. Matthew Prior, 'Predestination, a Poem', 85–88.

after, a real sink of iniquity; but he also found, and this disturbed him very much, that the Romans were justifying their behaviour in terms of the Augustinian doctrine of the total depravity of man and the bondage of the will to evil. Granted the truth of this doctrine, why make any effort to behave a little bit better?

Pelagius was evidently an early example of British practicality and empiricism, and he decided that what was necessary was a reform of social institutions and self-help. He was convinced that man could improve himself, both by individual effort and by making respectable and decent social institutions. He denied the originality of original sin, and this was his profound heresy. He denied that the sin of Adam affected anybody but Adam himself; he denied that it went on affecting the entire human race, and he insisted that all children were born innocent even as Adam had been born innocent. This was the opposite of the doctrine of St. Augustine, who affirmed that children were born in original sin and, unless baptised, would certainly be damned. St. Augustine even asserted, in very picturesque terms, that hell is paved with a mosaic of infants less than a span long—which we find a somewhat frightful doctrine, but which nevertheless follows logically from the assumption of the originality of original sin.

We cannot go into the details of the controversy, which was extremely important in the history of Christian dogma, but it is worth pointing out certain peculiarities in the Pelagian doctrine. Pelagius insisted that men are born without any inherited characteristics. He said they are born *'non pleni'* (not full) and without a character; that they are born *'sine virtute, ita et sine vitio'*,[2] that is to say without virtue even as without vice, without inborn tendencies either to good or to evil; and that each man becomes what he is, for good or for evil, in virtue of his surroundings and of his reactions to them. These ideas were

2. Pelagius, *De Libero Arbitrio*, quoted in St. Augustine, *De Peccato Originali*, xiii. 14.

profoundly at variance with the Augustinian doctrine and with the orthodox view of the Church of the time and were condemned; but for the next twelve centuries or so theological compromises had to be worked out between Pelagianism or semi-Pelagianism on the one hand and extreme Augustinianism on the other.

The next important Pelagian figure who appears is Helvétius, one of the thinkers of the eighteenth century, when people began to believe in inevitable progress—a belief which entails the conviction that man is determined primarily by the nature of his environment and can advance by improving it. Helvétius was extremely influential in his time, though very little read now. He reaffirmed the Pelagian doctrine that man is born without any hereditary characteristics and that he becomes what he is in virtue of what he learns and of how he reacts to the influences around him. Helvétius made the somewhat astonishing statement that any shepherd boy of the Cévennes could be turned into an Isaac Newton by suitable education. This sort of view prevailed to a considerable extent among the thinkers of the so-called Enlightenment of the eighteenth century, and certain elements of it were still to be found among the utilitarians of the nineteenth.

On the biological level we find, again in eighteenth-century France, the interesting figure of Lamarck, who insisted that environment could create hereditary factors—in a word, he insisted on the heritability of acquired characteristics. This view was controverted in the nineteenth century first by Darwin and then, in their detailed study of genetics, by Mendel and his followers. Today I don't think any geneticist accepts Lamarck's view, except possibly certain geneticists in Russia, followers of Lysenko, who claim that they can modify a plant species by environmental changes in such a way that the changes within the individual plant will be inherited. These claims, as far as I know, have never been substantiated, and the great majority of geneticists remain completely opposed to the idea.

Somewhat before Lysenko began his preaching in Russia, we had the phenomenon in this country of J. B. Watson's behaviourism, in the early days of which Watson made some quite remarkable statements which exactly parallel those of Helvétius. He affirmed, for example, that he could find no evidence of inherited human faculties of music or mathematics, and that man's behaviour was entirely determined by environmental causes. I think there has been some modification of this point of view, but even today the behaviourists tend to play down hereditary factors to an extraordinary extent. In Professor Skinner's monumental *Science and Human Behavior* there is exactly one page devoted to hereditary factors, and all the rest is devoted to the determination of behaviour by environmental conditioning. In theological terms, we may say that people with the behaviourist turn of mind tend to be Pelagians, whereas those with the geneticist turn of mind tend to be Augustinians. The truth as usual lies somewhere between the two extremes. It seems perfectly clear that hereditary factors—nature—and environmental factors—nurture—are equally important and that in point of fact we can never isolate the two.

In view, however, of the fact that there has been for a long time a down-playing of hereditary factors, I think it is worthwhile to go into what is original—inherited—in the human individual. In general we find that as we go up the evolutionary scale, the variability of species increases, and there is no question at all that when we reach man we find the highest level of variability of any species that we know. There are extraordinary inherited differences, such as anatomical differences, between human individuals. Perhaps the best of the recent atlases of anatomy, Anson's, published in 1950,[3] is probably the first to stress the profound variability of human beings on the anatomical level. Anson uses eight different plates to show the common variations of human hand. He has to use no fewer than twelve

3. Barry Joseph Anson, *An Atlas of Human Anatomy* (Philadelphia: W. B. Saunders, 1950).

to show the human heart in its commonest variations (there are people who have written of the heart who say that it is if anything more variable than the human face—an amazing statement when you consider how variable is the human face).

There are many other ways in which human beings vary anatomically. Take, for example, that very important organ, the intestine. In long and skinny people, as compared with round, soft people, the difference between the weight and length of the intestine is something fantastic: the intestine in the fat person may weigh twice as much as in the thin person and may be at least 50 per cent longer; it is consequently a great deal more efficient in doing its job, which is why the fat person tends to become fat even when he eats little, whereas the thin person does not become fat even when he eats a great deal. We find the same kinds of differences in the ductless glands. The pituitary can weigh from 350 milligrams to 1100 milligrams in perfectly normal people. The thyroid can vary from 8 to 50 grams, the para-thyroid from 50 to 300 milligrams, the male gonad from 10 to 45 grams. The ovaries may range in weight from 2 to 10 grams, and the number of ova contained in normal ovaries may vary from a few as 30,000 to as many as 400,000. The pineal gland can weigh as little as 30 or as much as 400 milligrams and a normal pancreas can have as few as 200,000 Islands of Langerhans, or as many as 1,800,000.

Similarly, there are great differences in physiological reactions. As experimenters in taste perception such as Albert Blakeslee recently pointed out, there are substances which some people taste as salt, some as sour, some as bitter, and some as sweet. There are also enormous differences in the acuity of peripheral visual perception. In general we can say that these indubitably genetic anatomical and physiological differences are of immense importance because they must be reflected to some extent in our mental and psychological life.

The enormous mental and psychological differences which we perceive among human beings are correlated, first of all, with differences in the structure of the nervous system. It is quite certain, for example, that brains are very different from one another in the number, shape, and arrangement of their neurons. Although we don't know exactly *how* these physical differences affect people psychologically, undoubtedly there is an effect upon our way of thinking and our character. The second genetic correlate of character and temperamental differences is the difference in the capacity of different individuals to produce various of the enzymes which control metabolism and nervous action. It is becoming clearer and clearer that this is a matter of immense importance. The third correlate is probably blood supply, which is likewise of great importance and which varies greatly among human beings: some people's hearts pump much more blood than others and much more rapidly, the arteries in some are more efficient in carrying blood to different parts of the body, and so forth. Thus we have here the genetic basis for many of the psychological differences which we see; they are not determined by environmental factors alone.

One of the reasons why modern psychiatry has so astoundingly neglected the genetic factor in psychology is precisely because it has neglected the bodily factor in man. If you examine the body it is perfectly clear that there are enormous genetic differences between human beings. But if you ignore the body and concentrate solely on psychological traits, then this is not so obvious, although by inference it is perfectly clear that the enormous physical differences between human beings must be reflected in psychological differences. I am always astounded, when I read the literature of modern psychiatry, to see that the founding fathers of the science, Freud and Jung and Rank, paid almost no attention at all to the physical side of human beings and therefore completely ignored the genetic side of their problems. You can read the so-called case histories, and never be told *who* the subjects are. You get a description of Mrs. X but you are never told if Mrs. X weighs 90 pounds or

250 pounds; yet there is obviously a considerable psychological difference between a woman who weighs 90 pounds and one who weighs 250. Here is Mr. Y, who is in a bad way, but you are never told whether Mr. Y resembles an ox or a daddy-long-legs, whether he is like a panther or like a jellyfish. This obviously makes a prodigious difference, but one can read book after book of modern psychiatric case histories without ever finding such obvious facts mentioned. Only in Adler do we find some references to the physical aspect of human personality.

As it is very important that the doctors of the body should realize that the mind has effects upon the body, so it is important that psychologists should realize that the body has effects upon the mind, that many of these bodily effects are obviously genetic in character, and that therefore there are hereditary factors in practically all psychological disturbances. The most obvious case in point, which as far as I know is never discussed in the psychiatric literature, is the question, If all our psychological troubles are due to traumatic experiences in childhood, why aren't we all crazy? We have all had very grave traumatic experiences, and yet only some of us are crazy and quite a number remain relatively sane. Again, it is quite obvious that such phenomena as Oedipus and sibling rivalry must act upon a biological substratum which is different in different cases.

There are certain people who have no psychological resistance, just as there are certain people who, undoubtedly for genetic reasons, have very little physical resistance to infection. This is of immense importance, for, as we can do something by biochemical means to correct a lowered resistance to infection, so it is perfectly possible that we might, by biochemical or nutritional means, do something to correct or to mask the genetic anomalies that make certain people much more likely to be affected by a psychological trauma than others are. Unfortunately, one finds almost no reference to this at all in the psychological literature; there is instead a kind of dogma, which may be called the dogma of environmental determinism, which almost systematically ignores the physiological factor.

This state of things is not universal and I am glad to say that within recent years there has been within psychiatry a strong unorthodox movement towards what is called constitutional psychology. The pioneer work in this field is being done by William H. Sheldon and his collaborators, as well as by George Draper and C. W. Dupertuis (in the field of constitutional medicine), who are investigating the relationship between disease and certain hereditary body peculiarities.

What Sheldon has shown is that we are perfectly wrong in thinking of 'types' of human beings. The trouble is that the nature of our language is such that we like to think in terms of pigeonholes and substantial types, and it is very difficult to talk about a continuum of any kind. In the world of physics, when people had to talk about the universe as a continuum, they had to invent a special ad hoc language, the language of calculus, and other forms of mathematical language. The same thing happens in psychological problems. As Sheldon has shown, and as is perfectly obvious must be the case, human beings do not vary by jumps and therefore cannot be put down as one type or another. Rather, there is a continuous variation among them; and this is not a variation between two poles—we always have a frightful tendency to think in terms of dichotomy—but it is much more realistically described as being a continuous variation within a three-pole framework.

I cannot go into the Sheldonian classifications today, but I do think they are extremely realistic classifications, and that his system does to some extent help us to see how the different genetic variations between body type and temperament—the relationships between physique and character—have always been intuitively understood by dramatists and story tellers. No dramatist is sufficiently idiotic to put the character of a Falstaff in the body of a Cassius; no story-teller would give the character of a Pickwick to the body of a Scrooge. The logic of Caesar's speech in *Julius Caesar* is perfectly obvious to us:

Let me have men about me that are fat,
Sleek-headed men, and such as sleep o' nights.
Yond Cassius has a lean and hungry look,
He thinks too much: such men are dangerous.[4]

Cassius thinks too much, but he is unlike what Sheldon would call the extreme ectomorph who thinks a great deal but never acts, or acts only feebly. He is one of those extremely dangerous persons who think a great deal and have enough of what Sheldon calls the 'mesomorphic factor' to act very strongly and efficiently—and too little of what he calls the 'endomorphic factor', the factor of geniality and of outgoing jolliness and kindness. Cassius is the typical fanatic, and I think we can imagine his physique to be closely related to that of Savonarola, who had the same tremendous power of thinking connected with terrific drive and a minimum of human kindness and compassion.

Take, for another example, a poet I happen to be very fond of, Chaucer, and read the prologue to *The Canterbury Tales.* You will be amazed at the amount of pure character drawing which comes through simply in the very accurate descriptions of the physique of each of the personages in the poem. It is an extraordinary example of how much can be done with a minimum of psychological analysis but a maximum of setting forth of the physical differences between people. We have a very good idea of who these people are simply because there has been an admirably vivid description of their outward characteristics.

Sheldon's tri-polar system is also interesting inasmuch as it corresponds very closely with the tri-polar system which we find in the religious tradition of India. (In the Christian system we have much more of a dichotomy between the way of Martha and the way of Mary, the way of action and the way of contemplation, although even within the Christian system it has been recognized that the way of Martha probably has more than one

4. William Shakespeare, *Julius Caesar,* I. ii. 192–195.

aspect to it.) One can read the full development of Indian psy-
cho-theological theory in the *Bhagavad Gita*. Human beings
are divided into three main classes: those who worship by
means of devotion and practice what is called bhakti yoga or
devotional worship; those whose worship is predominantly in
the field of action, in performing duty in a selfless way, and who
practice karma yoga; and those who worship through contemplation or through knowledge, the practitioners of jnana yoga.
These correspond closely to the Sheldonian three poles. The
extreme endomorph would inevitably be led toward the practice of emotional devotion; the mesomorph would be led toward a path of action dictated by duty; and the extreme ectomorph would be led toward the life of introversion and
contemplation.

Here we may remark on a very curious thing, that insofar as
the psychiatrists have recognized these kinds of temperamental
differences they have recognized only a dichotomy. Jung's insistence, for example, on the difference between the introvert and
extrovert is a division into two. He failed completely to see that
there are two very different kinds of extrovert: there is the
driving extrovert, who wishes to dominate either things or people—the Sheldonian mesomorph; and there is the emotional,
kindly extrovert—the Sheldonian endomorph—who wants to
spill the emotional beans and to bring everybody into his confidence, to be on good terms with everybody. These two kinds
of extrovert are as different from each other as both are from
the introvert—the Sheldonian ectomorph—who does not want
any of those things.

The tendency at the present time to underplay the importance of genetic factors generally is related to certain political
and philosophical doctrines. Orthodox Marxism, for example, is
based upon the idea of environmental determinism, and it does
not like the idea of congenital differences. In this country, possibly because of a wrongly interpreted view of democracy, it is
felt that too much stress upon the congenital and unchangeable

differences between people is somehow undemocratic—and also very depressing. I remember years ago my brother telling me that he had been asked by one of the slick magazines to write an article on genetics. He wrote the article; and I am glad to say he was paid for it, but the editor said that he was sorry, that he couldn't use it because the conclusions in regard to the ingrained and inborn genetic differences between people would be found too depressing by readers.

Unfortunately the nature of nature is that it is not particularly democratic in the Napoleonic sense of the word—where he said that what he was doing was opening the careers to talents. It is interesting that the Russians, in spite of the fact that Lysenko is allowed to go around saying that he can turn barley into wheat, which he certainly cannot, have decided that for the sake of finding men and women capable of exercising efficient leadership they must make a careful selection of genetically highly endowed people. We see that Russian education, as it has developed now, is essentially an aristocratic education concentrating on the people with the highest IQ and the greatest drive and not making much effort to impose a veneer of universal education on everybody. The universal education, in fact, stops fairly soon, but there is a most intensive education of the upper crust for the sake of creating an efficient oligarchy. It is a curious thing to find that, although Marxist theory is opposed to stressing genetic factors in man, the demands of practical life in a Marxist country have made it necessary for the Russians to devote more attention to the highly endowed than is being given at the present time in the democratic countries. But this kind of aristocracy or, more accurately, meritocracy—a word which has been used recently in Britain by anthropologists, who speak about its gradual emergence there—will certainly develop everywhere as technological societies demand it. We will have stratified societies based mainly upon the different capacities of people to pass examinations and go through more and more specialized and intensive forms of training.

These have been more or less factual discussions; we must pass now to the other end of the bridge. What are the consequences in the world of values and the world of thought of the enormous genetic variability among human beings? One consequence of the fact of variability is that liberty is a very precious thing. After all, if we were all the same, as Helvétius, Pelagius, or Watson in his early days believed, then there would be no point in liberty; what would be good for one would be good for all. It is human variability—the fact that one man's meat is another man's poison—that imposes upon us the duty of preserving individual liberty and of encouraging tolerance, of preventing majorities from repressing minorities, of permitting people to have a certain measure of self-determination in their lives.

In the religious tradition, inherited variability has been expressed in the doctrine that individual human souls are of infinite value, although this has not prevented the organized churches from trying to dragoon the faithful into a single pattern. We always have this tension between the fact of genetic variability and the fact that society does on the whole like to create a single manageable pattern of human life. The problem, as usual, is to make the best of both worlds, to find out how we can have a stable and viable society which yet gives scope to the enormous variations which, as a matter of empirical fact, do exist among human beings.

The extent to which societies have imposed patterns upon their extremely unlike individuals has varied greatly at different times in history and at different levels of culture. In the more primitive cultures, where societies are small and bound by very tight traditions, the pressure to conform is naturally very high. Anyone who reads the literature of anthropology must be astounded by the fantastic nature of some of the traditions to which men have had to conform. The advantage of a large and complex society such as ours is that it does permit the variability of human beings to express itself in a great many ways; there does not have to be the kind of intense conformity which we find in small primitive societies. Even so, in every society there is always a drive for conformity which is imposed from without by law and tradition and which individuals impose upon themselves from within by trying to imitate what the society regards as the ideal type.

I recommend in this context a very valuable book by the French philosopher Jules de Gaultier, which was published about fifty years ago, called *Bovarysme*.[5] The name is derived from the heroine of Flaubert's novel, *Madame Bovary,* in which this unfortunate young woman was always trying to be what in fact she was not. Gaultier generalizes this and says we *all* have a tendency to try to be what we are not, to be what the society in which we are brought up thinks is desirable. He says that everybody has a 'Bovaric angle'. That of some people is fairly narrow; what they intrinsically are by heredity is not too different from what they try to make themselves by imitation. But some people have Bovaric angles of 90 degrees, and some even of 180, and are trying to be exactly the opposite of what by nature they are. The results are generally disastrous. Nevertheless, one of the mechanisms by which society gets people to conform is to set up an ideal and rely on individuals to imitate it voluntarily. (It is not for nothing that what is probably the most influential and most widely read book of Christian devotion is called *The Imitation of Christ.*) Unfortunately, as we see only too clearly from the study of juvenile delinquency, the ideal imitated by many of us is not the highest ideal. There is imitation of Al Capone, unfortunately, and imitation of the young tough who goes around beating up people; there is imitation of rock-and-roll performers; and so on and so forth. The process is always present in any society, and it always has to be present. What we have to discover is some method of making the best of the social drive towards conformity while at the

5. Jules de Gaultier, *Le bovarysme* (Paris: Mercure de France, 1902).

same time safeguarding the genetic variability of individuals.

It is important to stress the fact that in order to make the most of genetic variability we have to improve the environment to the greatest possible extent. It is only when everyone has equal nutritional and educational opportunities that we shall be able to see to the full what his native capacities are. For these capacities will not then be masked by the effects of bad nutrition or by the absence of any educational facilities, and they will have the possibility of developing to their fullest extent. Contrary to what many of the earlier eugenists said, it is not enough just to sterilize the unfit or to try to breed differentially from the more fit; it is absolutely necessary to have a society which shall stress the importance of good environment, so that we may be able to see what the full genetic possibilities of individual men and women, boys and girls, are.

We can sum up then by saying that what these facts about human variability seem to show is, first, that liberty and tolerance are of immense importance and, second, that a decent environment—equal for all and being equalized upwards for all —is of immense importance. It is vital not to bully people who are genetically different into being like everybody else, and, within the limits of law and order, to try and permit each individual to develop according to the laws of his own being and in accord with the principle laid down by religion that the individual soul is of infinite value. Our ideal should be what Charles Morris, the Chicago philosopher, described in his book *The Open Self:* an open society composed of open selves.

WAR AND

NATIONALISM

I PROPOSE to talk in this lecture about one of the more disturbing features of our present human situation: war and nationalism.

It is probably worthwhile to begin with a few words about war and nationalism in the abstract and more general context of biology and semantics. We often hear it said that war is inevitable because man is a fighting animal, but biologically speaking war—a conflict between organized groups of members of the same species—is a very rare phenomenon. There is, of course, continual preying of one species upon another, but in fact there are only two species of creatures which make war: one is the harvester ant and the other is the human being. These two creatures have in common the institution of property. The harvester ants from one nest collect large quantities of foodstuffs; the members of a neighbouring nest come in genuine armies and fight for the possession of these foodstuffs. In spite of the fact that harvester ants do not possess a language and therefore have no conceptual system of principles or ethical notions, these wars can last for a considerable time. Some have been observed to last for as much as five or six weeks, which is a very long time for an animal without a language system to keep a war going.

Delivered on April 13, 1959

The human being, when he makes war, can go on far longer than the ant precisely because he possesses a language and a conceptual system. We are able, even when the passion of the moment has subsided, to keep on fighting and killing because we can goad ourselves with our concepts, our principles, our categorical imperatives, to do whatever we feel we have to do. One thinks of the phrase of Matthew Arnold, 'tasks in hours of insight will'd, Can be through hours of gloom fulfill'd.'[1] This is true not only of positive tasks, tasks that we would regard as constructive, tasks willed in hours of insight, but it is also true, unfortunately, of tasks willed in hours of passion and prejudice and often of a profoundly destructive nature.

It is because we possess a symbol system and can formulate ideals and categorical imperatives that it is possible for human beings to achieve both sanctity and pure diabolism—to persist at the highest level of charity and understanding and also at the lowest level of wickedness and folly. The animal can never be an angel or a saint, a lunatic or a devil, for it lives so to speak in a condition of intermittence. You can see this when two dogs fight; they will begin with tremendous frenzy and then suddenly one will sit down and start scratching fleas and they will forget all about it. But this is impossible for human beings because they have motives for fighting; they have words that say that it is right for them to fight; they have categorical imperatives by which it is their duty to fight and not to run away.

Conflict—not war—is frequent among members of the same species. But natural selection has taken great care that conflict between animals of the same species shall rarely be pushed to the fatal conclusion. We always think of the wolf, for example, as a peculiarly ferocious and sinister animal. Actually, as naturalists have observed—you will find a full account of this in Konrad Lorenz's book, *King Solomon's Ring*—wolves never fight to the death. The wolf that feels it is going to be beaten exposes its throat to its adversary in such a way that if the

1. Matthew Arnold, 'Morality', 5–6.

adversary chose to do so, it could immediately sever the jugular vein and kill its enemy; but, owing to the benevolent action of natural selection, the vanquishing wolf finds it psychologically impossible to bite. Instead he starts growling and then turns away. One can see that there are very good evolutionary reasons for this; if male wolves habitually fought to the death over females, the species would very soon come to an end. And it is interesting to find that the injunction to turn the other cheek, which is very rarely practiced by men, is constantly and instinctively practiced by wolves.

War, which may be described as a culturally conditioned state of affairs based upon the natural condition of conflict, is precisely the opposite of this because it consists in pushing organized conflict to the limit of destruction and is not instinctive. It is very important to remember that both war and the motivating power which drives men to war are socially conditioned because it makes us realize that there is nothing biologically inevitable about the terrible thing that menaces us. Because it is a socially conditioned phenomenon, we can, if we want to, de-condition and get rid of it.

War is conditioned by human symbol systems, and in our modern life the symbol system is that of nationalism. One can say that nationalism is a kind of theology—a system of concepts and ideals and ethical commandments—based upon a natural and instinctive attachment to our place of origin and to familiar people, but extended, by means of our capacity for abstraction and generalization, far from the natural piety of the native place and the familiar folk. Nationalism uses all the devices of education to create an artificial loyalty to areas with which the individual is quite unacquainted and to people that he has never seen.

We have now to briefly consider the question, How is a nation to be defined? Many attempts have been made to do this, and it is very curious that none of the most obvious methods covers all the cases. We cannot say that a nation is a population occupying a single geographical area, because there are cases of nations which occupy areas widely separated, such as Pakistan at the present time. We cannot say that a nation is necessarily connected with the speaking of a single language, because there are many nations in which the people speak many languages—even in so small a nation as Switzerland there are three main languages, and in India there are hundreds, with twenty or thirty being quite important. (There is a very considerable linguistic patriotism within the national frame of India which does tend to produce strong centrifugal forces.) There is the definition of a nation as something composed of a single racial stock, but this is quite obviously inadequate; even if one ignores the fact that nobody knows exactly what a race is, in this country alone 10 per cent of the inhabitants belong to non-Caucasian stocks and yet are quite clearly Americans in the fullest sense of the word. Finally, the only definition which the old League of Nations was ever able to find for a nation (and I presume the same definition is now adopted by the United Nations) was that a nation is a society possessing the means of making war. Thus the feeblest and smallest nation which has some kind of a war-making machine—Libya, for example—is a nation, but an immense geographical unit with a huge population, such as California, is not a nation because it does not have a war-making machine.

It is most curious to see how profoundly this oddly arbitrary definition of the nation as a society which is capable of making war has affected history. I remember being greatly struck twenty years ago, when I was travelling in Central America and reading the history of the region, by the extraordinary story of nationalism in that part of the world. It is worth looking at this history in some detail because in a certain sense it is like a small-scale laboratory experiment which can be studied more easily than large-scale events which take place in Europe and other parts of the world. Nationalism came to Central America after 1821, when the Spanish colonies revolted against the crown of Spain because the idea of the divine right of kings had been smashed by Napoleon when he imposed his brother Joseph on the throne of Spain. (Napoleon's brutal extraction of this keystone of the great arch of Spanish loyalty led to the collapse of the whole arch.) In Central America the result was that each province of what had been the Spanish empire declared itself a nation, and even some of the departments within the provinces declared themselves nations and had to be reconquered by the provinces as a whole. It is only by chance that there is not a small state between Guatemala and Mexico called Quezaltenango; such a state did declare its independence, but then was re-conquered by the rest of Guatemala.

What happened when nationalism was suddenly born into this area? We have there a population fundamentally the same overall: a minority of Spaniards and, underneath them, the Mestizos, the Ladinos, and the Indians, who were politically quite untouched and had no relationship with the general march of affairs. Their religion—a mixture of Catholicism and the ancient Indian religions—and their economic interests were also much the same. The people had lived at perfect peace with one another for three hundred years because they took for granted that they were all subjects of the king. Then, overnight, the provinces became nations—which are by definition war-making machines—and they spent a considerable part of the following century in savage struggles one with another. These struggles were not economic in character; they were almost always ideological struggles between federalists and non-federalists, liberals and conservatives.

This, then, presents an extraordinarily interesting small-scale and simplified picture of the arbitrary nature of the whole national set-up. At one moment you are not a nation and the next moment you are. In Germany, before 1870, Germans were not Germans; they were subjects of the kingdom of Saxony or of Bavaria, etc., and Germany was not Germany, it was the Germanies. Abruptly, overnight, the Germanies were welded into a single country and German nationalism was systematically encouraged. (The beginnings of German nationalism may have been earlier, under Napoleon, but it was not until the country was politically united that the theology of nationalism was officially taught.)

The history of modern nationalism begins with the French revolution and the rise of the self-conscious nation-state. The curious and ironical feature about this is that the tremendous fervour which was aroused among the revolutionaries for the new nationalist theology was the thing which helped Napoleon to extend his conquests far and wide over Europe. By 1811 he had the intention of setting up a new Holy Roman Empire, with its capital in Paris and its second city in Rome, and of consolidating it through a most elaborate system of legitimacy and nobility. But he completely left out of account the fact of nationalism. In the process of winning the empire he had aroused the nationalistic feelings of the people against whom he had committed aggression, and suddenly his whole internationalist dream was smashed by the rise of nationalism in Germany, in Austria, in Russia. The very thing which had helped him to win his victories turned against him and finally destroyed him.

Nationalism played an incredibly important part in the history of the nineteenth century. It is interesting to see that Karl Marx, who was after all a man of extraordinary intelligence and ability, seems to have greatly under-estimated its power. In this respect, this extremely astute and penetrating mind was much less realistic than the otherwise rather woolly-minded Giuseppe Mazzini, who built up a kind of idealistic theology of nationalism but at any rate saw the enormous power latent in it. Marx seems really to have supposed that national patriotism would very soon be replaced by class patriotism. History has shown that he was entirely wrong, and he would be profoundly surprised to find that today the ideology of Communism is the principal instrument of Russian nationalism.

Nationalistic fervor still persists and has recently overtaken a number of new converts. All the ex-colonial nations exhibit an ardour of nationalism which is certainly equal to the ardour which was displayed one hundred and fifty years ago in Europe. It is an ardour which is proportionate to their hatred of the ex-colonial powers but wholly out of proportion to their capacity to be efficient, modern nation-states. This is one of the tragedies of the situation today; we find an immense desire for national independence and a tremendous, almost quasi-religious fervour with regard to it which are quite unrelated to economic and cultural facts. This is certainly going to lead in many cases to a sense of frustration, to social chaos, and probably to various forms of dictatorship.

With nationalist feeling still as strong as it ever was, we would even be justified in saying that nationalism is the prevailing religion of the twentieth century, as it was during most of the nineteenth. It looks as though it is going to remain the prevailing religion for a long time. It is as though we had reverted from the monotheism which arose in Judea and was developed under Christendom to a religion of a particularly disastrous kind—a divisive religion that places absolute value in fragmentary parts of humanity and positively condemns those who accept it to chronic strife with their neighbours. In 1862 Lord Acton said about nationalism that it does not aim at liberty or prosperity; it aims solely at making the nation, which is a kind of abstract idea, the norm and mould of the political state. He added that the results of this would be not merely material but also moral ruin, and I think this was a remarkably astute prophecy.[2]

We must bear continuously in mind that everything that is happening now, such as the explosive increase in population and the advancing technicalization of every aspect of human life, is happening in the context of nationalism. Consequently,

2. Sir John Emerich Edward Dalberg-Acton, 1st Baron Acton, "Nationality," *Home and Foreign Review*, I (July 1962), 146–174. The essay was reprinted in the collection of Lord Acton's work, *The History of Freedom and Other Essays* (London: Macmillan, 1907), pp. 270–300.

it all takes on a very dangerous quality, precisely because it is taking place in the context of what appears to be the strongest quasi-religious fervour of our period, and in a world order which by definition commits those who believe in its theology to war with one another and to continual preparation for war.

This war ethos has been reduced to a kind of absurdity, as innumerable people, including those who are now preparing for war, are never tired of pointing out. War has reached a point where there can be no victors and where the only purpose which can be achieved by entering upon it is the complete destruction of the combatants and probably the destruction of large areas of not only civilization but life itself. Everybody knows this, and yet all the people in decision-making positions in the world today—and there are not very many of them—are so completely the prisoners of the theological-nationalistic system that they find themselves under a compulsion to go on willy-nilly preparing for something which they know must be disastrous. One has this extraordinary and paradoxical spectacle of unprecedented skill and knowledge and devotion and work and money being poured out on projects which can lead not to life, liberty, and happiness, but only to misery, to servitude, and to death.

The rationalization of this is in all cases the old Roman adage, *'si vis pacem para bellum'* (if you want peace prepare for war). Unfortunately, everybody has been acting on this adage for the last two thousand years or so, with the result that, as Pitirim Sorokin of Harvard has pointed out in his most elaborately documented book, most of the great nations of the world have spent from forty to sixty years of each century in war.[3] Preparations for war have always led to war, and there seems to be no particular reason to suppose that the present armaments race can lead anywhere else.

One of the most alarming things that has happened under the

3. Pitirim Sorokin, *The Ways and Power of Love* (Boston: Beacon Press, 1954).

present dispensation is that this piling-up of armaments has come to play a vital part in Western economies, particularly in the American economy, which depends completely on the expenditure by the government of approximately forty billion dollars a year on the manufacture of armaments. It seems to me one of the most tragic things which has happened, that this preparation for something which can only be a preparation for death has become the basis of Western prosperity. This is not a new phenomenon; the recovery from the Great Depression of the thirties was not complete until rearmament had begun in a systematic way. In England an enormous housing program was put into effect in the late thirties but this did not completely eliminate unemployment; nor did the very elaborate pump-priming of the New Deal eliminate it in the United States. It was only in response to Hitler's menace, when armaments began to be manufactured on a very large scale, that the unemployment bogey was finally banished. It is a dreadful, grotesque paradox that the prosperity of the West was due to the phenomenon of Hitler. And today we see the same thing: the fear of Russian competition, which entails the putting out of vast sums of money for armament, is the cornerstone and foundation of the prosperity which we are enjoying at present. There is a kind of vested interest in the preservation of this system and it will take a great deal of thought and courage to break away and to find some alternative means for keeping the economy going.

How easy is it going to be to get this change on the way? There is one school of thought which says that war is inevitable, that this is our fate. But what is the definition of fate? I don't think we can speak in such old-fashioned terms of some sort of external influence which foresees what is going to happen to us and creates a kind of plan to which we have to conform. The sociological idea of fate is very close to that which was elaborated by Tolstoy in *War and Peace*, the idea that historical events are determined not by the choices of individuals or small groups, but by the summation of innumerable small decisions taken by countless anonymous human beings, which add up to a general tendency in one direction. At present, however, owing to the remarkable concentration of power in the modern world, this is not true; on both sides of the iron curtain there are relatively few decision-making persons. We see now that something like two-thirds of the entire assets of the American manufacturing economy is in the hands of five hundred corporations and that, among these five hundred, a smaller number actually possess the decision-making power. Members of this corporate élite are to be found in decision-making positions at the head of the pyramid of rule in this country, where we see a sort of triumvirate of power: the highest political powers plus the highest military powers plus the highest economic powers represent an extraordinary concentration of force and economic power which makes it possible for us to imagine a way out of our difficulty.

It is quite clearly very dangerous when power gets into the hands of very few people. As Lord Acton said, 'Power tends to corrupt and absolute power corrupts absolutely.'[4] But in another way the concentration of power is encouraging because it means that the problem of war is not out of our hands; it has not become a problem of completely inhuman forces, and human will can still play a very large part in it. If the people with the enormous powers are men of reasonably good will, and if it is possible to influence their decisions, then we are in a better position than we would be if we were wholly at the mercy of non-human forces pushing us inexorably in one direction.

Now we have to inquire, What can we do in the present situation? How are we to get out of this push toward catastrophe? We walk and walk, we know the precipice is going to be there. Are we going to fall over the edge? I don't know; but I don't think it is necessary. The most obvious means which pre-

4. Sir John Emerich Edward Dalberg-Acton, 1st Baron Acton, Letter in *Life of Mandell Creighton*, vol. 1, p. 372.

sents itself whereby we can get out of this dreadful situation is moral exhortation, begging people to behave, to be good, and to be sensible. Unfortunately, moral exhortation doesn't go very far in changing a political trend—although it would be quite wrong to disregard its value. It is terribly important that we should try to combat the strange kind of moral insensibility and indifference to the fact of large-scale violence which seems to have fallen upon so much of the world. We accept as natural and inevitable an immense wholesale destruction to be wreaked on entire populations. We accept as inevitable the existence of absolute weapons and of genocide, as though there were no alternative.

There seems to be in this matter of moral sensibility a kind of dual standard. I remember that just after the Korean War a number of articles appeared pointing to the fact that during the war a majority of American infantrymen never fired their rifles, and that the actual killing was done at long range by artillery and by airplane bombardment. This seems to show that there is an intense moral sensibility in face-to-face relationships which disappears when the relationship is distant and, so to speak, abstract and generalized. The age of saturation bombing and H-bombs is also the age of the welfare state; the age of massive preparation for biological warfare and the most dreadful kind of indifference to mass extermination is also the age in which violent protests occur when dogs are sent up in sputniks, and people are particularly alive to the dangers of cruelty to children.

It is very curious to see the difference between today's attitude toward mass atrocities and what used to happen in the past. I remember during the Second World War, after the saturation bombing of the city of Magdeburg, which had been largely reduced to flaming ruins, being struck by the remark of a knowledgeable commentator that the last time this had happened to Magdeburg was during the Thirty Years' War, when the armies of Tilly had sacked the town. I happened to have been reading something about it at the time, and I remember the account of the shudder of horror which went through Europe when the news of the sack of Magdeburg was published and became known in various countries of the West. How different that reaction was from the reaction during the Second World War, when similar destruction was regarded as something which had to be done—a standard procedure—and there was no particular object in being very much upset by it.

I feel that there has been a profound change even in my own lifetime. When I was a boy we still believed, with a kind of extreme Victorian optimism, that anybody who wore a top hat and took a bath every day and went to church on Sundays would be perfectly incapable of the sort of atrocities that the Turks had committed against the Armenians. But in the First World War we discovered that even people who took baths every day and wore top hats were capable of that kind of thing. The goodness of civilized man, which had been taken for granted while I was still a boy, was changed into a taken-for-granted native badness of man, for whom anything was possible. Since then we have been taking the destructive side of human beings for granted more and more, and talking in the most light-hearted way about large-scale destruction. Even children, with the kinds of toys they play with now, take it for granted. I was greatly struck the other day, meeting a group of children in the street—the smallest of them was crying bitterly, and I heard him say to the others, 'Give me the machine gun.' It gave me rather a turn.

It is extremely important for anybody connected with education and with writing and with religion to attempt to close this schizophrenic breach in our moral sensibility. We cannot go on separating the welfare state from the genocidal absolute weapon; we have somehow to bring the sensibility which works in the former into the area of the latter, where it doesn't work. Although I don't think its immediate effects are going to be very striking, this is a most important task to be done. We have to create the right kind of atmosphere in which suitable political action can be taken.

Now let us pass from morals to politics. Here we are confronted immediately by the fact that most of the people involved in the armaments race regard any alternative to it as utopian. But, after all, aren't *they* being a little utopian? Isn't a policy which everybody admits is a policy of complete destruction a utopian policy? They call themselves realists, but I would say that they are utopian realists. They are realistic about the means they employ—nothing could be more realistic than the way they approach the problem of the absolute weapon and the methods of delivering it—but nothing could be less realistic than the ends proposed, because there are no ends except the end of the human race. On the other hand, the utopian idealist lives in the stratosphere and implores everybody to be good and kind and sensible, but offers no practical method of implementing his good intentions. What we need is a kind of realistic idealism or idealistic realism which can offer some sensible alternative, to make it possible to transfer the conflict onto another level which does not involve these horrors.

Let me quote something which I wrote in 1946 in a small book called *Science, Liberty and Peace,* where I discussed these issues and pointed out that it was absolutely necessary to try to shift the whole attention of politics from the insolvable problems of power to the solvable and even more urgent problems of human needs. This is what I wrote apropos the San Francisco conference:

> At the San Francisco conference the only problems discussed were problems of power. The basic problem of mankind—the problem of getting enough to eat—was relegated to an obscure international committee on agriculture. And yet it is surely obvious that if genuine international agreement is ever to be reached, it must be an agreement with regard to problems which, first, are of vital interest to the great masses of humanity and which, sec-

ond, are capable of solution without resort to war or the threat of war.[5]

I still think this is true and I am glad to see that more and more people are taking the same line—that the only acceptable mode of conflict with the other great power bloc, which will be to the immense advantage of both power blocs and the great masses of humanity, will be precisely a conflict as to who can provide the two-thirds of the human race who now live in misery and undernourishment with the means of assuring some kind of decent life for themselves and their children.

Unfortunately, the decision-making people are always extremely well-fed and are not particularly concerned with the problem of subsistence. They subsist a great deal too well, probably, in many cases, and their first question is a question of power: Who shall bully whom? But the masses of the people are concerned with the problem of subsistence, and their first question is: Where is my next meal coming from? Two-thirds of the human race belong to this undernourished mass of people who are in general completely disregarded. The decision-making people never really consult these masses on what they would like. If they were consulted, if a referendum of the whole world population, a Gallup poll, were instituted, we could ask them the question: Do you prefer the present system of power politics and armaments races, or do you prefer to have enough to eat? You cannot have both, because it is quite clear that countries which are spending 40 or 50 per cent of their revenue on non-productive armaments are not in a position to improve the agricultural situation of the backward nations or to help to industrialize them. As long as the current system of power politics and of preparation for war within the context of nationalism goes on, so long will persist the misery of these two-thirds of the world, who are increasing at an enormously rapid rate, and who

5. Aldous Huxley, *Science, Liberty and Peace* (New York: Harper & Row, 1946), pp. 73–74.

will soon be more than two-thirds.

In this context I would like to read a few passages from a letter which was sent by President Sukarno of Indonesia to the English periodical the *New Statesman* last summer. The *New Statesman* had carried a series of very interesting letters, the first from Bertrand Russell, then one from Nikita Khrushchev, and one from Secretary John Foster Dulles. Finally President Sukarno wrote:

> We of Asia are but pawns in the game of nuclear powers . . . However, it would be most unwise to disregard Asian opinion. In all sincerity, I tell you that we are growing increasingly resentful of the present situation. Asians are the chief victims of the West's failures and moral bankruptcy.
>
> We in Asia do not see you as saviours of civilization or as forerunners of the future; we see you as agents of death—our death . . .
>
> We utterly deny the right of the West to continue imperilling us and our future . . . It is past time for the West, Communist and anti-Communist alike, to draw back from the edge of complete moral bankruptcy. It is explicitly your task to utilize the skill and technique of your science for peaceful purposes. One tenth of the treasure and skill used in making your hydrogen weapons could transform my country . . .
>
> There can be no question now of the West giving moral leadership to Asia. Your moral leadership has, for us, meant first colonialism and now the philosophical, moral, political and social bankruptcy of a nuclear arms-race . . .
>
> You in the West are causing more gaps between humanity; you are also losing the battle for the hearts and minds of men.[6]

I think it is very valuable for us to see ourselves as others see us, and to realize that this is what the leaders of the unfortunate two-thirds of the world think of us and what they expect of us.

I cannot go into the details of the kind of policy which should be pursued. Such a policy has been set out, lucidly and ex-

6. *New Statesman,* 28 June 1958, p. 828.

tremely well, in a very valuable book by Professor Wright Mills of Columbia University, *The Causes of World War Three,* which I heartily recommend to everybody. He sets out what he thinks an idealistically realistic policy for the West would be, and also guidelines for changes in American policy and modes of thought, which would permit pressure to be put upon what he calls the 'power élite', the decision-makers at the top of the social pyramid. Meanwhile, he calls upon his fellow intellectuals and educators and writers to do all they can to help prepare the moral atmosphere in which such a change could take place.

I will close these remarks by pointing out that perhaps now is a fairly propitious time to come to some kind of agreement, not because I think anybody has had a change of heart, but because the advances of technology are making the present situation exceedingly precarious, and they are making it precarious in a new way. As a recent article in the *Bulletin of the Atomic Scientists* pointed out, it is now possible for at least twelve nations, some of them quite small, to produce the hydrogen bomb within five years or, if they carry out a crash program, even sooner; and the last thing that any of the three great nuclear powers wants is for the hydrogen bomb to get into the hands of anybody else. Obviously the world situation would become fantastically precarious, and the power of the great powers would be very seriously compromised. If Lichtenstein and Monaco had the bomb, they would be in a certain sense on a level with the United States and with the Soviet Union, which is obviously a situation which neither of these countries could possibly tolerate. For this reason I do think that there is a better chance for making a beginning in disarmament; this would consist in the banning of nuclear tests, which would make it very difficult or impossible for any other nation to produce a bomb. I think that such a test ban is now more likely to be negotiated than it has been recently, and it will become increasingly likely as the capacities of the small nations to reproduce the bomb at a cheap rate become greater.

I also think that if we attack this problem on all fronts at once
—on the moral front, the political front, the persuasion front,
the technological front—there is some considerable hope that
we may get ourselves out of this dreadful situation into which
we have, by our folly and also by our good intentions, alas,
succeeded in putting ourselves. We can see some prospect of
making the decision not to go to the edge of the precipice, but
to draw back in time.

THE WORLD'S

FUTURE

BEFORE beginning on any se-
ries of forecasts, I think it is worthwhile to say a few words about
man's different conceptions of the future. Most of us do not
realize that our view of the future is a fairly recent phenomenon or that the ways the future has been looked at by people
both within and outside our tradition are very different from
the way in which we look at it. The Indians have a cyclical idea
of time—the notion that there is an eternal recurrence and that
time repeats the same pattern over and over again. According
to the Indian idea, we are now at the last phase of one of the
great cycles, in the Kali Yuga, the Age of Iron. We have been
in it for about two thousand years, and apparently there are
about thirty-five thousand years more to go, during which
things will get worse and worse all the time—we 'ain't seen
nothing yet,' according to the Indians. After that, there will be
a general explosion, and we may then, after several million
years, start again on an Age of Gold. A similar view of time was
taken by the ancient Greeks: there was a great year which
repeated itself continuously.

Our present view of the future is entirely different. The notion of an eternal recurrence, which as late as Nietzsche was

Delivered on April 20, 1959

preached by some philosophers, has really gone out of the picture altogether. We think of time not as going round and round, but as moving irreversibly in one direction. The whole idea is expressed in the scientific notion of increasing entropy: we are continually moving in one direction, and life is a temporary reversal of entropy within the larger system.

In the Christian tradition, instead of eternal recurrence there was the idea of a definite creation in time (according to Bishop Usher, in 4004 B.C.) and a definite ending, which would take place probably very soon—and hence, a complete lack of interest in the future. This is how Professor J. B. Bury, who has written perhaps the most interesting book on the subject, sums up the Christian idea: 'According to the Christian theory, which was worked out by the Church Fathers, and especially by St. Augustine, the whole movement of history has the purpose of assuring the happiness of a small portion of the human race in another world. It does not postulate a further development of human history on earth.'[1]

We have also changed very much in relation to this Christian tradition. One can say that the early Christian notion of the future, insofar as it was a happier and progressive future, was a notion of what is vulgarly called 'pie in the sky'. This changed profoundly during the eighteenth and nineteenth centuries to a new conception of what might be called 'pie on the earth'— the idea of a world improving through indefinite periods of time. This idea of a progress, which some thinkers regarded as absolutely inevitable while others regarded it as conditional, but which in any case goes forward and may be expected to reach a pitch of perfection in a distant time, replaces the ancient idea of an Age of Gold in the past with either a sudden fall (as within the Christian tradition) or a gradual deterioration (as within the Oriental traditions).

Just as in the past the old conception of 'pie in the sky' jus-

1. J. B. Bury, *The Idea of Progress* (New York: Macmillan, 1932), p. 56.

tified both resignation to an intolerable lot upon earth and persecution, so in exactly the same way this idea of 'pie on the earth' has fostered both resignation and persecution. Under the old dispensation, it was right, in St. Augustine's delicious phrase, to use 'benignant asperity' toward heretics in order to safeguard their eternal bliss in the next world. To destroy them in this world was as nothing compared to the good you were doing them by saving them in eternal life. In the same way, we see in the modern world the most appalling persecutions and liquidations going on, not in the name of Heaven, but in the name of the extraordinarily good time which our great-grandchildren will have in the twenty-second century. The idea is that if we liquidate enough people now, then there will be this magnificent time, two hundred years from now which will go on forever, getting better and better. People used to compensate themselves for the miseries of life in this world by reflecting on life in the world to come; this same resignation to present misery is found today among people who reflect about the much better times that are coming in the future upon earth.

The compensatory idea of a better life in heaven has played an enormous part in the social life of the world. Historians agree that the Wesleyan movement in the eighteenth century was instrumental in guaranteeing England against a violent revolution. The intolerable conditions created in the first generations of the industrial revolution were made tolerable to the labouring masses, who were living in conditions of indescribable wretchedness, by this ardent preaching of the happiness which was going to be theirs after death. In the same way there seems to have been a real feeling during the nineteenth century, among the oppressed and the miserable, that this wonderful good time which was going to come on earth in two or three centuries was in some way a compensation for the miseries being suffered in the present. We have some very interesting literary expressions of this idea from the nineteenth century. One of the first is to be found in Tennyson's poem 'Locksley

Hall', which was published in 1842. This is a very curious poem. The hero is a young man who has been bitterly disappointed in love and who consoles himself not with philosophy, and not with religion, but by reflecting on the march of progress and on the wonderful things which will happen in the future. He talks about the increase of knowledge and of virtue and finally about the parliament of man, the federation of the world.

A few years later, in the same year as the publication of the *Origin of Species*, you find Victor Hugo, in France, talking even more lyrically about progress and what it means to man. He has the most fantastic passage where he speaks of man sailing in a kind of magic ship through the ether. The ship is the calculus of Newton mounted upon the odes of Pindar—a mixture of inspiration and science—and man is sailing clothed in light into the pure and divine future, into virtue, into shining knowledge, into the end of plague and disaster, into abundance, into calm and laughter and happiness, into union with heaven. This goes on for hundreds of lines. It clearly was Victor Hugo's brand of religion, and perhaps a majority of the great literary figures of the nineteenth century felt rather the same way. There are, however, a few exceptions. You will find in Alfred de Vigny, for example, an extremely sceptical reaction to the first railroads. He was by no means convinced, as Victor Hugo and the French historian Jules Michelet were, that railroads were going to transport the human race into universal peace and universal virtue. On the contrary, he spoke of the potential danger of new machinery to man, the danger that the machinery might actually enslave its creator. It is interesting to see this dark picture appearing just at the time when there was the most unbounded optimism in regard to technical progress.

Outside the world of literature, you find these same ideas very strongly expressed at the time of the first of the universal exhibitions, the Great Exhibition of 1851 in London. This was opened by the prince consort on May 1, 1851; he spoke of it as the realization of the unity of mankind. In the staid columns of the London *Times* there were equally enthusiastic editorials which said the Exhibition foreshadowed universal peace, that this May 1 was the first morning since the Creation in which all the peoples had assembled from all parts of the world to perform a common act.

This tremendous enthusiasm did infect almost everybody, but it is interesting to find that the new religion of progress was regarded at the time by the guardians of Christian orthodoxy as extremely dangerous and heretical. In the *Syllabus of Errors,* published in 1864, Pope Pius IX lists as one of the grave errors (which must be pointed out and condemned) the idea that the Roman Pontiff should come to terms with, and reconcile himself to, progress, liberalism, and modern civilization. This was definitely a heresy which must not be accepted. Thus we see the incompatibility between the new view of time and of human development on earth, and the traditional Augustinian view of time on earth as quite unimportant, with future betterment existing only for a few and in another world.

In 1859 we come to the crucial year of the publication of the *Origin of Species,* which introduced the new scientific conception of the world as an evolutionary world which began in the immensely distant past and, without any breach of continuity at all between the lower forms and the highest human forms, will go on indefinitely into the future. The evolutionary theory as such is neither optimistic nor pessimistic, but it can be interpreted either way. There *have* been progressive movements within evolution—it is absurd to say that a human being is not superior to an amoeba. He clearly *is* superior. At the same time, however, it is quite clear that the evolutionary process has not been progressive along *all* lines; many have become extinct or completely stagnant, and the world today is full of what might be called living fossils.

Therefore, although there has been quite clearly a line of progress within the line of evolution, it cannot be said that the theory of evolution, when applied specifically to human beings, justifies neither pessimism nor optimism.

The prevailing interpretation in the latter half of the nineteenth century was optimistic. There were pessimists, such as Eduard von Hartmann, but they were much less influential than someone like Herbert Spencer, who developed a most elaborate and essentially optimistic evolutionary philosophy. The inevitability of progress seemed almost self-evident to Spencer; he regarded it as a law of equal validity with Newton's law of gravitation. (Unfortunately, his whole theory assumed as its basis the inheritance of acquired characteristics, which we now have every reason for believing to be untrue.) There is no question that Herbert Spencer did exercise a prodigious influence in the second half of the nineteenth century, and that there was generally an extremely optimistic view of the future, a belief that progress was happening all the time and would almost certainly go on happening. I remember the golden glow of this optimistic theory when I was a child, the notion that we, who were fortunate enough to live in the more civilized parts of the world, were really incapable of doing the sorts of things that people had done in the remote past or that people were doing in the uncivilized parts of the world. If somebody had asked me as a child, or my parents, if they thought that within my lifetime we should see large-scale revival of slavery, of torture, of persecution for heretical opinions, of mass deportations, we would have said, 'It is absolutely impossible!' Nevertheless, we have seen these dreadful things, and our hope in regard to the inevitability of progress has been very much shaken. We are convinced that we live in a world of incessant change, but we are not at all convinced now that this change must necessarily be in the direction which our system of values would regard as excellent. If we use enough intelligence and goodwill, we probably *can* achieve a high degree of progress, but it is up to us to see that this happens, and there is nothing in the processes of change themselves which is going to compel it to happen.

This tempered optimism is the most prominent view of the

future, but another interesting fact is that with the coming of the hydrogen bomb human technology has reintroduced into the thinking of the West the old eschatological idea of the end of the world. The sudden and catastrophic ending of the world about which the Apocalyptic literature talks—a notion we had come to regard as untenable and absurd—has become once more a real possibility. Again, whether there shall be an indefinite future or whether there shall not is up to us.

Let us now consider, from our present viewpoint, what is likely to happen in the future. We begin with the very long-range view taken about four or five years ago by Sir Charles Darwin, the grandson of the naturalist, who is himself a physicist, in an interesting little book called *The Next Million Years*. It would seem at first glance that it is quite impossible to foresee what is likely to happen within a million years; and yet, in a certain paradoxical way, it is easier to make prophecies about very long spans of time than about shorter ones. The reason is quite obvious. When we deal with great spans of time we deal with huge numbers, and the average behaviour of great numbers of things or persons or events is more predictable than the behaviour of small numbers or of individual events. We see evidence for this everywhere around us. No fortune teller of our acquaintance has ever made a fortune by telling fortunes, but no insurance company has ever gone bankrupt. The reason is that the insurance company foretells the future for millions, and therefore can always be sure of making a profit, whereas the fortune teller tells a fortune for only one person and is likely to be much more often wrong than right. The same is true in regard to forecasts over great periods of time. The ups and downs tend to level themselves out and a general line may perhaps be projected into the future.

Sir Charles Darwin's view is simply that man is a wild species —he has not been domesticated. A domestic animal is one which has a master who teaches it tricks and controls its breeding, either by sterilizing it or crossing it with certain definite types, and therefore makes sure that future generations follow a particular pattern. But man has no master, and even his attempts at self-domestication are doomed to frustration inasmuch as the ruling minority which does the domestication itself remains a wild species. For this reason, in Darwin's opinion, man will never transcend the limitations imposed upon a wild species. Whatever may happen in short periods of history, in the long run the human species, like all other wild species, will live up to the very limits of its food supply with a large proportion in a state of semi-starvation all the time. This will go on, with ups and downs, Golden Ages and Iron Ages, during the ten thousand centuries he is envisaging. After a million years we may expect the species either to be extinct or to have evolved into quite a different species.

This is rather a gloomy point of view, and I don't think it is entirely justified. Sir Charles Darwin does not give credit to the human race for the extraordinary amount of ingenuity it has and its ability to get out of the extremely tight corners which it gets itself into, and perhaps he does not give credit to the human race for its exceptional toughness. The human species is probably the toughest species of all animals. It can exist in every conceivable kind of environment, and it can stand the most appalling strains and stresses, apparently better than almost any other species. Therefore, it may be that this long-range view, which has certain philosophical justifications, may prove to be wrong, owing to the remarkable capacity of man to spring surprises.

Meanwhile, we have to consider the short range, which is more interesting to us. What are our short-range prospects? Let us begin with the military and political prospects immediately confronting us. These were discussed a few years ago by Bertrand Russell, and it seems to me that his conclusions are extremely realistic and sensible. He says that there are three possibilities. First of all, if we get into a nuclear war, there is the possibility of the complete extinction of the species—and perhaps of all life upon earth if the nuclear war is sufficiently prolonged and waged with sufficiently deadly weapons. This is improbable, however, in the present state of technology.

The second possibility is that the nuclear war would result in a return to barbarism. Under present circumstances, this second alternative seems to have a good deal of probability, for the reason that a complex industrial system such as we depend upon now has very close analogies to an ecological system in nature. In nature, if we disturb one element in an ecological system, we throw the entire system out of gear. Analogously, if we were to destroy pretty thoroughly even one or a few elements in the complex industrial system, and if there were to be, for any reason, high mortality among the specially trained personnel on whom we depend for the functioning of the system, then it seems extremely probable that the whole industrial system would break down—it would be virtually impossible to run without one or another part of it—and the result would probably be a return of barbarism. For what we must remember is that the present enormous populations of the world are enabled to live solely in virtue of possessing this very complicated industrial and communications system. If it were to break down, enormous numbers of people would probably die of starvation and the survivors would naturally indulge in civil wars in order to get the few resources remaining. The very great number of deaths immediately following the explosion of the H-bomb would thus be followed by an even greater number of deaths and an immense chaos.

It would also be extremely difficult ever to rebuild the system because, after a serious atomic war, mankind would not start from scratch, it would start several hundred years behind scratch. When the system was originally built, with rather primitive machinery and tools, resources were plentiful. Metallic ores were extremely rich and quite easy to get at. Today, after one hundred fifty years of exploitation, this is not at all true. It would be very difficult for any people which had been reduced

to a primitive level to rebuild a complex civilization on the basis
of the rather impoverished resources left, particularly in those
countries which have been highly developed up to now. You
would have the paradox that it would be easier to rebuild an
industrial civilization in those parts of the world which had not
been previously industrialized and more difficult to rebuild it in
those parts of the world which had been previously industrialized and which had greatly reduced their resources of ores.

The third alternative which Lord Russell looks forward to is
the creation of a single world state, which could occur in one
of two ways: by force, as the result of one power being victorious
in a nuclear war—that is to say, if one power could ever be
victorious—which in fact is the way that previous empires have
always been build up; or under the threat of force, under the
fear of what might happen, and as the result of reason and
considered enlightened self-interest and humane ideals. This,
naturally, would be the desirable way of creating what Wendell
Willkie called 'one world'; but it must be confessed that the
historical precedents are not very encouraging. Take the case
of Italy. From the time of Dante onward, every intelligent
Italian saw that it was absolutely essential to have a united Italy,
but Italy was not in fact united until 1870, and then it was
united only by military force, by the Piedmontese. And to this
day you can meet Italians in Southern Italy or Sicilians who will
speak rather bitterly of the time when the Piedmontese de-
scended upon Italy and forcibly drew it together into a single
country. The same thing is true of Germany. The final unifica--
tion of Germany came after the Franco-Prussian war and was
essentially an act of force. One sees the same thing in the building up of a unified France through the use of force and cunning
by Richelieu in the seventeenth century. If there is a unification
by conquest in the future I would say that, should the West win,
we should see a kind of very superior, up-to-date Roman Empire as it was at the time of the Antonines; if the East should
win, we would see a very much more unpleasant kind of em-

pire, in which Western people would find themselves living on the wrong side of the tracks and thoroughly discriminated against.

Can we expect the coming together of the nations into a single world government, which is obviously infinitely desirable? And can we expect it to happen by democratic means? Can one expect a course of action which is manifestly good for everybody in the long run, but which in the short run causes discomfort or even suffering to a good many people, to be taken by a democratic society in time of peace? It seems to me rather dubious that this should be the case because there are enormous vested interests involved—and not merely the vested interests of the rulers, although rulers of a sovereign state do not wish to become merely officials in a province. Similarly, the owners of factories do not want to subordinate the interests which flourish under a tariff system or to subordinate themselves to the interests of a much larger unit outside the present borders of the country, where there will be more efficient factories which will throw their own out of business. There are the vested interests of many workers, who might be displaced from their work or thrown out of employment altogether and forced to migrate to other parts of the country. There are also the vested interests of intellectuals, who don't wish to change their ideas, and indeed the vested interests of everybody—no one wants to alter the conditioning which he has had in childhood.

In general, one can say that it is only when human beings are threatened by somebody else that they are ready to unite and to accept short-range privations for long-range goods; they are ready to unite under the threat of war and catastrophe. Undoubtedly, the best thing for world government under law would be an invasion from Mars. Unfortunately, this is rather unlikely to take place. But is it possible to persuade ourselves that after all human beings are their own Martians, that with over-population and over-organization and over-technicalization, we are committing immense aggressions against ourselves? Can we unite against ourselves for our own higher interest? It might be possible, by suitable education and propaganda, to put this view across, that what we regard as a piping time of peace is not, in fact, a piping time of peace, but that there is a real threat overhanging us all the time against which it is enormously in our interest to unite. This is rather remote speculation, but it is possible that some such argument might finally persuade people to take the step of getting together and forming a government in which all should live together under law.

These seem to be the immediate military and political possibilities in front of us. Now we have briefly to consider the technical and industrial prospects. Here the problem is one of resources. For those who wish to know more about this, I would advise them to read Harrison Brown's *Challenge of Man's Future*[2] and Brown, Weir, and Bonner's book, *The Next Hundred Years*, where all the figures are given.[3] When one considers that the amount of planetary capital consumed by the United States since the end of the First World War is greater than the entire amount of metals, fuels, and minerals consumed by the entire human race before that, one realizes what a fantastic drain upon resources is now going on. In order to carry on our present civilization, we require 1000 pounds of steel per head per annum, 23 pounds of copper, 26 pounds of lead, 3.5 tons of stone, gravel, and sand, 500 pounds of cement, 400 pounds of clay, 200 pounds of salt, 100 pounds of phosphate rock—in all, about 20 tons; and then, added to this, each member of the population requires the equivalent of 8 tons of coal to provide energy for him per year.

One sees that the amount of resources which is being used in the modern technical civilization is incredibly great. One of the consequences, as I hinted before, is that the easily accessible rich ores have to a large extent been exhausted. Fifty years ago

2. Harrison Brown, *Challenge of Man's Future* (New York: Viking).
3. Harrison Brown, John Weir, and James Bonner, *The Next Hundred Years* (New York: Viking, 1966).

a good copper ore contained 5 per cent of copper; today, ores are being worked with hardly more than 0.5 per cent of copper. And this is certainly going to continue. We are going to have to work poorer and poorer ores until finally we are exploiting granite and sea water to get the metals and minerals that we require. Theoretically this can perfectly well be done, and even in practice one can see how it could be done, but it will undoubtedly require far more work to get our raw materials than we put into it now, and it will entail an immense mechanization far beyond anything that we envisage today.

How long will our planetary resources last? The estimates vary greatly, from a few hundred years to a few thousand, but it is quite clear that sooner or later the richer ores will be exhausted.

Here Dr. Harrison Brown has posed a question: What likelihood is there of man's being able to make the transition from an industrial life based upon rich ores to an industrial life based upon the poorest ores, a transition that will require an incredible amount of ingenuity and skill? Dr. Brown, like Bertrand Russell, offers three alternatives. One is that we will succeed in making the transition, but that we shall then have a world-wide industrial civilization completely controlled by a totalitarian authority. The second possibility is that the transition will be made and that we shall then have a world-wide free industrial society devoted to the full development of human beings; but this alternative, while obviously the most desirable, is extremely difficult both to achieve and to maintain. The third possibility, which Dr. Brown thinks the most probable of the three, is that within the next thousand years or so, provided we escape war, we shall find ourselves gradually reverting to the agrarian state.

Let us consider now some of the more immediate possibilities and prospects in front of us. We begin with biochemistry, where such great authorities as Albert Szent-Györgyi are convinced that means will be found for controlling population, thus stabilizing world conditions and making some kind of reasonable development possible. He leaves out of account that the problem is not merely biochemical but sociological, psychological, philosophical, and religious, though on the biochemical level at least, I think we can look forward to such developments. In regard to food production, there seems to be no doubt that this can be enormously increased by the development of new varieties of plants through directed mutation, by the creation and domestication of various types of bacteria and fungi for producing different kinds of edible substances, and by new methods of finding water. Stephen Riess is working on methods of finding what has been called 'juvenile water', thus making possible the irrigation of vast areas which at present are completely barren. It seems fairly clear that if we can stabilize the population, it should be possible to feed it at an adequate level—although, inasmuch as the meat diet is extremely wasteful, probably with a vegetarian diet.

There will also certainly be advances in chemistry. I expect one of the most important will spring from basic research in photosynthesis, in the field of what may be called radiation chemistry. It will certainly be found that an enormous number of chemical processes can take place in controlled radiation— not merely in sunlight, but in the harder radiations possible now that we have large atomic piles. Quite unprecedented kinds of chemical synthesis will become possible.

Incidentally, all this will happen entirely as a result of basic research, not ad hoc research. We still tend to be obsessed with doing research to solve a particular problem, but the basic discoveries come only as a result of basic research. I read the other day a very amusing remark by Dr. Szent-Györgyi about the nature of basic research. He said,

> When I first came to this country ten years ago, I had the greatest difficulty to find means for my basic research. People asked me, what are you doing, what is it good for? I had to say, it is no good

at all. Then they asked, then exactly what are you going to do? I had to answer, I don't know, that is why it is research. So the next question was, how do you expect us to waste money on you when you don't know what you do or why you do it? This question I could not answer.

Such questions are not asked as often any more. All the same, there is plenty of room for improvement.

From the biological and chemical worlds, let us pass to the human world. In the field of psychopharmacology we shall probably see extraordinary developments as the result of research in basic metabolism, with the creation of a better environment for the central nervous system and the consequent elimination of a great many mental disorders and psychophysical diseases. We may also see the kind of scientific application which the eminent geneticist Professor Hermann Muller speaks about—the application of eugenic methods to the improvement of the human stock. Muller speculates about what he calls 'foster parenthood' and the possibility of the creation of a new kind of morality, by which people would think it more important to bear children who were the best possible in the field of nature rather than children who exactly reproduce their parents' idiosyncrasies and weaknesses. This would be possible through foster parenthood of children conceived by the union of reproductive cells derived from stocks representing the parents' highest ideal. Sooner or later eugenics will be practiced, although it is certainly going to take a tremendous revolution in our present ethical ideas on the subject. It may be added that the first nation that does practice such eugenic methods as Professor Muller advocates will in a few decades be enormously superior to all its rivals—which seems to me yet another reason why we should, as quickly as possible, by hook or by crook, achieve the 'one world' ideal; in the context of nationalism eugenics could become an instrument of extraordinary power and extraordinary danger.

Then we come to purely psychological processes. Psychology is, quite obviously, still in its infancy, and we can foresee remarkable developments. It may become possible within two or three generations to understand the processes of creative thinking, to find out how these processes can be systematized, how they can be taught, how human beings can be educated so as to live to the height of their potential instead of using only a small part of their capacity. Such purely psychological advances, added to those in the field of psychopharmacology, will probably greatly improve the performance of human beings. If these are conjoined with eugenic procedures, we can foresee with considerable confidence a remarkable improvement in the human creature. What Emerson said long ago, that all men plume themselves on the improvement of society but no man improves, will cease to be true. It may even be possible now to get men to improve and thus to improve society. Though no one knows whether this *will* be accomplished or not, we are perfectly justified in saying that it *can* be accomplished now.

Let us very briefly talk about mechanical advances. Probably the most important of these will be connected with the great electronic computing machines, which will enable us to perform feats of thinking and problem-solving of which we were never capable before, and which will, therefore, open up to rational action areas in which it was quite impossible in the past. It may be possible even to conceive of making rational policy decisions—knowing what all the possibilities in a field are and choosing the best. Such decisions have been left entirely to the intuition of politicians in the past, but they now may come under the control of fact and of reason based upon fact. I was reading just the other day in a recent number of *Harper's* magazine about a fascinating new electronic device used for doing research in the back numbers of scientific periodicals. This is an appalling job at present; there are many thousands of papers published every year, there is a backlog of literally millions of them, and it is incredibly difficult to discover what has, in fact, been done in this jungle of material. Now a machine has been developed into which you can put magnetic tape to which the subject matter of the papers has been transferred, and in a very short time the machine will tell you where you can find out what you wish.

And we mustn't forget our friends the Sputniks and satellites. These will be exceedingly useful, not so much in regard to outer space as in regard to the earth. They will give us extremely good information about weather. (I was appalled to read a statement from Dr. Werner von Braun the other day saying that satellites will be sent up and a number of them connected together by radio into a kind of electric relay which will permit TV programs to be globally transmitted at any moment. This is a grave menace, but there it is!)

In conclusion, it seems quite clear that enormous possibilities lie open to us, that we are on the threshold of profound discoveries within our own nature and in external nature. If we can solve the basic political and demographic problems, we could produce a world of the most incalculably superior nature. Whether we shall do so or not, I don't know, but it is very important to realize that the immediate future is probably immensely important in regard to these possibilities. Harrison Brown has summed it up by saying that the next hundred years will undoubtedly prove to be more critical than any that mankind as a whole has been called upon to face. This is a very sobering prospect, but I think it is perfectly true.

More than fifty years ago Tolstoy said that in a society which is badly organized, as ours is, where a small minority rules over the majority, every scientific advance and conquest of nature strengthens the hand of the minority against the majority. It is up to us to decide now whether these conquests of nature and accessions of knowledge are to be used for frightful and inhuman ends, or whether they are to be used to create the kind of progress of which we have dreamed—and, indeed, the kind of progress of which nobody has ever dreamed, because the potentialities which are now opening up before us have never been present in the history of the world before.

THE INDIVIDUAL

LIFE OF MAN

In this lecture I shall discuss the relationship between man on the macroscopic level and man on the microscopic or individual level. What is the relationship between the individual and his society and the historical process in which both are involved? This seems a fairly obvious and trivial question, but I think it is actually a question of considerable importance; there is nothing self-evident about the relationship between the individual and the greater mass of historical and social life within which he is embedded.

I shall start with a physical analogy, not with a biological analogy, because the biological analogies so frequently used in discussing sociological matters are essentially false. I don't think, for example, that society is an organism, as many people have said. An organism is a creature having its own life, able to direct itself, having sense organs and some sort of central nervous system; society does not seem to have any of these characteristics. We shall be much nearer the truth if we say that society is an organization within which individual organisms have their place.

The analogy I want to use is a very simple one: the analogy of gases and the individual molecules which compose them.

Delivered on September 21, 1959

The laws of gases deal with the interdependence of volume, pressure, and temperature. They are quite simple laws and extremely instructive and helpful in regard to our dealing with gases in any considerable quantity. The molecules of which gases are composed, however, possess neither temperature nor pressure, and almost no volume, so that the laws which apply to gases do not in the least apply to molecules. The only attributes of molecules which are relevant to the behaviour of gases are kinetic energy and the tendency to random movement. It is the combination of these two attributes which, when the molecules occur in sufficient numbers, leads to the characteristic behaviour of gases according to the formulations of the gas laws. The point that we have to stress is that gas laws are entirely different from molecule laws and that what holds true in one sphere has almost no relevance in the other.

In the same way we see that there is a profound difference between the generalizations which we can make about societies at large and the generalizations we can make about individuals. We cannot, by exercising empathy in relation to individuals, say anything about society; and conversely, we cannot, from the generalizations which we can infer from the observation of society, say anything about the behaviour of particular individuals. We see this very clearly in the statistics which are constantly being printed in the papers. We know that, according to the actuarial statistics of life insurance companies, the average age of death is sixty-seven for men and seventy-two for women. But this tells us nothing about when Mr. or Mrs. Jones is likely to die. There is then this gulf: the life of the individual, which is a life of self-consciousness, a life of feeling, a life of will, a life of urges and intentions, does not apply to society. The generalizations which can be made in the larger, social sphere are possible only because very large numbers and very considerable durations of time are involved.

In general we find that the greater the numbers involved in any natural event, the more precise are the generalizations—

the so-called natural laws—which we can formulate. This was one of the great discoveries of the nineteenth century, which Ludwig Boltzmann made very clear in his classical work on heat. The same basic notion underlay the whole Darwinian theory, which was in fact the statement of the average behaviour of enormous numbers of individuals. Within societies the numbers of individuals are extremely small when compared with the numbers of molecules within a unit of gas or of atoms within a human body. Consequently, the generalizations which we can make from the observation of a society have many more exceptions than the laws of physics and chemistry (and they are not so precise and accurate). Nevertheless we certainly can make some generalizations about society as a whole, and, although many sociologists have attempted to go much too far in formulating them, such laws have real value and are capable of giving us some power to predict the future. However, when we come to the behaviour of individuals, we find that a knowledge of these laws is not particularly helpful—it doesn't help us to predict what Tom, Dick, and Harry are going to do. There is a basic differentiation between the natural sciences and the historical sciences. The natural sciences seek to reduce diversity to unity by finding the similarities between objects or events and by making a generalization about them, whereas in the study of history on the small scale, and in the study of biography, we remain concerned with particular cases. In the world of natural science it would almost be necessary to leave out of account a miracle, if it were to take place, because a miracle is something which can never be repeated and which occurs outside the general law of averages; but within the sphere of history, if a miracle took place we should certainly have to take account of it.

Let us now consider the relationship of the individual to history. Every individual life span obviously runs parallel to a sector of the general historical movement of the age in which the person lives. But to what extent do we *exist* in history? To what extent is an individual *in* the history of his time? To start with we must ask the question, What is history? Ideally, history is the record of everything that happens; clearly there could never be such a record because it is much too complex to set down and, anyhow, the changes and chances of the past have eliminated practically all information about earlier periods. In fact, what historians describe as history is simply those aspects of the past which, according to their own philosophy of life, they regard as particularly important and significant. Let me take an example from what a philosophical historian, Arnold Toynbee, says about the history of our time:

> What will be singled out as the salient event of our time by future historians, centuries hence, looking back on the first half of the 20th century and trying to see its activities and experiences in that just proportion which the time-perspective sometimes reveals? Not, I fancy, any of those sensational or tragic or catastrophic political and economic events which occupy the headlines of our newspapers and the foregrounds of our minds; not wars, revolutions, massacres, deportations, famines, gluts, slumps, or booms, but something of which we are only half-conscious, and out of which it would be difficult to make a headline . . .
>
> Future historians will say, I think, that the great event of the 20th century was the impact of the Western civilization upon all the other living societies of the world of that day.[1]

But if the impact of the West on other cultures is the really important historical fact of our time, then virtually none of us is in history. For we are not subjectively cognizant of this impact of the West upon other cultures or of the impact of other cultures upon the West.

A similar case in point is the thirteenth century, which is generally regarded by modern historians as one of the great golden ages of the human spirit, the age of scholasticism and the great cathedrals. Yet if you read the works of any of the moral-

1. Arnold J. Toynbee, *Civilization on Trial* (New York: Oxford University Press, 1948), pp. 213–214.

ists, the people who were the contemporaries of St. Thomas Aquinas and the cathedral builders, you find that all of them are agreed that their age was an age of decadence, that never were men so immoral and delinquent as they were at that time, that they were much stupider than they had been in the past, and so on. Who is right? Were the people who actually lived through the age of scholasticism and of the cathedral builders correct in thinking that theirs was an age of decadence, or are we correct in thinking that it was a golden age when the spirit of man developed in an extraordinary way? This is a question that remains open; probably in a sense both are correct. But what is brought home very clearly is that what we live through subjectively is very far from being the essence of history as perceived by the historians of a future time. We have to be aware of the curious fact that we are living in two worlds and that our individual world does not correspond to the large-scale one with which the philosophical historian deals.

To what extent is individual life, which runs parallel with the great stream of history, in fact within that stream? The most startling fact about every individual life is that a third of it is passed entirely outside of history and even outside of space and time, so far as subjective experience is concerned: a third of our life is passed in sleep, in which we are neither in space nor in time, from an internal point of view. Nor are we in history; we just pass out of the world of history into a state of temporary not-being. It is a state which is absolutely essential to us because in it we take refuge from our hideous egotistic activities in order to regain a certain amount of the health and sanity which we are always undermining by our conscious activities.

Shakespeare has a wonderful passage about sleep in *Macbeth:*

> Sleep that knits up the ravell'd sleave of care,
> The death of each day's life, sore labour's bath,
> Balm of hurt minds, great nature's second course,
> Chief nourisher in life's feast.[2]

2. William Shakespeare, *Macbeth*, II. ii, 37–40.

This is exactly what sleep is—the extraordinary accession of new life and new insight which come in during those eight hours out of the twenty-four when we can escape from ourselves. Even the most violent fanatic or the most delinquent gangster is, for a third of his life, in this moment of complete unconsciousness when he can forget his ego, in some way reconciled with the deep, divine source of all being. It is a beautiful thought that even a Hitler, even a Himmler, even a Genghis Khan, even a Jay Gould, even a Richelieu can forget for a moment his fearful daytime preoccupations.

A very interesting fact, when we come to social organizations, is the discovery that they never sleep. Social organizations live, so to speak, in a state of chronic insomnia; they never depart from themselves nor open themselves up to new accessions of life and insight. They are corrected from time to time only by individuals—who do get the benefit of sleep and therefore can reform social organizations in a rational way. As Mr. Bumble said, 'the law is a ass'—for the reason that the law never sleeps.[3] The Church suffers similarly. There was a hymn which I used to sing very frequently at school, one of whose verses goes,

> We thank Thee that Thy Church unsleeping,
> While earth moves onward into Light,
> Through all the world her watch is keeping,
> And rests not now by day or night.

This watchful sleeplessness may account for the deplorable facts of ecclesiastical history. The Church is periodically reformed by people who get inspiration from sleep and from the deep mind, and because of this it remains as sane as it does. But it suffers from the defects of all organizations inasmuch as, not being an organism but merely an organization, it does not have the capacity to retreat and take holidays from itself; it never sleeps and cannot recuperate.

To come back to the individual and the extent to which he is in history, we find that there are a great many periods in his

3. Charles Dickens, *Oliver Twist*, Chapter 51.

life besides those spent asleep when he is out of history. These include infancy and most of childhood. During those periods he is living an almost wholly private life in which public affairs have very little influence at all. The same is true of old age and decrepitude, and periods of sickness, too; here the individual is so much diminished that he falls out of public life altogether, and because of his narrowed attention and the chronic pain and frustration, he lives quite out of all relationship with the public world. Finally, the most private and non-historical act of all is the act of death, in which there is a narrowing down of attention until the individual is taken totally out of the world of history. It is true that there have been eminent men who have tried to remain historical even on their death bed. There is a very painful story about Daniel Webster, who talked excessively to his friends while he was dying and wound up by asking, 'Have I said anything unworthy of Daniel Webster?' It seems to be a terrible thing that a man at this moment of life should feel it necessary to be still a public, historical figure, to worry about whether he was still worthy of his own reputation.

When we add up all the periods during which we are out of history—the period of sleep, the period of infancy, the period of extreme old age and decrepitude, and the period of sickness —we find that out of the average seventy-year life span the individual probably spends about forty years completely outside of history. He just isn't there at all in relation to the grand historical generalizations which sociologists and historians make.

Even as a mature and self-conscious being, however, the individual spends a great deal of time in a life which is purely private and not historical. The definition of private life which I like the best is one given by the Russian essayist Vasili Rozanov about thirty or forty years ago. He said that private life is 'picking your nose, and looking at the sunset.'[4] This is a very beauti-

4. Vasili Vasilievich Rozanov, *Solitaria* (New York: Liverright, 1927), p. 96.

ful definition; if you interpret it in a more general way, you see
that what it really means is that private life consists in enjoying
your purely physiological reactions and your aesthetic and in-
spirational reactions. Naturally we tend to rationalize and explain these experiences in terms of the prevailing culture.
Nevertheless they do remain amazingly private and apart from
the general historical movement of the time in which we live.

It seems to me worthwhile to look at the case histories of some
poets and other artists in relation to the time in which they
lived. Wordsworth wrote his *Lyrical Ballads,* the whole of *The
Prelude,* and the great odes (including the 'Ode. Intimations of
Immortality') between 1795 and 1807, that is to say, at the
height of what was until very recent times the most overwhelming period of change in European history—the period of the
French Revolution and the Napoleonic Wars, which inaugu-
rated the modern epoch. Although Wordsworth talks in *The
Prelude* about his reactions to the French Revolution, the really
significant thing about all this mass of poetry is its nature mysticism, which is what appeals to us, what makes Wordsworth live
and seem important in the modern world.

One of Wordsworth's contemporaries was Jane Austen; *Pride
and Prejudice* was written in 1796 and the other novels between 1811 and 1816. Yet not only was Jane Austen's life hardly
affected by the considerable events going on in the world
around her, practically all her characters remained completely
unaffected. Once or twice there is a faint hint—some of the men
may be in uniform—but that is about all. It is remarkable to
think that these novels, with their immensely intimate and
ironical analysis of the family life of every day, should have been
written in the midst of the most fantastic upheaval of modern
times.

Another example—a man I happen to have been much inter-
ested in at one time, was the French philosopher Maine de
Biran, the greatest metaphysician of the eighteenth century.
We know a great deal about his private life because he left a

very detailed diary covering almost every year of his adult life. It is interesting to find what was going on in Maine de Biran's mind in the early summer of 1794, which was the year of the execution of Danton and the year Robespierre's power was at its height and the Terror in full swing. Maine de Biran was living in his own house in the country, a good way from Paris. He wrote, 'Today, May 27, I had an experience too beautiful to be ever forgotten. I was walking by myself a few minutes before sundown . . .'. There follows a rather long passage about how the night of nature filled him with a kind of Wordsworthian ecstasy, and ravishment succeeded ravishment, and, he continued, 'if I could perpetuate this state I should have found upon this earth the joys of heaven.'[5]

Biran came closer to history during the hundred days. At the time of Napoleon's first abdication, he had gone over enthusiastically to the royalist side—he had always been a loyal supporter of the King—so when Napoleon came back from Elba he was in a very awkward and unpleasant position. But even then he was able to escape into the world of pure intellectual speculation: 'I live in this world of speculation foreign to all the interests of the outside world. These speculations keep me from thinking of the actions of my fellow men, and this is fortunate, for I cannot think of them except to hate them and despise.'[6] In the same way, in an earlier century, we get the testimony of Montaigne, who says in his marvellously frank and honest way, 'I cannot too much stress with how little an expense to my peace of mind I have lived half my life in my house, while my country was in ruins.'[7]

Such facts are of enormous significance. They show that

5. Maine de Biran, *Oeuvres* (Paris: Librairie Felix Alcan, 1920) vol. I, pp. 52–53.
6. Maine de Biran, *Journal intime inédit,* 1815, quoted in A. de la Vallette Monbrun, *Essai de biographie historique et psychologique: Maine de Biran* (Paris: Fontemoing, 1914), p. 265.
7. Michel de Montaigne, *Works,* trans. G. Hazlitt (Boston: Sheldon, 1862), vol. 3, p. 376.

even this small-scale, short-range, catastrophic history, which goes on all the time in its violent and brutal way, and which, as Toynbee says, occupies 'the headlines of our newspapers and the foregrounds of our minds,' does not very much engage us. Although at certain moments we may be painfully involved, for the most part we can continue to live our intensely private lives.

This was certainly the experience of a great many people during the catastrophes of recent years, although a very important point which has to be stressed is that in contemporary times—above all in totalitarian countries, but to an increasing extent in democratic countries as well—the governmental authorities have gone out of their way to prevent people's escaping into their private lives during moments of crisis. Hitler had the strongest objections to permitting people to live in their private world, and the Russians still do, insisting upon everyone's becoming engaged and enmeshed in short-range history. It would be very difficult now for a Maine de Biran or a Jane Austen to live quite so completely apart from the historical moment, largely because wars and revolutions involve entire populations rather than small bodies of professional fighting men.

Nevertheless the difference between private life and public life, between biography and history, still remains a very strong one. We see clearly in the nature of our newspapers the fact that most people are not much interested in the public life of their times. Most of the space in newspapers is given up to the more sensational events of private life, such as murders and divorces, and a relatively small amount is given to the consideration of the great historical events of our time. This is the most striking difference between newspapers in the Western world and newspapers in the totalitarian regimes, where almost no space is given to the adventures of private life and the ideas on which public life is based are drummed in continuously in propagandist articles. This makes the newspapers, I imagine, incredibly dull, but it serves the purpose of the rulers, which is to indoctrinate their subjects and to make them go single-minded in a certain direction.

One of the best ways of looking at the divorce between private and public life is to consider the idea and the fact of progress. To what extent is it a fact of our subjective life? Progress is a modern myth which arose in the time of the Renaissance and came to its flowering in the eighteenth and nineteenth centuries. Previously the whole idea had been that man had had a golden age in the past and had been going steadily downhill since. From the time of the Renaissance onward the golden age was in the future and man was going up. There have been several versions of the myth. There was the idea, which was very popular in the eighteenth century, that if you got rid of priests and kings, then automatically the golden age would appear. Then there was the myth of the nineteenth century, that industrialization would bring universal peace. This expression of the myth died rather painfully during this century; the First World War and the Russian Revolution gave it a serious blow, and it was polished off by the more recent events of the Second World War and the Atom Bomb.

But although the myth is no longer tenable, we can nevertheless say that progress is a fact. There is quite clearly a trace of progress recognizable within the natural order—the fundamental basic progress from the inorganic to the organic, the evolution of giant molecules which could reproduce themselves and which made life possible, the passage from extremely simple forms of life to more complex forms capable of adapting themselves to different kinds of environments and finally even controlling the environment. We see progress from the animals which produce their young with eggs to the animals which produce embryos and control temperature within the body and then to the animals which develop a highly organized nervous system. Although it is quite clear that within the biological range everything which has developed in the past persists to this day—the giant molecules still persist in the form of viruses; so do the single cell organisms still persist—nevertheless at the leading edge of the development there is something which can quite clearly and legitimately be described as progress. The same thing seems to be true even within the human sphere, where evolution has ceased for the most part to be biological and hereditary. We still have the same kind of innate capacities which our ancestors had, but—owing to the facts that we have language and can accumulate knowledge—we use those capacities in a much more effective way for controlling our environment today than in the past. We are perfectly justified in saying that there has been genuine progress, although one can still go about this world and find neolithic and even palaeolithic people.

The question, then, is: While this progress can be observed objectively, to what extent can it be experienced? Obviously the original biological progress was never experienced, partly for the good reason that for about two billion years there was nobody to experience it in a conscious way. Even after man arose, for almost all of his time on earth he was, as an individual, completely unable to experience progress, for the simple reason that progress took place extremely slowly.

Now, however, progressive changes in the field of technology and the field of ideas are taking place in spans which are measured by decades or less. Thus it should at least theoretically be possible for the individual to have a direct subjective experience of progress. And, to some extent, he does. Nevertheless it remains true that we don't experience progress subjectively very much, although we observe it, we read about, we see the signs of it in buildings and new types of airplanes and so on.

There are many reasons why we don't experience progress as much as we might expect that we should. To start with, human life is not a progressive action. It rises to a certain level, proceeds on a plateau, and then sinks down. Inasmuch as human

life is intrinsically non-progressive, we cannot expect that there
will be in many phases of it a very strong subjective experience
of the progress which we can objectively observe. It is very
difficult to ask old people to be aware of the world going up and
up when they themselves are going down and down. In the
second place, man has an almost infinite capacity for taking
things for granted. When something new comes in, it is rather
astonishing for a day or two, and then it is accepted as part of
the order of things. What today is a golden ceiling overhead
becomes—when we make the climb and get to it—a disregarded floor under our feet. Then, too, we must remember that
every child is born into the world as it exists at that moment and
has no experience of the world as it was before. To a child born
into the world at the present time, TV and jet planes are a part
of the order of things. He has no idea of the sort of world in
which I was brought up, which was a world of horses and trains,
although these curious (to him) neolithic survivals still exist.
This is another reason why it is as exceedingly difficult for us to
experience progress subjectively as it is to experience other
aspects of public and historical life: most of us are concerned
only with the facts of our private lives, with family relationships,
with squabbles, with jealousies, with pity for the people around
us, with envy, with sex, with gossip. We are involved only in the
life of the molecule, not in the life of the gas.

For all these reasons, then—because our life span is so short
and progress in the past has been so slow, because we take
things for granted, because human life is itself non-progressive, and because we live and want to live so much in our
isolated, insulated private life—these great objective facts are
very little experienced by us, and we find ourselves living in a
strange amphibious world. Man is a multiple amphibian, living
in many double worlds and leading many double lives, and
one of them is undoubtedly this life of being a private individual embedded in a history which one can see objectively but
which one doesn't experience. Dr. Johnson, who was ex-

tremely hardboiled about idealism and pretensions, has a couplet which expresses it all very clearly. It is not good poetry, but it is a good epigram:

> How small of all that human hearts endure,
> That part which laws or kings can cause or cure.[8]

We can add to kings and lords such items as technology and scientific invention, and we shall find that the same thing remains true: there is a very small part of history which is felt subjectively to be of supreme importance to us. As Dr. Johnson says, 'publick affairs vex no man'[9] and the news of a lost battle never caused any man to 'eat his dinner the worse.'[10] Conversely, the news of a scientific breakthrough or some immense discovery never makes any man eat his dinner the better.

This state of amphibiousness between society and the individual, between history and biography, is an odd and uneasy kind of existence. But we have to accept it, and in any process of education we have to prepare young people to live in both worlds—to live as best they can in their individual world and, if possible, to take an intelligent interest in the historical one. They probably can never feel the historical world subjectively as they should—or perhaps they shouldn't; I think it is a great blessing that we *don't* feel it subjectively most of the time. Anyhow, they should be aware of it intellectually and objectively, so as to be able to be useful citizens. For this is always the problem of human beings—to realize amphibiousness and to know that they must make the best of this world and of that.

I will conclude this brief sketch of our amphibiousness with a passage which has always touched me very much, from a strange late Elizabethan poet, Lord Brooke:

8. Lines contributed to the end of Oliver Goldsmith's 'The Traveller or, A Prospect of Society' Cf. *The Poems of Samuel Johnson* (Oxford: Clarendon Press, 1941), p. 380.
9. James Boswell, *Life of Johnson*, 15 May 1783.
10. Ibid., 18 September 1760.

Oh wearisome Condition of Humanity!
Borne under one Law, to another bound:
Vainely begot, and yet forbidden vanity,
Created sicke, commanded to be sound:
What meaneth Nature by these diverse Lawes?
Passion and Reason, selfe division cause.[11]

11. Fulke Greville, Lord Brooke, 'Chorus Sacerdotum' from *Mustapha*.

THE PROBLEM

OF HUMAN NATURE

In the last lecture we discussed the rather curious relationship between the individual life and the public, historical life of man. In the lectures which follow I shall talk about the individual. I shall try to pose and answer the question, Who precisely are we? What sort of creature is the human being? Are we, as Descartes said, a completely individualized ego, whose essence is consciousness, and who is related only to one part of matter within the body? And is matter entirely of another class of reality, having as its essence only extension? Or are we, as modern empiricists are inclined to believe, a monistic mind-body? Is the self completely insulated from all other selves, or is there some kind of psychic medium in which all selves bathe, so that the individual is not totally cut off from other minds?

I want to start with the manner in which people in the past have thought about human nature. The terms in which they discussed the problem are of course very different from the terms in which we discuss it; they dealt with fundamentally the same facts in terms of different frames of theoretical reference. Nevertheless, I think it is worthwhile making this historical detour because when we examine what people have thought in

Delivered on September 28, 1959

the past about the nature of man, we find that it does throw a great deal of light on the problem.

I shall begin with the theory of man as we find it in the well-spring of Western civilization, that is to say, in the Homeric poems. The best way of starting is to read a passage from the nineteenth book of the *Iliad,* where the terrible quarrel between Agamemnon and Achilles is made up. Agamemnon apologizes to the enraged Achilles for having taken away his girl, Briseis, and explains why he did it. He says,

> I was not to blame. It was Zeus and my lot and the Fury that walks in the darkness, that blinded my judgement that day when I confiscated Achilles's girl. What could I do? At such moments there is a power that takes command, Ate, the eldest daughter of Zeus, who blinds us, the cursed sprite that she is, flitting through men's heads, corrupting them, bringing down now this one, now that one. Why, even Zeus was blinded by her once, and Zeus is known to stand above all men and all gods.[1]

Instead of regarding this as a way of shirking responsibility, Achilles accepts the explanation wholeheartedly and says, 'how utterly a man can be blinded by Father Zeus!'[2]

The creature Ate which Agamemnon speaks of in this passage is a very interesting personage. In the later Greek tragedians the word 'Ate' stands for disaster in general, but in the Homeric poems 'Ate' means the state of mind that *leads* to disaster—the kind of infatuation, the moral blindness, the fact of being carried away, which leads men to do things against their better judgement and even against their rudimentary interests.

We see here that what we should call unconscious urges and drives is explained in the terms of the ninth century B.C. as intervention from without by supernatural forces. In a word, the whole theory of Homer is based upon the idea of demonic or divine possession. The gods either intervene directly or else they intervene by some agent such as Ate—who is herself a

1. Homer, *Iliad,* XIX. 87–100.
2. Ibid., 282.

divine being—and they cause us to do preposterous and dreadful things.

Besides the bad interventions, there are in Homer also good interventions, where the supernatural powers suddenly come and help us. The word *menos* occurs very frequently in the *Iliad* and in the *Odyssey;* it means power, strength, the accession of some new insight or ability, the capacity to do something difficult or impossible. *Menos* will suddenly come upon a man in battle, or it will come upon him in counsel, giving him wisdom and intelligence. Even animals are capable of *menos;* a horse can suddenly have a great deal of *menos* and gallop at a much greater rate than it could before. So we see that the two sides of what we shall call the unconscious self are represented by two kinds of supernatural interventions.

In Homer, an intervention may be either by some known god —Zeus, or Zeus's immediate agent, or Athena, or any of the other gods—or else it may be by some supernatural being whom one doesn't know. In this case the intervention is spoken of as being caused by a *daimon,* an anonymous god of some kind. The *daimon* idea comes right down into Classical Greece. Socrates's monitions—the little voice that he heard, telling him to avoid doing things which he ought not to do—was the voice of a *daimon,* a divine being. An interesting aspect of what Socrates has to say about these irrational interventions coming from what we call below the threshold of consciousness is the idea that there are several kinds of madness. There is a natural madness due to disease and there are two kinds of supernatural madness: the destructive madness brought about by Ate, or by one of the gods who wishes to bring us down, and the helpful madness, which Plato divides into four categories—the prophetic madness (as illustrated by the Oracle of Delphi); the Dionysian ritual madness of the orgiastic catharsis; the poetic madness; and the erotic madness. Socrates says in one place that 'the greatest blessings come to us by way of madness,'[3] provided

3. Plato, *Phaedrus,* 224 a.

always that the madness be given to us by divine gift.

It is worth remarking that the idea of supernatural possession went on exercising a tremendous influence on men's minds, and was accepted as a rational explanation of many peculiar forms of human behaviour, until well on in the seventeenth century. I happen to have made a study of this matter as it occurred in the seventeenth century; I wrote a book on the celebrated case of the Devils of Loudun, which is a story of the so-called possession of an entire convent of nuns. One sees in reading the theologians, the moralists, and even most of the doctors of the period, that the idea of demonic possession seemed absolutely obvious in those days. Until one has an adequate theory of the subliminal self, the idea of possession is completely logical and sensible. It seems to be about the only way in which these strange phenomena can be explained.

It is interesting in this context to see how the Greeks dealt therapeutically with many of the psychological problems which we treat either with drugs or by psychotherapy. Anxiety states, they found, could be dealt with very satisfactorily by getting people to participate in the Dionysiac orgies, which were great dances that went on for hours and hours until people went into a kind of ecstasy and even fell down in a state of exhaustion. Later on came the corybantic dances, which were diagnostic as well as cathartic. As far as one can make out, the point of the corybantic dance was first of all to listen to certain types of music, each of which expressed the personality of some god, and then, by seeing which music the sick person reacted to, learn which was the god responsible for his possession. Not only did one enter into the cathartic dance; at the end of the dance one performed the requisite rituals and made the proper sacrifices and so obtained an absolution which undoubtedly helped toward the consummation of the cure.

This kind of thing still goes on at the present time. Last year in Brazil I had the opportunity of witnessing several *Macumba* dances (they are called *Macumba* dances in Rio, *candomblé* in

Bahia). These are Brazilian adaptations of West African tribal rites; they are practiced by the Negroes, who are in an extremely poor economic position, and who lead pretty intolerable lives of great frustration. They work off their accumulated frustration on Saturday nights, not by getting drunk, but in a much more satisfactory manner: by dancing from sunset to the following sunrise. I would say that the therapeutic results of these Saturday night dances are at least equivalent to six months on the psychoanalytic couch at fifty dollars a time. And the Greeks did this regularly—what may be called group therapy, in Greek terms.

Most educated people ceased to believe in possession towards the end of the seventeenth century, and there was a curious interregnum during the eighteenth century and a good part of the nineteenth when there was really no satisfactory explanation of these very odd phenomena. Either they were simply disregarded, or they were explained as the French Commission which sat on the Mesmer case (in which Benjamin Franklin took part) explained what was then called mesmerism and what we now call hypnotism—in terms of something vaguely called 'imagination'—and as such dismissed.

It was not until the latter part of the nineteenth century that the theory of the unconscious as a dynamic force was developed in order to explain the facts of experimental hypnosis and of hysteria, which were being systematically studied in Paris by Jean Martin Charcot and in Vienna by Josef Breuer and Sigmund Freud. This theory provided for the first time a really satisfactory alternative to the possession hypothesis.

I think it is important to remark, however, that in his own way Homer was extremely realistic subjectively, if not objectively. For many of the sudden urges or hunches or insights which even normal people have are felt as though they were invasions from the outside or supernatural interventions. Among people in an abnormal state of mind, the sense of being possessed by external forces is extraordinarily strong. These people hear voices and see hallucinations, and it is almost impossible for them not to believe that some alien force is attacking them.

As a matter of cultural history, it is interesting to see how the 'explanation' of this universal and everlasting human phenomenon—what people 'see' and 'hear'—has varied at different ages, in terms of the different *Weltanschauungs* which have been accepted at the moment. The idea of supernatural possession lasted from the time of Homer right through the Christian epoch until at least the seventeenth century. Then, in the middle years of the nineteenth century, after the rise of spiritualism, many people regarded phenomena such as those produced by the Fox sisters in 1848 as due not to possession by supernatural beings but to possession by departed spirits.

In modern times, the explanations are in most cases very different. Like most people who have published books and have become to some extent public figures, I receive a great many unsolicited letters, some of which come from what I suppose is the lunatic fringe (sometimes one has the sense that the fringe is like that on a Spanish shawl—that there is more fringe than shawl). I have had in the last few years at least a dozen of these pathetic letters, and I am reminded of it because just the other day I received one from Sweden, from a gentleman who has written me as long ago as 1952 about the same problem. In exactly the same way as in many of the other letters, he complains that he is being subjected to bombardment by some new kind of radio, which he says is in the hands of a group of (as he describes them) 'homosexual-fascist-communists' who are sending out messages and pumping them into his mind; and the poor man is in this terrible state and can get no relief because the Swedish police are in league with his enemies, and so on and so forth. This is a very common phenomenon. These experiences which are felt as invasion, and which would have been interpreted in the past as possession by supernatural beings, or possibly as possession by departed spirits, now appear to be possession by an electronic device. Nothing changes, but everything changes. The fundamental experiences remain the same, but the cultural frame of reference in which we explain them varies profoundly from age to age.

Now we have to go back again for a moment to Homer, to see what exactly is the nature of the self. We have talked about deep irrational drives which are produced (in Homer's terms) by the intervention of supernatural beings. But what is the human personality on which these interventions take place? The interesting thing in Homer is that, as far as he is concerned, there is no such thing as a permanent soul. The word 'psyche' is used by him, but never in relation to the mind of a person during his lifetime. It refers only to the thing which leaves the body at the last breath and which then becomes a ghost, like the ones seen by Ulysses in Hades. These ghosts are insubstantial— they are not personalities at all—and, if you remember, they can only communicate with Ulysses after he has fed them with blood. He makes a sacrifice and pours the blood into the trench; the ghosts drink a little of it, take on a little materiality, and are able to talk with him.

This is the only use of the word 'psyche' in Homer. For the rest, the personality is seen by Homer very much as many modern empirical psychologists see it, as a kind of bundle of symbiotic complexes. There is the *ego*, which is more or less equivalent to what he calls the *noos*, the rational side of man. Other forces within the personality include *thumos*, the organ of feeling, which is one of the most important; it is located in the chest and mounts up very often into the nostrils and the head. Then there is the midriff, the *fren*, which means mind, organ of passion, life. The belly also plays an important part, rather as in the Jewish tradition, where the bowels are the seat of compassion and the heart of affections.

Homer's psychology is curiously like the psychology of early Buddhism, although Homer is not so incredibly and painfully systematic. The early Buddhist idea is that man is *anatta*, without a substantial soul. He consists of a group of *skandhas,* which are complexes, partly physiological, partly emotional, consisting partly of the appetitive and partly of the reflective and intellectual side of man. All the facts of human behaviour can be explained in terms of this *skandhas,* just as Homer thought that all the facts of human behaviour could be explained in terms of the *thumos, fren, noos, ego,* and so on.

One of the most interesting facts about Homeric psychology, in which it also resembles very much the older Indian psychology, is that there is virtually no reference to the will. It seems to us extremely strange that these older psychologists don't talk about the will, but if you don't have a unitary controlling soul, then the idea of will doesn't seem to be so very important, and it seems to be possible to get on without it. In the marriage service, to the question 'Dost thou take this woman to be thy wedded wife?' we would answer 'I will'; but the Homeric hero, if he was being fully logical, would say, 'Well, my *thumos* and my *fren* are all for it, and in spite of the fact that my *noos* has certain reservations, I will go along with my viscera, all the more so as I can feel definitely the symptoms of possession by Aphrodite.'

The idea of a multiplicity of semi-independent forces loosely bound together within the mind-body, whose symbiosis constitutes the personality, has been commented upon by Professor Martin P. Nilsson, who wrote a few years ago in the *Harvard Theological Review* that 'Pluralistic teaching about the soul is founded in the nature of things, and only our habits of thought make it surprising that man should have several "souls." '[4] Homer was not a philosopher, but he was an extremely acute observer—what may be called a kind of palæo-empiricist—and in a certain sense he anticipated the judgement of Hume on the nature of the human being. For Hume insisted that there is no

4. Martin P. Nilsson, "Letter to Professor Arthur D. Nock on some fundamental concepts in the science of religion," *Harvard Theological Review,* vol. 42, no. 2, p. 89.

observable self. All that we observe is a 'bundle or collection of different perceptions, which succeed each other with inconceivable rapidity, and are in a perpetual flux and movement.'[5]

So much for the position of Homer, that man has no substantial, detachable soul, but is a bundle of semi-independent symbiotic forces, half physiological and half psychological. This was the current notion about 800 B.C. About 400 years later the Greek notion of the personality was entirely different. We find in Socrates and Plato that it is completely self-evident that man has a unitary soul and that this soul is detachable and can survive after the death of the body. The question arises, What is the reason for this profound change? It used to be fashionable to say that maybe there had been influences from India, but recent scholarship inclines to the belief that the important influences during that period were from the North. It was in the seventh century that the Greeks first began penetrating into the area of the Black Sea and founding colonies upon its shores. There they came into contact with the Scythians, who practiced a form of shamanistic religion such as is still practiced in Siberia and Central Asia—or *was* practiced until the inhabitants of those parts of the world were converted to Marxism.

The shaman was a medicine man who established contact with the gods, but he did it in a way fundamentally different from the way in which the Delphic Oracle, the Pythia of Delphi, established her contact with the gods. The Pythia of Delphi was what the Greeks called *entheos:* she had the god inside her, she was filled with the god—from *entheos* comes our word 'enthusiasm'—and the god spoke through her in the first person. Apollo, when he spoke through the Pythia, said 'I' in precisely the same way as the modern medium speaks with the voice of her control. The shaman, on the contrary, did something quite different. He didn't wait for the god to come into him. He went out to look for the god. He practiced what in

5. David Hume, *A Treatise of Human Nature*, I, iv, 6.

modern mediumistic jargon is called 'travelling clairvoyance'. He went into a trance and got out of himself and moved about the world and came in contact with divine beings and saw what was going on in other places.

Whether clairvoyance is a fact or not, I don't know. But it is absolutely undoubted that certain people believe it to be a fact. They have a capacity for apparently going out of themselves, getting information from distant places, and getting into contact with what appear to be divine beings. They also seem to have the capacity of getting into contact with previous existences. One of the interesting things about the shamans is that they remembered their earlier existences as shamans of an earlier date, and the fact that they were reincarnations of people who had had the same power in the past was one of the things which gave them their power to be shamans in the present.

Modern scholarship inclines to believe that the rise of the Orphic holy men in Greece was essentially due to shamanistic influences from the Black Sea and that in fact such Orphic holy men as Epimenides were shamans. And there is no doubt at all that Pythagoras was profoundly influenced by the Orphic holy men and took on from them many features of his system, which in turn influenced the later philosophers.

In the Pythagorean system reincarnation was no longer regarded as the privilege of very few exceptional people (the shamans). It was democratized and made available to all. This had a very profound theological and psychological effect because reincarnation ceased to be a reward and a source of power, as it had been for the shamans. Instead the implication was that reincarnation was a kind of punishment and that each person was living out a life that was in fact the hell of previous lives, a kind of misery and horror from which the one desire was to escape. Thus we get already among the people influenced by Orphic thought the idea of original sin, that no one is innocent, that all men are evil—*poneroi,* as the Greeks said.

And so we find ourselves, from the time of Pythagoras on,

with this new notion of a substantial unitary soul imprisoned in a body for offenses which have been committed in earlier lives. The phrase *'soma sema'* (body equals tomb) begins occurring in Greek in the fifth and fourth centuries, an idea which is absolutely opposed to anything that had ever entered the mind of Homer, to whom the body wasn't a tomb, but a part of the personality. With a sort of canonization of these ideas by Socrates and Plato, we get the beginning of the mind-body dualism which then was systematized and made scientific very much later on by Descartes, and which has haunted Christian thought ever since. This distinction between mind and body, and the sense that the body is very bad, that the spirit is in some way alien to the animal side and to nature in general—this semi-Manichaean point of view—is very far from the Hebrew tradition, which completely accepts the life of the body. Nevertheless, in spite of the fact that Christianity derives from the Hebrew tradition, this Greek dualistic and puritanical side, which springs from the Orphics and goes on to Plato, often predominates.

It is worth spending a moment to discuss the Hebrew point of view with regard to the soul. In the earlier parts of the Old Testament there is no immortal soul. Man is rewarded on this earth, and soul and body are completely joined. The personality is a mind-body, and just as Homer has no word for the substantial soul, so Old Testament Hebrew has no word for the general conception of body. It seems so obvious that the two go together that it is not necessary to make the distinction. On the other hand, there were numerous words for the various organs of the body, and we find in the Old Testament, and also in the New, that psychological ideas are constantly expressed in physiological terms. Joseph's bowels 'did yearn upon his brother' (Genesis 43:30) and God's mercy is equated with bowels by Isaiah. St. Paul urges the Colossians to put on 'bowels of mercies, kindness, humbleness of mind, meekness, long-suffering' (Colossians 3:12). In Philippians he exhorts his correspondents by the bowels of Christ (1:8) and speaks of the 'bowels of mercies' (2:1). In the Psalms we get constant references to the kidneys, which have a deep psychological meaning. God 'trieth the heart and reins' (Psalms 7:9) and he tests man's faith; 'my reins also instruct me' (Psalms 16:7), 'Examine me, O Lord, and prove me; try my reins and my heart' (Psalms 26:2), 'Thus my heart was grieved, and I was pricked in my reins' (Psalms 73:21), and so on.

This constant reference to the bodily expressions of personality and conditions of behaviour runs through the Old Testament in the most realistic way. There is a kind of proto-empiricism here which, as in Homer, stresses the great importance of the physiological side of man. And with modern developments in endocrinology we now realize that these things are perfectly true. The reins, or rather the little glands on top of them, the adrenals, are of enormous importance to us. The fact of having more or less adrenalin or no adrenalin in the blood makes a profound difference to our personality. We have discovered that many of the violent and sudden experiences which seem to us completely irrational and which are experienced subjectively, as though they were interventions from outside, are in fact due to sudden physiological uprushes of chemical materials created within the body.

While we are talking of these chemical mind-body changes we should also mention the external chemicals that are taken in from the outside and can produce profound effects upon the mind. As Housman said,

> Malt does more than Milton can,
> To justify God's ways to man.[6]

And there are many chemicals a great deal more effective than beer. Incidentally, one of the most fascinating by-paths of the history of religion is the one that traces the use of chemicals in various religious traditions for the purpose of changing the state of mind and producing enthusiasm, the sense of god within.

6. Alfred Edward Housman, *A Shropshire Lad*, lxii.

Almost all religious traditions at one time or another made use of some such chemical mind changers, from wine in the rites of Dionysius to beer in the rites of the Celts, and to peyote in the rites of many North American Indians. It would take me too far afield to go into this, but these religious traditions, which we are today beginning to investigate, make us much more sympathetic with the empirical and semi-physiological way of looking at the mind which was current among the Hebrews and in the time of Homer.

Let us now try to sum up what has been happening. We may say that the history of psychology since the time of Homer has taken the form of a kind of spiral. We begin with the mind-body, this personality which hasn't got a single controlling soul. We pass then to the idea of a detachable soul as it was developed by Plato. And in recent years we seem to have come around again to a position which is 'above' the Homeric one—a kind of scientific empiricism, where we are inclined to accept the idea of an inseparable mind-body composed of rather loosely associated elements which don't necessarily form a single unitary soul.

The question remains whether beneath this Humean or Buddhistic arrangement of *skandhas* there is some kind of pure ego or *atman,* as the Indians say. This is something which we shall have to discuss in later lectures, but I would like today to quote a few words of Bertrand Russell on the subject: 'it does not follow [from Hume's view of human personality] that there is no simple Self; it only follows that we cannot know whether there is or not, and that the Self, except as a bundle of perceptions, cannot enter into any part of our knowledge.'[7] I would be inclined to dispute this. I think that there probably are methods by which the pure ego or self or *atman* can enter into our consciousness, and I shall talk about them in later lectures. But meanwhile we have to bear in mind that, as Russell says, the

7. Bertrand Russell, *A History of Western Philosophy* (New York: Simon and Schuster, 1945), p. 663.

existence of a loosely conjoined aggregate of powers does not necessarily mean that there is no simple soul or *atman*. It merely means that it is extremely difficult, but not impossible, to contact it.

THE EGO

I N this lecture I want to start giving an answer in contemporary terms to the extremely difficult question of who we are.

Let us begin with the notion of 'I.' The 'I' remains very much what it was in Homer's time—that is to say, the self-conscious being who uses verbal symbols, who is able to employ reason, who looks before and after. This 'I' was defined in its essential form by Descartes as the creature who thinks: *'cogito ergo sum'* —I think, therefore I am. More recently, beginning with Maine de Biran in the eighteenth century and going on with Schopenhauer, Nietzsche, and, later, Henri Bergson, William James, and John Dewey, the 'I' has also been defined as the creature who wills. Instead of *'cogito ergo sum'* the phrase should be *'volo ergo sum'*—I will, therefore I am.

I would say that, in fact, the 'I', the self-conscious being, is the creature who wills and who thinks. This creature finds itself habitually confronted by what Maine de Biran called 'organic resistances'. In a word, the 'I' finds itself surrounded by a number of 'not-I's' within its own organism; it is only one among a considerable number of very important and dynamic factors.

We will begin thinking of these 'not-I's' on the level of the

Delivered on October 5, 1959

137

body because this is quite clearly the basic level on which the unconscious functions. At its deepest level, the unconscious *is* the body. We are dictated to by this strange intelligence within our physical organism which carries on and does extraordinary things without our knowing how. An obvious example of what the body can do apart from the 'I' is what happens when the 'I' gives a command. I will that my hand shall go up into the air. I will it all right, but I haven't the faintest idea how the act is performed. We have discovered, as a result of very long and arduous research, that the processes involved in lifting my hand are incredibly complex, but I have, as a self-conscious being, absolutely no idea of what they are. I merely give a command and leave it to 'somebody else' to carry it out. Furthermore, this 'somebody else' works in an almost infallible way, if we leave him alone, to carry on the main processes of our bodily existence. The heartbeat, the digestion, the respiration, the glandular secretions, the healing process—all these things go on without the 'I' being in any way able to help them. In fact, what are called psychosomatic diseases are the consequences of the 'I' and the personal unconscious interfering with the otherwise almost infallible proceedings of this deeper self within us.

What on earth is this 'deeper self' on the physiological level? We have no really satisfactory name for it at present, although in the past we had some names. In the Aristotelian psychology and physiology there was a kind of trinity of soul: there was the rational soul, which was the soul belonging to the 'I', and there were also the vegetative and the animal souls, which looked after the physiological processes in the body. We have, then, to think in terms of this strange kind of physiological intelligence, which is looking after us without our knowing how it does its work, and which we can't help, but which we can interfere with.

We can observe this physiological intelligence in certain animals. There is, of course, the intelligence of the instincts, which is remarkable enough and which has been developed by evolution in the course of millions of years. But over and above instinctive purposive actions, there are actions carried out by the 'not-I'—the vegetative soul or entelechy—which are not instinctive at all and which yet betray the most exceptional degree of intelligence and purpose.

Perhaps one of the most fantastic examples of this kind of physiological intelligence is the ability of the parrot to imitate the human voice. The parrot presumably listens to the human voice; is conscious, insofar as parrots are conscious—and I suppose they are conscious; takes some kind of interest in what is being said; wishes—heaven only knows why—to reproduce it; and then something else takes over. The remarkable physiological intelligence within the parrot, which is infinitely more intelligent than the parrot itself, proceeds to manipulate literally hundreds of muscles in the parrot's speaking apparatus—a noise-making apparatus which is utterly different from the human one: The parrot has no teeth and no soft palate, its tongue is perfectly different from ours, its vocal chords are different, and it has a beak. Yet it is able to reproduce articulate human speech so well that sometimes human beings are actually deceived by it. And very often parrots, with their curious sense of humour, will annoy dogs by imitating their masters and calling them. The more one thinks of this extraordinary behaviour, the odder it becomes; it has nothing to do with instinct and it has nothing to do with biological survival. But parrots, for some unknown reason, desire to imitate, and their physiological intelligence is able to arrange the relevant muscles so as to. reproduce the sounds it hears with a precision which no merely conscious mind could possibly equal.

Something similar occurs in very small infants. The fact that infants at a very early age will smile back at a smiling face is the result of an imitative process. When such infants see a smile, there is something within them which proceeds to arrange the muscles of the face in such a way that the smile is reproduced.

We see then that over and above the merely vegetative faculties—the power of keeping the heart beating, the respiration and the digestion going—the physiological intelligence is capable of very remarkable ad hoc performances. In our conscious life these take place all the time. We visualize something we want to do and it is done—not by the 'I', but by this extraordinary thing we carry about inside us. It is one of the basic physiological facts with which the 'I' is associated, one of the powers with which it has to live.

Another physiological fact with which the 'I' has to live is the body's morphology, its actual shape and structure. What influences do these have upon our psychological life? Here obviously the most remarkable fact about human beings is that they are very different from one another—which illustrates the general evolutionary tendency that the higher up in the scale of evolution a species is, the more profound the variations within it: the most highly variable species is homo sapiens.

Along with these morphological variations, there are also very remarkable biochemical variations within the human species, and it is possible to carry on human life with quite different biochemical arrangements. This biochemical variability is one of the things which annoys pharmacologists very much, because unfortunately different human beings will react in entirely different ways to the same drug; the one desire of any scientist is to have a standard that he can work upon, and the human being is very, very far from standardized. It is this tremendous variability within the physical organism which is at the basis of all our moral ideas about the goodness of democracy and the value of such things as tolerance and living and letting live.

It seems pretty obvious that creatures which are so extremely different from one another physically are probably different from one another psychologically. It would be very surprising if hereditary differences as great as we can observe between one individual and another should not be correlated with very considerable differences in their behaviour and in their general psychological set-up. Indeed, the realization of the interdependence of mental behaviour and physical structure goes back to great antiquity. It was formulated by Hippocrates, the father of Western medicine, who spoke about two main physical types—what he called 'phthisic' habitus and 'apoplectic' habitus. The apoplectic habitus is the sort of big, burly, rather fattish, typical businessman or politician, who is going to have the renal-cardiac syndrome in later life. This is still a variety of human being we clearly recognize. The phthisic habitus was a slight mistake. Hippocrates evidently thought that the thin, slender type was particularly subject to phthisis or tuberculosis, but there is no particular evidence to show that this is the case.

Aristotle had a very curious approach to the mind-body problem: He tried to correlate mental characteristics with only one physical characteristic. For example, he was very interested in the shape of the nose. He was also interested in the resemblance of human beings to certain animal types, and he would classify them in this way, so that leonine-looking people were leonine in character—or, rather, like what he supposed lions to be like; we are not sure what they are like at all. There is something in this; if you look at a photograph of Garibaldi, you see he looked exactly like a lion, and he was a leonine man. But this is a very crude system of correlation.

With Galen, in the beginning of our era, we get a much more elaborate typology, a correlation between mind and body in terms of the four humours—blood, black bile, yellow bile, and phlegm. It is interesting to see that this very ancient psychophysical theory has left its trace upon our current vocabulary. We still speak of people with a sanguine temperament, a phlegmatic temperament, people who are choleric, people who are melancholic with a preponderance of black bile, and so on. These were fairly adequate notions—doctors and physiologists went on speaking in these terms right through the eighteenth century—and they did help people to think about the fundamental correlation between mind and body.

In more recent times—from the very end of the eighteenth

century on—we get a more scientific approach to the problem. The French were pioneers in this field: Leon Rostan spoke of three types of people, the *type digestive,* the *type musculaire,* and the *type cérébral*—the digestive, muscular, and cerebral types. It is an extremely acute observation. Later in the century there was G. Viola in Italy, also talking about a tripartite division into what he called macro-splanchnic, normo-splanchnic, and micro-splanchnic body types. These terms are very much the same, when they are explained, as those used by Rostan; they refer to the short trunk of the long-legged thin person, the medium trunk of the muscular person, and the heavy, relatively long trunk of the bulky person.

In our own time we have the important studies of Ernst Kretschmer, who made some very interesting correlations between body types and different kinds of insanity. He started with a tripartite division—the athletic, the pyknic, and the asthenic type—but reduced it (unfortunately) to two, the pyknic, or fat, bulky type, and the leptosome, or thin, light type.

More recently, and more scientifically and thoroughly, the matter has been gone into by Dr. William H. Sheldon and his collaborators, whose powerful technique for analysing and quantifying the physical differences between human beings in terms of a tri-polar frame of reference we discussed briefly a few days ago.

Sheldon calls the three poles endomorphy, mesomorphy, and ectomorphy. Endomorphy is the pole which at its extreme gives very big, fat, soft people with slow reactions and with a tendency to put on weight and become extremely fat in old age. These people are in a sense 'gut people'. Their gut is very often twice as heavy and twice as long as the gut of an extreme ectomorph. They have an amazing power of assimilation, and they are at home on the earth inasmuch as they have an immense capacity to absorb food and to remain alive. The mesomorphs are 'muscle people' with heavy bones and powerful muscles. You can see their pictures any day in the sporting pages of the newspaper; the professional footballers all belong to this terrific type. They tend to have a powerful neck and a rather coarse skin with very heavy folds showing in the face. They have great endurance and striving force, and, as we shall see when we come to the correlations of temperament, they tend to be aggressive—politicians, businessmen, soldiers, and so on. The ectomorphs are the thin, light, stringy-muscled people whose ratio of surface area to mass is extremely high and whose nervous system is consequently much closer to the surface than either the mesomorph's or the endomorph's. They are, so to speak, built around a nervous system which is much more vulnerable, being nearer the outside, and much more sensitive than those of the other two.

Sheldon devised a method for quantifying the different amounts of each component in every human being. The amount varies on a 7-point scale between 1 and 7, and any individual's pattern can be expressed in terms of three digits. I happen to be a 1-2-7. That is to say, I have a minimum of endomorphy, a little mesomorphy, which permits me to get around, and the maximum of ectomorphy. This is not a very common type; the types near the middle are commonest. Sheldon once told me that most members of my type are in asylums —I am extremely lucky to be out.

Something which Sheldon stresses as being very important in the physical set-up is what he calls 'dysplasia', a disharmony between different regions of the body. Certain regions of the body may exhibit a proportion of the three factors quite different from that of other regions. This is a typical sort of would-be athlete's tragedy: a boy who has enough mesomorphy to feel the desire to become an athlete may unfortunately have much more ectomorphic extremities, so that he simply doesn't have the strength in his arms and wrists and ankles to support his athletic ambitions; he would like to be an athlete but he just cannot be. These dysplasias probably play a very important part in juvenile delinquency. There is another dysplasia, which is also very common, and which may likewise cause very severe psychological disturbance. It can probably be found in Elizabeth Arden's Arizona Maine Chance, for ladies who have a classical torso but unfortunately complete dysplasia in the hips, which tend to bulge out and which have to be treated locally as strenuously as possible. Another factor which Sheldon emphasizes is what he calls 'gynandromorphy'. All of us display some degree of resemblance to the opposite sex, but some of us may have a good deal of it. A high degree of gynandromorphy acts as a kind of total dysplasia and may cause, again, great psychological trouble.

We have now to consider the relationship between these physical differences and the temperament of the people who have them. Sheldon has been able to establish a fairly high level of correlation between the physical pattern of any given individual and a pattern of temperament which he measures on a point scale in terms of intensity. Using about sixty different fundamental psychological traits, twenty for each of the three components, he has found that there is a fairly close relationship —the deviation is usually no more than one point—between the physical and the temperamental patterns. In cases where the deviation between the temperamental pattern and the physical pattern is as much as two points, the person is under very great permanent stress. Deviations of more than two points apparently are never found except in mental institutions.

The reason for the deviations is that sociological pressures demand that people behave in a certain way which doesn't happen to be the way in which their physique would normally 'ask' them to behave. Anthropologists have shown how powerful this trend can be, particularly in primitive societies which exercise a prodigious pressure upon their members. For example, Margaret Mead showed in her study of the Pueblo Indians that the Pueblos have a profound disapproval of anybody who shows a typical mesomorphic pattern of behaviour. They don't like people who, in our terms, are aggressive, show leadership, have drive. They want people who conform, who behave as other people in the tribe behave.

In our own culture, progressive education represents an almost exclusive valuation of the mesomorphic, and to some extent the endomorphic, points of view. Unfortunate children who were born with introverted tendencies are made to share and to rush around with others, and they are absolutely miserable, because what they want is privacy, and not to be pushed around with a great herd of other people. But this has become fashionable now, just as it was fashionable in an earlier age to try to repress the mesomorph and the endomorph, to impose stoical restraints upon the overflowing, spill-the-beans endomorph and to impose quasi-physical restraints on the exuberant energy of the mesomorph. You can look at earlier civilizations and see the social patterns which were created for doing precisely this.

There has always been a great problem of what to do with powerful muscular men with a tremendous drive for domination. One of the answers in the Middle Ages was to put them into religious orders of knighthood and send them out to fight with the Mohammedans. This kept them out of the way as far as Europeans were concerned, and they were bound and kept in very good order by all kinds of traditions and codes. At the same time means were found for protecting the introverted people without much muscular energy by establishing convents into which they could retire. This permitted the various people to find the niches in society most suitable to them, and the more violent were prevented from doing a lot of mischief to their fellow men.

It does happen that the internal categorical imperatives of temperament and physique are so strong in certain individuals that in spite of profound sociological pressure they start trying to behave like Napoleons, with the result that they get severely slapped down by the rest of society. This shows that even under the greatest sociological pressures the fundamental, physically determined drives of temperament may carry people into very great social trouble. And the moral is that we shouldn't try to mould or squeeze people into the procrustean bed of our popular conception of human virtue of the moment, but permit them as far as possible to develop along their own temperamental lines.

Let us now give a very brief account of the main temperamental traits connected with the three physical traits, endomorphy, mesomorphy, and ectomorphy. Endomorphs—the round, fat, gut people—are distinguished by relaxation, by a love of comfort, a love of ceremoniousness, and a love of eating —above all, eating in public. They are good routineers and they have a universal, indiscriminate amiability. They are very good mixers, they like people, and they have no difficulty in communication. In fact, they communicate all the time. They have an extreme extroversion of affect. Under the influence of alcohol, they become even more genial and amiable than they were before.

The extreme mesomorph is a driving person who loves power, is indifferent to others, and tends to be callous and to trample on other people. He is the typical aggressive go-getter. He may do it very politely, but he is still an aggressive go-getter. He tends to make a great deal of noise. He laughs loudly. He snores loudly. He speaks loudly and he has all the traits of an effective soldier and politician. If you look at the photographs of the gentleman (Nikita Khrushchev) who visited our shores recently, you will see that he is quite clearly an endomorphic mesomorph. He has enough endomorphy to be very genial when he wants to be and to get on with people and to communicate, but he also has the terrific driving force of the somatotonic temperament which goes with mesomorphy. *In vino veritas;* under alcohol the highly somatotonic person tends to become even more aggressive than he is ordinarily. These are the people who get into fights in bars and make themselves very unpleasant; they are extremely different from the genial drunks on the endomorphic scale.

The ectomorph, the cerebrotonic, is essentially an introvert and lives in a permanent state of restraint. His actions are restrained. He has great difficulty in communication. He is not a good mixer. He feels that the endomorph, with his pouring out of what he is feeling, is very shallow, very trivial, and vulgar in many ways, and he is horrified by the driving energy of the mesomorph. He is very fond of privacy and doesn't make much noise. Under the influence of alcohol he just feels ill.

So much for what seems to be the most highly developed scientific correlation yet made between physique and temperament. I find it extraordinary that this should have been so totally neglected by Freudian and by neo-Freudian psychology, but unfortunately, among many schools of psychology at the present time, the importance of hereditary physical differences in the whole study of the human psyche is sadly under-estimated. I want to read a brief passage from a recent book by Professor Norman Brown, *Life Against Death*. He is speaking very critically of the neo-Freudians and blaming them for thinking too much in purely psychological terms, and he sets up against them what he calls the 'materialism' of Freud himself. He says, 'With the loss of the Freudian materialism of the body, psychology becomes in neo-Freudian hands, as also in Jungian hands, once more what it was before the Freudian revolution, a psychology of the autonomous soul.'[1] But when we pass from this generalization to the specific facts of the case and see what Professor Brown, who is an ardent Freudian, has to say about 'Freudian materialism of the body', we find that the materialism consists almost exclusively in a preoccupation with events in only two parts of the body—the mouth and the anus. It is an absolutely extraordinary fact that the 'Freudian materialism of the body' boils down to this incredibly limited preoccupation with such an infinitesimal part of the total physical organism. After all, we are much more than these two aspects of the body, and we do know that our bodies have the most profound influ-

1. Norman Brown, *Life Against Death* (Middletown; Conn.: Wesleyan University, 1959), p. 204.

ence upon our behaviour and upon other people's behaviour.

Psychologists proceed as though we were disembodied souls or souls connected only with one or the other end of a digestive tube, as Freud would have us believe, and nothing else. And it is all the more remarkable when one reads that so extremely acute and philosophical a psychiatric writer as Erich Fromm, one of the neo-Freudians, defines temperament as the psychic qualities which are rooted in a constitutionally given soma. This is an admirable definition. Then he says that it is extremely important that psychologists should take account of these temperamental differences. And he says that undoubtedly in the future this will take place. But he himself pays no further attention to them at all, ignores the fact that there is already a very large literature on the subject, and proceeds as though nothing whatever had been done.

Not only are the main schools of psychiatry today indifferent to the relationship between the psyche and the physique, but we find the same sort of indifference in behaviourism. We have, for example, in B. F. Skinner's *Science and Human Behavior*, a very fully developed science of human behaviour which is exactly like, say, the science of the laws of motion. But the laws of motion are illustrated in very different ways by a breaking wave, a flying arrow, and a butterfly. It seems to me self-evident that the laws of behaviour are illustrated in very different ways according to the physique and temperament of the person who illustrates them, yet there is the minimum of reference to the fundamental physical and temperamental differences between people.

Sheldon has also done very valuable work in the field of mental illness. On the basis of standardized photographs of three thousand schizophrenics in various mental hospitals, he has come to some very interesting conclusions. He found, first of all, that Kretschmer's earlier insight that schizophrenia was very largely correlated with a high degree of ectomorphy is true. But he goes on to say that what Kretschmer did not make clear is that in a very large proportion of these cases there was not merely ectomorphy but also a high degree of disharmony within the body, which was clearly reflected by a disharmony within the temperament. Consequently, one has to consider the idea that while schizophrenia may be precipitated by traumatic experiences, these experiences are felt to be traumatic because they occur to people in a high ectomorphic region with a high degree of dysplasia. There wouldn't have been such disastrous effects if these people had been shaped differently.

Here again we see the enormous sociological importance of Sheldon's ideas. If there are people who can be identified as, so to speak, predestined to go toward schizophrenia, then there is quite a lot we can do in the way of prevention by means of differential education to shield them from disturbing shocks. And there is probably also something which can be done on the pharmacological level, for it seems to be pretty clear that most schizophrenics have some biochemical anomaly. Presumably the traumatic experience accentuates the biochemical anomaly, which in turn makes people schizophrenic mentally, which in turn makes them more subject to these traumatic experiences—and so a vicious circle is set up. The importance of finding a way to check this most serious of all the scourges which now affect civilized men becomes clear when we realize that more than 50 per cent of all hospital beds in this country are occupied by schizophrenics. It is our major health problem at the moment, and it is simply not being solved by the kind of psychotherapy which is at present available, largely because this psychotherapy has ignored the physical correlates of the disease.

A very interesting case of the correlation between physique and character is to be found in the traditional image of Christ. Christ has been painted now for nearly two thousand years and if we look at his traditional image we find that he is always represented as a personage with a high degree of ectomorphy. On the basis of a study of many hundreds of these images,

Sheldon says that the average figure of Christ in Christian art is a 2-3-5, that is to say, there is a certain amount of endomorphy, which gives the power of communication and sympathy; a bit more of mesomorphy, which gives the messianic drive and the power to carry through the message; and a high degree of ectomorphy, which gives the inward-looking life and the doctrine of restraint which has run through the whole orthodoxy of Christianity. What to do with the extreme mesomorphs has been one of the great problems of Christianity. They have in the past been controlled by the various orders of chivalry and by elaborate educational procedures, all based upon a cerebretonic view of life, with its idea of restraint and control.

It is quite clear that there has always been an intuition among Christians that this was the inevitable physical form of the Saviour. In fact, it is very interesting that in the rare cases where artists have departed from this traditional norm we are often rather shocked by the representation. Certain artists have represented the form of Christ as a much higher mesomorph. There is a very famous picture of the resurrection by Piero della Francesca which shows this tremendously athletic figure rising from the grave. It is a magnificent picture, but it is curiously out of the traditional view of Christ. There are also muscular, powerful figures of Christ in many of the paintings of Rubens. When he had seen some of these paintings William Blake made the little rhyme which says,

> I understood Christ was a carpenter
> And not a brewer's servant, my good Sir.[2]

We should remark here that no artist whatever has represented Christ with a high degree of endomorphy. In this Christianity differs very much from Confucianism, for some of the Chinese sacred figures are typical endomorph figures—big, soft, and comfortable. Actually, the Confucian system is essentially endomorphic. It is a system of relaxation, of great preoccupa-

2. William Blake, *On Art and Artists*, xxvi.

tion with family, of ceremoniousness, and it is thus not at all like the Christian system. It has a different kind of temperamental background to it.

We see, then, that on the deepest level our unconscious equals our constitution: we are determined by what we physically and temperamentally are. Naturally the environment plays a very great part, but it plays the particular part it does because we are the particular people that we are. It is important to bring out this deepest physical level of the unconscious because it is quite pointless to talk about the unconscious unless we see it rooted in the constitutional differences which make us the individuals we are.

THE UNCONSCIOUS

THE unconscious can in all circumstances work either to our advantage or to our disadvantage—it is both negative and positive, creative and destructive. In orthodox Freudian theory there is much more concern with what may be called the negative side of the unconscious than with the positive. This was inevitable, seeing that the theory was developed in a therapeutic context; Freud, after all, was working with neurotic people in the Vienna of the late 19th century.

Quite recently a collection of Freud's papers, called by the editor *Creativity and the Unconscious,* was published. When one looks into the papers one finds that there is remarkably little on the subject of creativity; even when he was discussing the positive side, Freud had very little contribution to make.

In dealing with the positive side of the unconscious I would say that the work of the pioneer psychologist F. W. H. Myers is much more illuminating than the work of Freud. Myers was about fifteen years older than Freud but died about forty years before Freud did. His great work, *Human Personality and Its Survival of Bodily Death,* published posthumously in 1902, still remains after nearly sixty years a mine of information on the

Delivered on October 12, 1959

subject, above all, of the creative and positive side of the unconscious. This is a book which I recommend very strongly to anybody who wants to know about the positive aspects of what Freud dealt with on the negative side.

Let us begin now with the negative unconscious and with certain idiomatic phrases which we constantly use. Language contains a great deal of fossil wisdom, and many idiomatic phrases throw a great deal of light on the insights of the ages into the problems of man. We use phrases such as, 'I don't know what came over me'; 'I must have been mad'; 'I must have been out of my mind'; 'He can't have been himself when he did that'; 'I don't know what possessed me.' In the last phrase we come straight back to the idea of demonic possession which we found in Homer and in the Bible. It is very significant that we find in these idiomatic phrases such a clear picture of an ego surrounded by irrational forces which are continually breaking in upon it and compelling it to do all sorts of things that it really doesn't want to do.

We find that the unconscious can be dealt with as the representation in the mind of certain physical anomalies, that one type of negative unconscious influence is due to congenital physical defects of one kind or another. The physical defect of extremely low IQ, or of some kind of malformation, leads on the unconscious level to terrible feelings of inferiority which have to be over-compensated. Defects in the endocrine system lead to all kinds of very strange psychological results which are felt as barriers and hindrances and compulsions on the unconscious level and which interfere with the conscious self doing what it wants to do.

Then we have to consider what happens to people who find themselves born with a certain kind of temperament but who live in a society where that temperament is undervalued or even regarded as abnormal or disreputable. In this context, it is worth quoting a very touching little poem by William Blake:

O! why was I born with a different face?
Why was I not born like the rest of my race?
When I look, each one starts! when I speak, I offend;
Then I'm silent & passive & lose every Friend.
Then my verse I dishonour, My pictures despise,
My person degrade & my temper chastise;
And the pen is my terror, the pencil my shame;
All my Talents I bury, and dead is my Fame.[1]

This is a very vivid picture of what happens to a person of one kind of temperament who finds himself living in a society in which that kind of temperament is greatly undervalued and where other kinds of temperaments are regarded as the only moral and reputable ones. Another example is the predicament in which an extremely introverted cerebrotonic child finds himself in a school where he is compelled to be a good mixer, to be constantly with other people, to join in the fun, etc.—all things which he finds completely opposed to his deepest ingrained nature. The result is that all kinds of disturbances go on in his unconscious and he very often develops a neurosis. Freud was in part responsible for this 'somatotonic revolution'; he says in so many words that the extroverted way of life is the way of health for every man. Freud himself was an extrovert of a rather aggressive type, and undoubtedly that way of life was the way of health for him, but it seems to be perfectly obvious from observation that this is not the way of health for many people and that any attempt to force these people into adopting this way of life against ingrained and congenital tendencies is bound to have the most disturbing effects upon the unconscious.

Next among the influences from the physique are the influences of sickness, particularly chronic sickness—and much chronic sickness is actually of psychosomatic origin. The conscious ego starts interfering with what Aristotle called the 'vegetative soul'—the wisdom of the body; the body then goes wrong, and the normal processes of psychology are thrown out.

1. William Blake, Letter to Thomas Butts, 16 August 1803.

The ego feels itself more than ever frustrated and in turn interferes with the normal functioning of the body still further, so that the whole process goes round and round in a terrible vicious circle, with mind and body making each other constantly worse and worse.

Human misery is greatly stressed by all the world religions. The Christian religion insists that this is a vale of tears, and the Buddhists say, 'I show you sorrow,' meaning the world which we find around us, and 'I show you the ending of sorrow,' which is the road to enlightenment. Now, probably about one-third of human misery is inevitable because it is due to the fact that we are sentient beings in a largely insentient universe which is not concerned with our well-being. But about two-thirds of our misery is strictly home-made and the product of ignorance, stupidity, and, to a less frequent extent, malice. The moral is, as the Duchess in *Alice* would say, to get rid of stupidity and ignorance, which naturally is a great deal easier said than done.

Now we have to consider that aspect of the negative unconscious which has been specifically the concern of the psychoanalysts and which is obviously an extremely important part of the whole picture. This is the side of the unconscious represented by repression. Freud himself said that we obtain our theory of the unconscious from the theory of repression. What happens is that we have, in childhood above all, certain urges, wishes, and purposes which do not conform with the cultural standards around us and which we soon learn to regard as highly discreditable. We therefore push them down into an area of the mind where we are no longer aware of them. However, repressed urges continue to exist, and they exercise a great and very pernicious influence upon our thoughts and feelings and actions on the conscious level. The age during which cultural pressure weighs upon us most heavily is infancy and childhood, and it is during infancy and childhood that most of the work of repression goes on.

It is not only the discreditable wishes and urges and purposes that we repress. We also repress incidents which are too painful for us to think about. We just cannot take the thought of certain things which have happened to us, and consequently we push them down out of sight. In neurosis, then, we are suffering the penalty of things which we did and things which happened to us many years ago, as well as the penalty of urges and wishes repressed.

Along with repression from the inside in the name of cultural ideals and of duty there goes conditioning from outside, and this is of equal importance in the history of the negative unconscious. Conditioning can take place no matter what the state of the subject, but, as Pavlov has shown, it is most effective when the subject is under great physical or mental stress. When the subject is in pain or is suffering from fear or is in the throes of some violent emotion—anger or even joy—he is peculiarly susceptible to conditioning. It is during these times of lowered resistance that conditioned reflexes are set up most easily and are most permanent. Pavlov found it exceedingly difficult to get rid of the conditioning which had been imposed upon dogs under a great state of stress. And precisely these Pavlovian techniques have been used in the so-called brain-washing both of enemies and of friends (brain-washing is probably used more intensively on Communist workers in China than it was even on prisoners during the Korean War). While it is quite clear that some conditioning is absolutely essential and very good, it is equally clear that plenty of conditioning is extremely undesirable and may lead in later life to very severe troubles.

We see then that a great part of our negative unconscious is due first to repression and then to the undesirable conditioning which has been put into us at an earlier period, often under conditions of stress, and which continues to act upon us very much as a post-hypnotic suggestion. Neurosis is the failure of the conscious ego to deal with the events of the moment in terms appropriate to the moment. Instead of dealing with what is happening now, the neurotic person deals with events in terms of repressed feelings and hidden memories from the past which are totally irrelevant to what is happening at the present time. In a certain sense it may be said that all psychotherapy is essentially a spring cleaning of the memory. It is not a question of getting rid of remembered facts—we do have to go on remembering the multiplication tables, our geography lessons, and so on. It is a question of ridding the memory of the painful emotional states which cause us to act in a completely inappropriate way in the present time. We are reacting not to now; we are reacting to then. Consequently, everything we do is completely pointless and senseless.

It has been realized for a very long time that the memory in its unregenerate form is a dangerous faculty which can put us very wrong. We find very interesting passages about this in Buddhist literature, and I was interested not long ago to find a passage on the problem of memory in the writings of St. John of the Cross, the great Spanish mystical writer of the sixteenth century. He says, 'This emptying of the memory, though the advantages of it are not so great as those of the state of union, yet, merely because it delivers souls from much sorrow, grief, and sadness, besides imperfections and sins, is in itself a great good.'[2] We may perhaps doubt whether the rather mechanical methods of emptying the memory employed in Catholic monasteries are likely to be very effective; nevertheless it is quite clear that these people were entirely on the right track. There is no doubt that really effective therapy would make use of some of the methods used in religion, combined with the various methods of analysis and abreaction therapy which can serve under modern conditions to cleanse the memory.

So much for the negative side of the unconscious—first the negative side due to physical influences and then the negative side due to repression and to conditioning from the outside. Let us now turn to what I would think is much more important: the

2. St. John of the Cross, *The Ascent of Mount Carmel*, III, i.

positive side of the unconscious. Here again, let us start with the colloquial phrases which indicate the nature of the positive contribution which the unconscious makes to our life. We use phrases such as, 'It has suddenly struck me'; 'It has suddenly occurred to me'; 'I have had a brilliant idea'; 'A wonderful notion has come into my head'; 'The violinist gave an inspired performance'; 'The preacher spoke as though he were inspired.' Here we are back with the old Biblical and Homeric idea of supernatural possession, this time a good possession and not a demonic possession. Homer makes an appeal to the Muses to help him and speaks about minstrels who sin 'out of the gods' —a very remarkable phrase—and later on in Greek history we get the accounts of the Pythia of Delphi, who received the oracles of Apollo.

Thus we see that when we use words like 'inspired', which we do without any particular thought, we are carrying on a very ancient tradition; similarly we find that the Bible is full of these same ideas. St. Paul in the Epistle to the Hebrews says, 'God, who at sundry times and in divers manners, spake in time past unto the fathers by the prophets' (Hebrews 1:1). When one looks at the works of the prophets themselves, one finds that they think of themselves as passive and very often reluctant instruments. They are not particularly anxious to undergo the tremendous influx of some non-rational and much greater power, but they have no choice. Later on, in early Christian times, we have accounts of the passive involuntary reception by the early Christians of what were called 'charismata'—gifts of the spirit which came involuntarily into certain people.

Let us now consider the positive unconscious in its relation to everyday life. When we look carefully into our everyday experience, we find that the conscious 'I' seldom comes up with a really brilliant idea—it is a kind of plodding faculty. We constantly get the impression that our best ideas come to us from an area of our mind which is not our conscious mind; phrases such as 'It occurred to me' are good representations of this fact.

The mechanism of the unconscious must be looked at more or less as follows: We consciously take in material which then is passed on to some layer of the unconscious (Freud speaks of this layer as the pre-conscious, but I would think there are deeper layers, beyond the repressed unconscious, where this material goes). There it undergoes a process of digestion and organization, and it is then represented to the conscious mind in the form of some idea which is often felt to be extremely brilliant and illuminating, which the conscious mind could not of itself have concocted.

As this is such an everyday phenomenon, we can take it for granted and not think too much about it. However, we are very decidedly amazed by the more unusual phenomena of the same kind such as artistic inspiration. It is a significant fact that in several of the Indo-European languages the word for 'poet' and the word for 'seer' are the same. In Latin the word *vates* means both seer and poet; the same thing is true of the Irish word *fili*. The whole idea is that the poet receives inspiration from some other source than the merely self-conscious mind, and it is re-markable that many great poets in modern times have felt exactly the same way. Goethe says, 'The songs made me, not I the songs.'[3] The French poet Lamartine writes, 'It is not I who think; it is my ideas that think for me.'[4] Alfred de Musset says, 'One doesn't really work, one listens. It is as though some stran-ger were whispering in one's ear.'[5] And Shelley makes a very curious remark, 'The mind in creation is as a fading coal, which some invisible influence, like an inconstant wind, awakens to transitory brightness.'[6]

3. Quoted in Albert Bielschowsky, *The Life of Goethe* (New York: Putnam, 1912), vol. 3, p. 31.

4. Quoted in Pitirim Sorokin, *The Ways and Power of Love* (Boston: Beacon Press, 1954), p. 108.

5. Quoted in Paul Chabaneix, *Le Subconscient chez les artistes, les savants et les écrivains* (Paris: Baillière, 1897), p. 201.

6. Percy Bysshe Shelley, 'A Defence of Poetry', in *Essays, Letters from Abroad, Translations and Fragments by Percy Bysshe Shelley* (London: Edward Moxon, 1852), vol. 1, p. 41.

There is a very striking phrase which sums up this whole idea in the writings of a romantic German philosopher, Frans von Baader, who says that Descartes was entirely wrong in saying 'Cogito ergo sum.' What he ought to have said was 'Cogit*or* ergo sum'—not 'I think' but 'I am thought, therefore I am.'[7] Insofar as I am a conscious ego, I think, therefore I am. But insofar as I am a creative unconscious, and insofar as my conscious ego requires the collaboration of the creative unconscious, I am thought, and therefore I am, on a more important scale than I would have been if I were merely a conscious ego doing my own private thinking—my own private thinking being strictly limited.

What may be called genius is the uprush of helpful material from the deep levels of the unconscious, which is then worked up by the conscious self into an appropriate form. Edison said that genius is nine-tenths perspiration and only one-tenth inspiration, but there has to be the inspiration first and then the work on it afterwards. Genius is the harmonious collaboration of the two parts of our being; it is openness to what lies below us on the unconscious level and the capacity to mould this material into forms which shall communicate to other people and shall carry over some of the meanings and feelings which the original artist had.

We must not imagine that all such uprushes are of the highest quality. Unfortunately, there can be uprushes from the unconscious of the utmost silliness and stupidity. A painful example of this is the case of Voltaire, who prided himself above all on being a tragic poet. Unfortunately, he was a very bad tragic poet. There is an extraordinary letter where he describes the writing of his tragedy *Catiline,* which is in five acts, in rhymed Alexandrines, and which he completed in a week. Nobody, he writes, who had not felt the afflatus of genius could imagine how such a feat was possible.[8] No doubt that is true, but unfortu-

7. Franz Xavier von Baader, *Sammtliche Werke* (Leipzig, 1857–1860).
8. Voltaire, Letter to Charles Jean Francois Henault, 14 August 1749, in

nately the play is perfectly unreadable. The mode of genius in this particular case did not produce the results of genius.

The most non-genius type of inspiration of this kind is shown by those people who have a gift of automatic writing, who sit down with a pen and let the scripts come pouring out. The vast majority of these scripts are completely uninteresting and non-sensical, but they do come up from the depths in the same kind of way that the inspirations of genius come to men of genius. The difference is that in the case of men of genius what comes up is originally of much better quality, and the work which they then put into it in their conscious state of mind brings the final creation to a pitch where it can be appreciated by other people and felt to be of great significance and importance.

Another particularly odd kind of intervention of the creative unconscious is illustrated by the cases of the so-called calculating boys. Every now and then we hear or read in the papers the story of a child who can perform the most astounding mental calculations—finding the cube root of seven-figured numbers in fifty seconds, etc. Let me quote the charming case of an English calculating boy called Blyth, who was born in 1819. This is a story which his brother tells of him:

The little boy, Benjamin, and his father were going for a walk before breakfast—the father liked taking a brisk walk before breakfast—and suddenly the little boy asked him, 'Papa, at what hour was I born?'

The father said, '4:00 a.m.'

'What o'clock is it now?'

'7:50.'

The boy walked on a few hundred yards in silence and then gave the number of seconds that he had lived (he was then six years old, roughly). The father didn't attempt to check the figure at the time, but when he got home he sat down with pencil and paper and worked it all out and then went with some

Voltaire's Correspondence, ed. Theodore Besterman (Geneva: Institut et Musée Voltaire, Les Délices, 1956), no. 3434.

triumph to the child and said, 'I regret to say you are 172,800 seconds out.'

The boy said, 'Oh, Papa, you have left out the two days for the leap years of 1820 and 1824.' Great collapse of Papa.[9]

Why on earth do certain children have this fantastic power, and what mind do they have that is capable of this sort of thing? In recent centuries there have been two calculating boys who grew up to be men of first-rate genius, André Marie Ampère in France and Karl Friedrich Gauss in Germany. There have been several other cases where calculating boys grew up to be very capable mathematicians and intelligent men, but there have also been many cases where they grew up to be either completely mediocre or even virtually half-witted. The oddest of all these cases is that of a German called Dase who lived in the middle of the nineteenth century. He was incapable of understanding the first book of Euclid, but he had such an incredible faculty for doing sums in his head that he was paid a lifetime salary by the Prussian government for finding the factors of all numbers between seven and eight million. He spent his life doing this with an incredible rapidity. He had absolutely no powers of ratiocination at all, and yet he was able to do these extraordinary sums (which would now be done by electronic machines).

Let us now briefly speak on the subject of sleep. We are as well and as sane as we are only because the ego takes a holiday for one-third of every day. If we remained awake all the time, we should undoubtedly all be extremely ill or quite mad. And while the ego is out of the way during sleep, we may say that what is called the vegetative soul is functioning, without interference from this intolerable self and from the personal unconscious, and keeping us well and sane.

There is, however, some activity during sleep: dreaming. Most dreams naturally refer to events which took place during

9. F. W. H. Myers, *Human Personality and Its Survival of Bodily Death* (New Hyde Park, N. Y.: University Books, 1961), p. 76.

the day before we went to sleep or in very recent times; but some dreams, as the Freudians have pointed out, refer in a symbolic way to buried material. Yet others seem to partake of the nature of what Jung calls 'great dreams' and to refer to what he calls archetypal material on a far lower level of the unconscious. Some dreams don't even seem to refer to that, but to something which doesn't have any particular relation to the human psyche.

These archetypal and completely otherworldly dreams bring us to another very strange phenomenon of the unconscious, the phenomenon of visions, which we will touch on today and take up in more depth in a later lecture.

Spontaneous visions seems to be fairly common. Blake had them all the time, and we have some very curious accounts of the nature of his visions—for example, of how he came to make drawings of Sir William Wallace, the Scottish hero, and of Edward I:

> [Blake] was sitting meditating, as he had often done, on the heroic actions and hard fate of the Scottish hero [Sir William Wallace], when, like a flash of lightning, a noble form stood before him; which he instantly knew, by a something within himself, to be Sir William Wallace. He felt it was a spiritual appearance; which might vanish as instantly as it came; and, transported at the sight, he besought the hero to remain a few moments till he might sketch him. The warrior Scot, in this vision, seemed as true to his historical mental picture, as his noble shade was to the manly bearing of his recorded person; for, with his accustomed courtesy, he smiled on the young painter; presently the phantom vanished and Edward the First, who also remained long enough to be sketched, took his place.[10]

Then there is a very interesting account by John Varley of Blake's drawing of the famous head of the ghost of the flea:

10. Postscript to the Appendix in Jane Porter, *The Scottish Chiefs* (1841), quoted in Mona Wilson, *The Life of William Blake* (London: Oxford University Press, 1971), p. 310.

I felt convinced by his mode of proceeding, that he had a real image before him, for at one point he left off, and began on another part of the paper to make a separate drawing of the mouth of the Flea, which the spirit having opened, he was prevented from proceeding with the first sketch till he had closed it again.[11]

Another celebrated visionary was the eighteenth-century Swedish scientist and man of affairs, Swedenborg, who had visions of life in the next world of an enormous elaboration and detail which must have come to him with a complete sense of reality. And then there is the whole series of visionaries within the tradition of the Church, beginning with St. Brigid of Sweden in the thirteenth century, who had visions of the Passion of Christ in the most elaborate detail, and ending with Catherine Emmerich, who died in the beginning of the nineteenth century.

Unfortunately these visions do not correspond with one another, and it is, therefore, impossible to say whether any of them are in fact veridical, cognitive visions. In most cases we probably have to put them down to what may be called the story-telling faculty which lies at the back of the mind. This very peculiar faculty seems to be present, to a certain extent, in all minds, and it can be evoked by various methods which we will describe later, although in certain cases it occurs spontaneously.

Here it is worthwhile mentioning that when Homer and the poets who followed him asked for inspiration from the Muses, they were not asking for poetical skill. They were asking for material. They were saying, 'Please tell me what really happened at the siege of Troy' (or what really happened during these mythical histories). Hesiod is delighted when the Muse provides him with some new names which he can bring in.

11. John Varley, *A Treatise on Zodiacal Physiognomy* (London, 1828), pp. 54–55. The head of the Flea with closed mouth is on Plate 6 of Varley's *Treatise*, and a composite head with open mouth on Plate 5. Blake's full-length drawing of the 'Ghost of the Flea' appears on p. 94 of *The Blake-Varley Sketchbook of 1819*, introduction and notes by Martin Butlin (London: Heinemann, 1969).

Appeals to the Muses can thus be seen as appeals above all to this story-telling faculty at the back of our minds. As for the actual stylistic execution, this the ancient poets knew well enough and could do with their conscious minds.

We now come to a very ticklish subject, the subject of parapsychology. This in many academic circles is regarded as a rather obscene subject, a kind of intellectual pornography. Indeed, there are some academic circles where, I would think, it would be more respectable to study the works of the Marquis de Sade than the works of Dr. J. B. Rhine. Nevertheless, I do happen to think that such phenomena as telepathy, clairvoyance, and precognition actually occur. I think it is impossible to study the enormous mass of evidence accumulated in the journals and proceedings of the Society for Psychical Research and the experimental work done in recent years at Duke and other universities without coming to this conclusion.

Why do so many otherwise open-minded scientific people refuse even to consider the evidence? The reason is that the facts, if they are facts, just don't make sense in terms of the *Weltanschauung* which we accept as more or less axiomatic. They don't make sense above all in terms of the view that we have of human nature and of its relation to the universe. In point of fact most of us are still influenced unconsciously by the hypothesis of Descartes about the nature of man and its relation to the world. Descartes insisted that the world was divided into two halves, one half matter and the other half mind, and that man was divided into a mind and a body. The material half of the world he regarded as being composed of one substance, but the mental half was composed of innumerable substances, every individual mind being a separate impenetrable unit of a substantial nature. One unit could never react directly with other units, and it could react with matter only in relation to the matter of its own body and, through the body, with other pieces of matter.

The essence of this mental substance, Descartes insisted, was consciousness. We have already rejected this idea, but it seems to me now that in the light of modern psychology, and I would say of parapsychology, we have to revise even further the Cartesian assumptions. We have to insist that not only does the mind have this great unconscious side, but the unconscious side is not enclosed at its lowest fringe. Rather, it touches a kind of psychic medium out of which individual minds are crystallized, and through this psychic medium it is enabled to establish contact with other minds.

The Cartesian idea of a pure dualism within man has to be supplanted. Instead, we have to think of man as a composite of three factors: a body; what Western philosophers call pure ego, Eastern philosophers call *atman,* and St. Paul called *pneuma;* and a psyche, which is not a separate, water-tight unity, but rather a thing composed. We may have to think of the elementary psychological particles out of which the psyche is composed as being, in the vaguest sense of the word, ideas; these elementary particles can then be built up into complexes, like what the Buddhists call *skandhas,* and the whole thing bound together in a rather precarious and unstable unity which we call the self, its instability being clearly proved by what happens to it in cases of mental disorder and even in stressful conditions of normal life.

We have then this picture of a precarious and rather unstable self in relation to an unconscious which is not shut in at the lower levels, or at the upper levels either, but is open at both ends, so that communications with other minds or a Mind outside itself are possible. This leaves us in an uncomfortable philosophical position, because such a conception just doesn't fit satisfactorily into the generally accepted world picture at the present time. The problem is being discussed by two eminent contemporary philosophers, C. D. Broad of Cambridge and H. Haverley Price of Oxford, neither of whom has come up with a satisfactory answer.

At the moment, then, we have to accept a kind of ambivalent

notion about human nature. For most practical purposes we have to think in terms of something like a neutral monism, with the mind and body being aspects of the same substance. But we also have to think in the light of the facts of parapsychology, that to some extent mind is independent of body and can exist in a kind of psychic medium; that ideas may have a life of their own and may enter our idea system in a way which is very peculiar and difficult to understand; and that ideas may perhaps persist in existing long after the bodies connected with the minds in which the ideas were originally invented have died. There may be a kind of reservoir of this mental life into which we plunge; and above this, enveloping it and interpenetrating it, we may also have to postulate something which William James spoke of as 'cosmic consciousness' and which Bergson called 'Mind'.

I will leave this subject on this very unsatisfactory note, as an unresolved philosophical problem, for the good reason that I don't know how to resolve it and I don't think at present anybody else knows how to resolve it. But I feel quite sure that it will be resolved sooner or later. Meanwhile, we have to go on as best we may with this oddly anomalous situation in which we find ourselves.

LANGUAGE

I WANT to begin this discussion of language with a certain number of extracts from different authors which cast a lot of light on the subject. The first is from the autobiography of Helen Keller, where she describes how she discovered language as a child. She writes:

[My teacher] brought me my hat, and I knew I was going out into the warm sunshine. This thought, if a wordless sensation may be called a thought, made me hop and skip with pleasure.

We walked down the path to the well-house, attracted by the fragrance of the honeysuckle with which it was covered. Someone was drawing water and my teacher placed my hand under the spout. As the cool stream gushed over my hand she spelled into the other the word 'water', first slowly, then rapidly. I stood still, my whole attention fixed upon the motions of her fingers. Suddenly I felt a misty consciousness as of something forgotten—a thrill of returning thought; and somehow the mystery of language was revealed to me. I knew then that 'w-a-t-e-r' meant the wonderful cool something that was flowing over my hand. That living word awakened my soul, gave it light, hope, joy, set it free! There were barriers still, it is true, but barriers that could in time be swept away.

Delivered on October 26, 1959

I left the well-house eager to learn. Everything had a name, and each name gave birth to a new thought. As we returned to the house, every object which I touched seemed to quiver with life. That was because I saw everything with the strange, new sight that had come to me.[1]

Let us now set a number of other quotations against this, beginning with some from Goethe. Goethe was one of the supreme masters of the word, and it is very interesting to find this great manipulator of words speaking constantly against language. He says in one place, *'Gefühl ist alles; Name ist Schall und Rauch*'[2] (Feeling is everything, name is merely sound and smoke). Then there is the famous quotation,

> *Grau, teurer Freund, ist alle theorie,*
> *Und grün des Lebens goldner Baum.*[3]

(Gray is all theory, green life's golden tree.) And, again:

We talk too much. We should talk less and draw more. I personally should like to renounce speech altogether and like organic nature, communicate everything I have to say in sketches. That fig tree, this little snake, the cocoon on my window sill, quietly awaiting its future, all these are momentous signatures. Indeed, a person able to decipher their meaning properly would soon be able to dispense with spoken and written words altogether. The more I think of it, there is something futile, mediocre, even foppish about speech.[4]

Talleyrand, the great French diplomatist of the early nineteenth century and one of the great masters of practical life, said that 'Speech was given to man to disguise his thoughts'[5]— which was undoubtedly true in his case. Another interesting

---

1. Helen Keller, *The Story of My Life* (New York: Grosset & Dunlap, 1905), p. 23.
2. Johann Wolfgang von Goethe, *Faust, I.* Marthens Garten. 3456–3457.
3. Ibid., Studierzimmer. 2038–2039.
4. Johann Wolfgang von Goethe, *Conversations with J. D. Falk* (1809).
5. This phrase was attributed to Talleyrand by Harel in his play *Le Nain Jaune.*

observation about language was made by the great Christian existentialist philosopher Kierkegaard, who said that the purpose of language is to assist and confirm people in refraining from action. This is, in a sense, a development of the phrase in the Gospel which says that 'not all of those who say "Lord, Lord" will enter into the kingdom of heaven' (Matthew 7:21).

What is required, then, is not devotion or theological speculation, but right action. On the other hand, we find that language can be most horribly effective in promoting action, especially bad action. As Hitler wrote, 'All effective propaganda has to limit itself only to a very few points and to use them like slogans.'[6]

We find a number of remarks about language in relation to religion in the epistles of St. Paul—remarks the more curious when one reflects that it is precisely the language of St. Paul's epistles which has dominated the whole Christian scene for nineteen hundred years. Paul says, in one well-known phrase, 'The letter killeth, but the spirit giveth life' (2 Corinthians 3:6). And, 'We should serve in the newness of the spirit and not in the oldness of the letter' (Romans 7:6).

Finally, here is a passage from the works of John Locke on language in relation to philosophy. Although written nearly three hundred years ago it is still very much to the point:

> Vague and insignificant forms of speech and abusive language have so long passed for mysteries of science and hard, or misapplied words have by prescription such a right to be mistaken for deep learning and height of speculation, that it will not be easy to persuade either those who speak or those who hear them that they are but the covers of ignorance and a hindrance to true knowledge.[7]

These quotations indicate very clearly the curiously ambivalent attitude towards language which we always have had and certainly still have, and which has prevailed throughout the

6. Adolf Hitler, *Mein Kampf* (New York: Reynal and Hitchcock, 1939).
7. John Locke, *An Essay Concerning Human Understanding*, 'Epistle to the Reader.'

ages. The phrase which opens the Gospel according to St. John, 'In the beginning was the Word' (John 1:1), is perfectly true in regard to the beginning of the strictly human world. There is no doubt at all that the strictly human form of life arose when it was possible for man to speak. Language is what makes us human. Unfortunately, it is also what makes us all too human. It is on the one hand the mother of science and philosophy, and on the other hand it begets every kind of superstition and prejudice and madness. It helps us and it destroys us; it makes civilization possible, and it also produces those frightful conflicts which wreck civilization.

Now human behaviour differs from animal behaviour precisely because of the fact that human beings can speak and animals cannot. And we find that even the most intelligent animals, because they cannot speak, cannot do things which to us seem absolutely rudimentary and which very small children, as soon as they learn to talk, would be able to accomplish.

There was a very interesting experiment carried out by the great German Gestalt psychologist, Wolfgang Köhler, who worked for many years with chimpanzees. Köhler found that his chimpanzees could use sticks as tools to pull down bananas which were hanging out of their reach. They were intelligent enough to see that this tool—the stick—could be used for extending their arm and getting the banana. But Köhler found that the animals only used the stick to get a banana when both stick and banana were in view at the same time. If the banana was in front of them and the stick was behind them, they could not use the stick; they could not bear the banana in mind long enough to look around and pick up the stick and then use it.

The reason for this is quite clear. We have words for banana and stick which permit us to think about these objects when they are not actually in sight. Even a small child, knowing the words 'banana' and 'stick', has a conceptual notion of their relationship and is consequently able to think of 'stick' in conjunction with 'banana' even when the stick is behind him and to remember this long enough to pick the stick up and use it on the bananas.

The fact that animals cannot retain their knowledge of things over a long period, and consequently lose interest in them, accounts for their (to us) preposterous behaviour in many situations. They constantly interrupt one line of action to do something else, and they may come back to the first activity or forget it altogether. Human beings, on the other hand, thanks to language, are able to pursue one purpose or to act in relation to a principle or to an ideal over long periods of time. In a certain sense we can say that language is a device for permitting human beings to go on doing in cold blood the good and the evil which it is possible for animals to do only in hot blood, under the influence of passion.

This continuity is illustrated not merely in the life of individual human beings; it is also illustrated very forcibly in the life of entire societies, where language may be described as a device for connecting the present with the past and the future. While it is clear that the Lamarckian conception of the inheritance of acquired characteristics is completely unacceptable, and untrue biologically, it is perfectly true on the social, psychological, and linguistic level: language does provide us means for taking advantage of the fruits of past experience. There is such a thing as social heredity. The acquisitions of our ancestors are handed down to us through written and spoken language, and we do therefore enjoy the possibility of inheriting acquired characteristics, not through the germ plasm but through tradition.

Unfortunately, tradition can hand on bad as well as good items. It can hand on prejudices and superstitions just as effectively as it can hand on science and decent ethical codes. Here again we see the strange ambivalence of this extraordinary gift. It is like the fairy stories in which there is a good fairy and a bad fairy, but in this case the good fairy's gift, which is this amazing gift of language, also turns out to be the bad fairy's gift. It is one of the ironies of our destiny that the wonderful thing which

Helen Keller so eloquently describes as a giver of life and creator of thought is also one of the most dangerous and destructive
things that we can have.

In the beginning of human life, as a strictly human adventure,
was the Word. But what happens when there is no language?
What happens in very small children and animals? What is the
life of what may be called immediate experience? Here it is
worth making a small digression to consider some of the ideas
of Indian philosophy. Indian philosophers have always affirmed
that the thing which creates our specifically human world is
what they call *nama-rupa* (name-and-form). Name may be
defined as subjectivized form and form is the projection of
name into the outer world, and the two create for human beings this world of separate objects existing in time. However,
the enlightened individual goes beyond grammar. He has what
may be called a 'grammar-transcending experience' which permits him to live in the consciousness of the divine continuum
of the world and to see the one continually manifest in the
many. The enlightened person is, so to speak, *after* the rise of
language; he lives in language and then goes beyond it. But
what sort of world is there *before* language is introduced? What
sort of world is the world of immediate non-verbalized experience?

William James spoke of the world of immediate experience,
in a very characteristic phrase, as a 'blooming, buzzing confusion',[8] the idea being that the animal and the small child live in
a chaos of sensations. But recent investigations in the ethology
of animals and the perceptions of small children have revealed
that immediate experience really isn't quite as blooming and as
buzzing as James supposed. What emerges most strikingly from
recent scientific developments is that perception is not a passive reception of material from the outside world; it is an active
process of selection and imposing of patterns. The nervous sys-

8. William James, *Some Problems of Philosophy* (New York: Longmans,
1948), p. 48.

tem of animals and of human beings is contrived in such a way that it automatically sifts out from the blooming, buzzing confusion those elements which are biologically useful. So far as animals are concerned, it selects out of the confusion precisely those elements which help them to survive; the animal sees only two classes of objects—the edible and the dangerous.

One of the things which has been revealed in the study of animal universes is how exceptionally limited and extremely odd many of them are. The great German biologist Baron J. J. Von Uexküll wrote a great deal about what he called the *umwelt* of the animals, the different universes in which creatures of different classes and species live. The subject is one of immense fascination. It makes one realize how extremely arbitrary our idea of reality is, though our idea of reality is incomparably greater than that of even the highest of the lower animals. Goodness knows what sort of a world a creature with more effective senses and a better mind than ours would live in!

As an example of the strangeness of some of these animal universes, let me cite the case of the frog, which was communicated to me recently by Patrick D. Wall of M.I.T. Apparently the recent researches on frogs indicate that, although the frog has mechanically very good eyes, it sees in a very limited way. Evidently the buzzing, blooming confusion comes in at its eyes, but what its nervous system selects out of the innumerable sensa which come in is limited to that which moves. One can imagine a frog sitting on a water-lily pad and looking down into the water. There is a minnow swimming, and as long as the minnow swims, the frog sees it; the minnow stands still for a little and immediately it disappears from the frog's universe; when it starts swimming again, it enters into the frog's world once more and goes on. The frog's universe must therefore be unutterably strange, a continuous emergence and disappearance of objects. What on earth would a frog's philosophy be— the metaphysics of appearance and disappearance? There may be frog Platos, for all we know, who would devise the most extraordinary systems to account for this fantastic reality.

Much more limited universes belong to animals of lower levels of organization than the frog. Even animals as high as dogs and monkeys quite clearly have entirely different kinds of universes from ours. They just don't notice certain things which to us are very important. The dog obviously doesn't notice the sunset or the flowers on the tree, which to us seem very beautiful. He just smells the trunk of the tree and finds something very satisfactory there.

When we come to human beings, we find that the nervous system selects from the buzzing, blooming confusion in the same way that the animal's nervous system selects, but it doesn't select anything like as rigorously. Much more comes through to the human consciousness than ever comes through to the animal, even to the higher animal. Such an enormous range of reality enters the human mind, there is such a great profusion of material, that here James is quite right: in spite of the neurological selection and abstraction which has gone on, the profusion is a confusion. And here is where language comes in. We proceed to a higher level of abstraction by means of language and select in this conscious and semi-conscious or pre-conscious way those materials which are useful to us biologically; and, since we are not entirely at the mercy of our biological necessities, we also select those materials which are valuable socially or valuable from the point of view of aesthetics or what not.

The materials which we derive through these acts of abstraction are immediately translated into symbols which we can understand. We evidently have this innate tendency to turn all our experiences into more or less equivalent symbols, as well as an innate urge to order and meaning. The symbols may be of many non-verbal varieties, but by far the most important and the most highly organized symbol system is language. And it is through language that we impose symbolic order and symbolic meaning upon a profusion which, as it is apprehended directly, seems to us terribly confusing.

This process of abstraction and selection is extremely useful to us from a biological point of view. In fact, it is quite clear that we couldn't get on without it. It is useful to us as scientists and technologists in our efforts to control environment. It is also useful to us as social beings. But here we come once more to the ambivalence of the linguistic and symbol-making process. As we impose order and meaning upon immediate experience, it is just as easy for us to impose bad order and bad meaning as it is to impose good order and good meaning. We enjoy the process of symbolization; it is as though there was a kind of art-for-art's-sake pleasure in the procedure. But we very often find that in our enthusiasm for imposing order and meaning through symbols upon immediate experience we have made an awful mess of the experience and created a symbol pattern which leads us into endless trouble.

It is worth quoting a few examples of how this urge to order and meaning has somehow gone astray. One of the areas in which human beings have tried to impose their own kind of order and meaning is the area of astronomy. Man, from earliest times, has looked up at the heavenly bodies, the sun, the moon, the planets, and the stars, and has been puzzled, as anybody in heaven knows, by the extraordinary mystery of their existence. He has tried to impose upon this mystery an order and a meaning which makes sense to him as an all-too-human being; and in many cases, as we see from the study of history, he has made profound mistakes in regard to the order and meaning of the heavenly bodies—mistakes which have cost him very dearly in his social and individual life.

Consider man's attitude toward eclipses. From time immemorial, eclipses have been regarded as portents which foretold disasters. They have been felt to be closely connected with human life—and always in an extremely dangerous way. On the 27 August 413 B.C. there was an eclipse of the moon. This particular eclipse of the moon was of great historical importance because it was observed by Nicias and the Athenians, who were at the time besieging Syracuse in Sicily. They had been in considerable trouble and it was quite clear that they ought to go home, that they would probably get into much worse trouble if they stayed on. An eclipse was profoundly unlucky in the symbol system of the Athenians; in their search for order and meaning in the universe, they had made the decision that a journey should never be started in the neighbourhood of an eclipse. So Nicias decided to postpone the return to Athens for at least a month, with the consequence that his entire fleet was destroyed and his entire army was taken prisoner by the Syracuseans. If you have this hunger and thirst for order and meaning and are not patient enough to look into the real nature of the order and meaning, but insist that the universe is meaningful in terms of your all-too-human wishes and desires, you will certainly get into trouble.

A similar example of the extreme danger of having turned the universe into the wrong kind of symbols was illustrated by the Aztecs. They, too, wanted to make some kind of sense and order of the celestial phenomena, and they concentrated primarily upon the sun. Unfortunately they anthropomorphized it and felt that in order to keep alive, the sun must be constantly fed—and one of the things that they thought the sun needed was the blood of sacrificial victims. As anybody who has read Aztec history knows, they had the peculiarly unpleasant method of sacrifice of ripping the heart out of the victim and holding it up to the sun. The necessity of providing the sun with a continual supply of human blood imposed upon the Aztecs the foreign policy of continually raiding their neighbours for victims. They did their best not to kill people in battles, but to take them alive; and they would bring them back to Mexico City and sacrifice them at the rate of twenty thousand a year. Needless to say, this procedure did not make them very popular with their neighbours; when the Spaniards arrived, a great many of the neighbours of the Aztec kingdom went over to their side, and this accounts for the almost miraculous success of Cortez and his tiny band in overthrowing the Aztec empire.

These two examples show how dangerous it is to try to impose symbolic order and meaning upon the world before you really understand what the world is like. Nevertheless, we shall always do this because it is very difficult for human beings to tolerate the mysterious as such—what theologian Rudolpf Otto calls the *Mysterium tremendum* of the world. It is so terrible and inexplicable that he has always had to put up a smoke screen of symbols between it and himself. In one of its functions, it may be said that language is a device for taking mysteriousness out of mystery. We have always done this, and unquestionably in future times historians will see that we are still doing it, perhaps not as flagrantly as the Aztecs or the Greeks did it, but probably very badly.

This tendency to impose premature order and meaning upon the universe is illustrated in the culture of the Middle Ages. As the great French historian of medieval art, Emile Mâle, points out, in the Middle Ages the *idea* of a thing was always more real than the thing itself.[9] The study of things for their own sake held no meaning for thoughtful men. The task for the student of nature was to discover the eternal truth which God would have each thing express. We may now ask ourselves what were the eternal truths expressed by individual things in the Middle Ages: They were not generalizations based upon the humble observation of facts; medieval scholars were simply not interested in the humble observation of facts. They were only interested in illustrating in the external world something that they had read either in the scriptures or in the Greek philosophers whom they regarded as authorities.

We may say that the proper relationship between words and things had been reversed during the whole of the Middle Ages. The proper relationship, I presume, is that words should be regarded as arbitrary symbols standing for things. But the men

9. Emile Mâle, *The Gothic Image* (New York: Harper & Row, 1958), pp. 27–28.

of the Middle Ages looked at it the other way around. They regarded things as being illustrations of some general abstract principle to be found in Aristotle or in some part of the scriptures. As one reads medieval literature, one begins by being highly entertained by the extraordinary phenomenon of allegorical botany, of parables in natural history, of astronomy which tells fortunes. But in a very short while—certainly I speak for myself—one becomes terribly oppressed by the awful humanization of nature. One has a sense of being boxed into a world where everything has a suffocating feeling of humanity instead of being other than humanity. To use a phrase of Gerard Manley Hopkins, the medieval world is one where everything 'wears man's smudge and shares man's smell'.[10] It was only when this reversal of the relationship between words and things was changed, as a result of the new interest in science, that we entered a world where nature is refreshingly other than in the all too human world.

In our own time, we find that all the most horrifying aspects of contemporary life have arisen precisely from this wrong relationship between symbols and worlds. All the totalitarian tyrannies of our time have been based upon the wrong relationship of things and words; words have not been regarded by them as symbols arbitrarily standing for things, but things have been regarded as illustrations of words.

Take, for example, the whole Nazi racial doctrine. This would have been impossible if individual Jews and gipsies had been regarded as what they were—each of them a separate human personality. But they were not so regarded. Instead each of these persons was reduced to being merely the illustration of a pejorative label; the word 'Jew' or the word 'gipsy' was regarded as a category. And the individual humans, who were of course the only realities, were assimilated to this category; they were made to be merely illustrations of a bad category, which

10. Gerard Manley Hopkins, 'God's Grandeur', I, 7 in *The Poems of Gerald Manley Hopkins* (London: Oxford University Press, 1967), 66.

as such could be exterminated with a perfectly good con-
science. What was being exterminated was not really a human
being; it was merely the illustration of an idea.

We see the same thing under the Communist regimes, where
individual human beings are lumped together merely as illustrations of capitalism, imperialism, cannibalistic bourgeoisie,
and so on, and as such are regarded as something sub-human
which it is permissible to destroy. There is no doubt at all that
this tendency is one of the most dangerous which we have to
face. It is one of the highest prices we have to pay for the
inestimable benefit of language. We are forced to accept—because we accept the grammar and syntax of our language—the
idea that whole classes of real individual things are in fact
merely the expressions of some diabolic principle.

After all, one can say that wars can really only be fought if the
purely human individuals engaged in them are disregarded and
the opposite side is simply equated with the concretization of
a bad abstraction. This is in fact what all war propaganda is: it
is making people on our side believe that people on the other
side are merely the concretization of very bad abstractions. I
think the democratic countries don't go quite as far in this as the
other ones have done, but it remains an appalling danger.

Now let us consider the dangers on an intellectual level of
having a wrong form of order and meaning in the world. A few
years ago I became very interested in the history of what used
to be called 'animal magnetism' and was later called 'hypnosis'.
When one examines the history of this very strange subject
during the nineteenth century, one is flabbergasted by the attitude of official medicine, and, to some extent, of official science
in general, toward the subject. Because the Victorian *Weltanschauung* had taken a certain form and the urge to order and
meaning had stressed the fact that material objects were somehow much more real than psychological events, it was quite
impossible for most medical men to behave in any kind of scientific or even rational way towards the phenomena of animal
magnetism and hypnosis.

The whole theory of hypnotic anæsthesia was fully developed by James Esdaile in 1846, before the invention of chloroform and ether, and before the invention of aseptic surgery and antiseptics. Not only was Esdaile able to perform a great number of major operations which had never been performed before, he was able to reduce the death rate following surgery, which was then 29 per cent, to 5 per cent. One would have thought that the medical profession would have sat up and taken notice, but all that Esdaile got for his pains was to be hounded out of the profession, called a quack and a charlatan, and forbidden to practice at all. It is extraordinary that the recently published textbook of Dr. Milton Marmor, the anæsthesiologist at Cedars of Lebanon in Los Angeles, really just takes up where Esdaile left off 113 years ago, that simply from pure professional and academic dislike of unfamiliar ideas, this immensely valuable procedure was allowed to remain completely or virtually unexplored for more than a century.[11] This wasn't merely a malignancy; the members of the medical profession who persecuted Esdaile and his followers were completely the prisoners of their system of order and meaning, which had been developed in the past century or two, and they could not escape from it.

Undoubtedly the future will show that there are plenty of semantic prisons in which we are confined today which do not permit us to think straight about all kinds of very important subjects. It will undoubtedly be clear to the historians a hundred years from now, but it is not clear to us what these prisons are. We can only be quite sure that there are plenty of them.

11. Milton J. Marmor, *Hypnosis in Anesthesiology* (Springfield, Ill.: C C Thomas, 1959).

ART

I'M going to try to talk in this
lecture about an impossibly large subject—the subject of art—
and how it relates to the human individual. When one comes
to think of it, the enormous part played by the arts in human
history—the great importance which man has always attached
to his arts—is one of the strangest things. One has to consider
why this would be so and what the relationship is between the
arts and human life. The subject is vast, and I can only touch on
various aspects of it in a rather tentative way.

We have seen that in general man has what may be called an
urge to order and an urge to meaning. We are given by our
nervous system a profusion of experience, and a profusion so
great that it seems to us confusion. Consequently, even after
our nervous system has done the selection from immediate
reality, we find ourselves bewildered, and we have, in some
way, to cure our bewilderment. We desire to think of ourselves
as coherent beings, living in a coherent world which makes
sense. But in order to live in such a world, we have to create
it by imposing upon the world of our experience a pattern of
order and meaning, and this we do by imposing a system of
symbols upon it.

Delivered on November 7, 1959

We can say that science, art, and philosophy are three ways of making sense of the world in which we live. Science and philosophy are concerned with explaining the world in terms of the fewest possible number of general principles which will give meaning to the profusion with which we are presented by our nervous system. The order and meaning sought by the artist and imposed by him upon the confusion-profusion of the world is of a different kind. He doesn't seek to explain it in terms of beauty. To use a phrase originally used by Clive Bell, which, although it is quite vague, is still a very useful phrase, the artist gives order to the world in terms of 'significant form'. What he does is to try and perceive the forms inherent in nature and to find a symbolic equivalence for these forms which he then imposes upon the world in order to produce the order which he feels to be so supremely important, and which, indeed, we all feel to be supremely important.

The artist seeks to impose this order of beauty and of significant form upon both the external reality and the internal reality within himself. He wants always to see himself in relation to the world and to create symbolically a harmony in which both fit. In this respect—in that it consciously takes into account the internal world as well as the external—art differs markedly from most types of science.

The orders and meanings which the artist imposes upon the world are naturally of very different qualities. There are good orders and there are bad orders. There are good meanings and there are bad meanings. An order may be either not orderly enough—and we have a chaotic work of art—or it may be too orderly—it may be rigid and conventional and boring in its formality. Or else we may have an order in which the elements out of which the symbol system is created are excellent, but in which the total arrangement fails. Conversely, we may have a good overall arrangement of rather inadequate elements. And occasionally we get an excellent arrangement of excellent elements, in which case we have a masterpiece. But as we all know, masterpieces of art are very rare.

In the same way, we can have different degrees of excellence in the meanings given by artists to the world. We can have meanings which are noble and meanings which are ignoble. We can have meanings which are true to nature and realistic, and meanings which are profoundly unrealistic. We can have low and unpleasant meanings, and we can have fine and important meanings. Here we see where the social importance of art comes in; one can say that the style of life in any given society within a given period is, to some extent at least, dictated by the quality of the art prevailing at that time. If the art is good and if people care for it, then on the whole what may be called the style of living will be good. If the prevailing art is bad, then the style of living may be extremely wanting in elegance and nobility. So we see that in a certain way aesthetic errors and shortcomings may have social consequences. A bad work of art may in a sense be a social offense; it can do a lot of harm—or anyhow fail to do a lot of good. The best works of art somehow help us to know ourselves and to know our relations with the world at our best and at the best of the world, whereas bad and inferior works of art encourage us in our weaknesses and encourage us to see the world in a completely uninteresting and insignificant way.

In a certain sense we can say that the citizen in *Julius Caesar* who kept shouting, 'Tear him for his bad verses,' was right, that the man who writes bad verses is committing some kind of crime against society.[1]

The great artist must proceed through understanding and sympathy. The greatness of the great artist depends precisely on the width and the intensity of his sympathy. There have been, of course, extremely gifted artists whose view was exceedingly narrow. They have produced remarkable works of art within a very small compass, but on the whole the artists

1. William Shakespeare, *Julius Caesar*, III. iii. 34.

whom the world has always recognized as the greatest are those with the widest sympathy. The people who combine intensity with wide extension are able, so to speak, to take in a greater amount of material and give order to it than the smaller artist.

Walt Whitman has some interesting remarks on sympathy. He says,

> The messages of great poets to each man and woman are, Come to us on equal terms, Only then can you understand us, We are no better than you, What we enclose you enclose, What we enjoy you may enjoy. Did you suppose there could be only one Supreme? We affirm there can be unnumbered Supremes, and that one does not countervail another any more than one eyesight countervails another.[2]

There is a line in 'Song of Myself' where Whitman says, 'whoever walks a furlong without sympathy walks to his own funeral, dressed in his shroud'.[3] And, another famous line, 'I am the man . . . . I suffered . . . . I was there.'[4] These lines about sympathy are followed by a striking series of identifications where the poet identifies himself with different classes of suffering humanity. He identifies himself with the hunted slave, with a victim of the massacre of the Alamo, with a sailor on the *Bonhomme Richard*. It is curious to compare this Whitmanian rhapsody, which is extremely beautiful, with the much more classical expression of the same idea which we find in Matthew Arnold's 'Strayed Reveller', where he speaks of the poet seeing the world as clearly as the gods see it, but seeing it also very differently inasmuch as he is identified and suffers with what he looks at.· The poem can be summed up in these words: 'Such a price the Gods exact for song, to become what we sing.'[5]

The process is one of becoming and then expressing what we become in terms of the most powerful and penetrating symbols

2. Walt Whitman, Preface to the first edition of *Leaves of Grass* (1855).
3. Walt Whitman, 'Song of Myself' (48) 1265.
4. Ibid. (33) 827.
5. Matthew Arnold, 'The Strayed Reveller to Ulysses', 103–105.

possible; it is a matter of finding a symbolic equivalent to the immediate experience of sympathy and putting it across in the noblest and finest form possible. And it is when the artist fails to put it over in the form which we recognize as noble that we are faced with the problem of bad art and the bad social consequences it may have.

Here I would like to make a little digression on two aspects of art which are always present: art as communication and art as therapy. All poets have stressed the fact that art is a therapy. They talk again and again about the power which art has to get rid of the painful emotions and thoughts which torment the poet—to get rid of them simply by paying attention to them and expressing them. This cathartic, therapeutic side of art has been found in modern psychotherapy to be extremely important. Innumerable people with psychological problems have found that they get great relief in making artistic expression of their ideas; the painful pressure within them is let loose, and they are able to carry on much more effectively as a consequence.

However, what we do find now, I am sorry to say, is that many people who take up art in an amateur way and get a great deal of pleasure out of it seem to confuse the two functions of art and imagine that, because the art they produce is for them therapeutic, it will give pleasure to other people. This, alas, is not necessarily true. The picture that I draw, which may be very good for me, may make you sick; this is something which, unfortunately, many people find difficult to understand. I think that we should make it quite clear that art as communication is a job for specially gifted people, but that art as therapy is something which probably everybody ought to practice for his own good. If we make this clear, and make it clear to ourselves that art as therapy is not necessarily the same as art as communication, then the distressing confusions and disappointments which greatly affect many amateur artists will be avoided.

Let us now go back to the problem of art as contrasted with science and philosophy. In science and philosophy there are probably two main methods of explaining reality. One is the method of concentrating attention on the atomic elements of reality. This is represented in classical antiquity by the work of Democritus and Lucretius and is the basic methodology of modern physics and chemistry starting with Galileo and Newton. We see it applied on the psychological level in behaviourism.

The other method is the formal one of concentrating attention on the gestalten of nature, on the forms which are presented on a large scale. In the classical period this formal approach was represented, in different ways, by Plato and Aristotle, and in modern science we see it in taxonomy, in comparative anatomy, and in morphology. Incidentally, the word 'morphology' was invented by Goethe, so it has a profoundly artistic and poetic overtone to it; in modern psychology we see it represented in the Gestalt school.

In most cases art has been more interested in the second approach to reality, although there have been atomic approaches. In modern literature we can find examples in D. H. Lawrence's *Women in Love,* in Dorothy Richardson's novels, and in parts of James Joyce's novels, where the concentration of attention seems to be on psychological elements so small—psychological atoms, so to speak—that they are below the level of character and narrative.

There is an analogy here with the smallest particles of physics and chemistry. In chemistry the molecule is below the level of color and of temperature. The atom and the sub-atomic particles are still lower—they are even below the level of chemistry. Nevertheless, in literature as in science, when they are used well the 'elementary particles' do give us remarkable insights into reality.

In the field of music we may find something analogous in the works of the French composer Pierre Boulez, where the tones are almost atomic—below the level of melody and the ordinary forms of construction. Something of the kind can also be seen in some manifestations of non-representational art. I would think that some of the paintings of Jackson Pollock may be seen in the same way, as being art in which the artist has concentrated on the atomic elements of form—which are below the level of pattern in the ordinary sense and certainly below the level of representation of natural objects.

These atomic approaches, if they are well done, can be extremely interesting, although I think we should get tired of them after a time. In general, art has concentrated on the formal elements; it has concentrated not on the atoms composing the reality, but on the general patterns. It has looked for these patterns in the outside world and it has sought, by means of symbolic equivalents of these patterns, to impose an overall order and meaning on the reality which it finds so confusing.

Here another brief digression must be made to consider the nature of the symbolic forms which artists have chosen. Art can be divided into two main classes: those forms of art which deal with spatial reality and those forms of art which deal with reality where there is a time element. We shall find in both these cases that the symbols used by artists have a relationship with patterns occurring in the external world.

Let us consider first one of the fundamentals of spatial art, which is also one of the fundamentals of living objects in the natural world: the question of symmetry and asymmetry. As we see when we examine living creatures, there are two main forms of symmetry. There is the symmetry of the free living animal, which is a bilateral symmetry: the two sides of the animal match one another, but it is different fore and aft; it has a head and a tail and it moves in one direction. This is radically different from radial symmetry, which we find in many flowers and in those kinds of animals which are either sessile or free— which don't have the capacity for moving purposively in any direction, but either stand still or just float passively about.

When we examine the way in which artists have used symmetry in their symbols, we see that where radial symmetry occurs as a symbol, it is always associated with ideas of repose and restfulness. The symbols having bilateral symmetry seem to have something dynamic and powerful and directed about them. This is strikingly illustrated when we contrast the domes and round arches of Byzantine and Romanesque architecture with the spires and pointed arches of Gothic. The first give us a strong impression of repose and stillness. The others give an equally powerful impression of dynamic purposefulness and movement and direction. We see, then, that there is here a strong, close relationship between the meaningfulness of symbols and the kinds of facts in the outer world which we observe and which we unconsciously transfer to our symbols.

The mathematical relationships within the patterns of the outside world are often very close to or identical with the mathematical relations within the symbolic forms which we find satisfactory in art. For example, the Golden Section, which underlies practically the whole compositional procedure of Western art, is frequently found in nature; and such mathematical relationships as the Fibonacci series and the logarithmic spiral occur both in nature and in art and are felt to be profoundly satisfying. The mathematical relations which are used by animals as what modern ethologists call 'releasing mechanisms' are very simple and striking patterns which are easily recognized even by animals on a quite low level, and they are felt by human beings to be æsthetically significant.

In the same way, we find that natural rhythms are used in temporal symbols. After all, in all forms of temporal art (poetry, drama, narrative, dancing, music) we find the same elementary. symbols being used: repetitions, variations on a theme, rhythms of a more or less circular nature, or rhythms proceeding, so to speak, in a straight or an undulating line. Analogies of all these are found in nature. The movement of the heavenly bodies, the cycle of growth, the rhythms of breathing, of heart activity, of peristalsis, and so on, and the more irregular rhythms such as hunger and satisfaction, all find their analogy in the various arts which contain an element of time. Man looks at the external world, sees the cosmic and physiological rhythms around him, makes an analogue of them in his temporal arts, and uses them to impose upon what Alfred North Whitehead calls 'the flux of perpetual perishing' a rhythmic and repetitive pattern. He gives meaning and order to something which, when it is not ordered, is apt to seem terrifying—the movement toward an inevitable darkness in the future. Man has to make these patterns to give a kind of sense and coherence and meaning to the flux of time; he derives them from elements in nature, strengthens them in his system of symbols, and then re-imposes them upon nature so as to make nature more coherent in his own mind.

Now we have to consider what happens when the artist decides to create. Psychologically, what he does may be described roughly in this way: he pays attention to something in his own mind or in the external world in which he is interested and which he wants to reduce to symbols and express. Then he leaves himself open to anything which may come into his mind and enrich his ideas about what he is paying attention to, permitting him to impose a more elaborate and subtle order upon the symbol system which he is going to make. Anything which drifts into his mind may be used in this process—associations with events in his past life, pieces of scientific or philosophical or historical knowledge, things observed here and there in the external world—all this is grist to his mill. These elements are then by the imagination harmonized into a whole and expressed in the symbolic terms appropriate to the particular art in question.

The definition of imagination given by Coleridge is a very famous one and you are probably familiar with it, but I think it is worth reading again. He defines it as

> the power which reveals itself in the balance or reconcilement of opposite or discordant qualities, of sameness, with difference; of the general, with the concrete; of the idea, with the image; the

individual, with the representative; the sense of novelty and freshness, with old and familiar objects.[6]

This bringing together of disparate and often apparently irrelevant or even mutually hostile objects of knowledge or experience, and fusing them together in a single whole, is extremely important in all considerations of artists.

On what may be called the 'molecular scale' of art, we see the power of imagination illustrated very clearly in literature by the metaphor. The metaphor is essentially a bringing together by the imagination of elements which are fundamentally disparate and irrelevant to make of them a new whole which strikes us when we read it as giving a new meaning and order not only to the elements which are brought together, but to the point which they illustrate.

Let me give a few examples of good metaphors. First, the metaphor in *Macbeth* about sleep: 'Sleep that knits up the ravell'd sleave of care'.[7]Here the metaphor is the ball of silk which is being tangled by a kitten playing with it; sleep smoothes it out and puts it to order again. This is an extremely powerful and beautiful metaphor.

Consider the metaphor we find in *The Tempest,* where Prospero says, 'The strongest oaths are straw/To the fire i' the blood.'[8] Again, a very powerful metaphor. And here it is worth remarking how these metaphors depend on a certain social and economic context. To a child brought up in a city apartment this metaphor would mean nothing at all. He has never seen straw, and if he lives in a well-heated apartment he has never seen a fire. If he were writing this he would probably say, 'The strongest oaths are celluloid to the short circuit in the blood.' Anyhow, if we have had the luck to be brought up in the old-fashioned countryside and to see fires, this is a very powerful and illuminating metaphor. The same kind of illumination of the

6. Samuel Taylor Coleridge, *Biographia Literaria* (London, 1817).
7. William Shakespeare, *Macbeth*, II. ii. 37.
8. William Shakespeare, *The Tempest*, IV. i. 52.

force and violence of desire is expressed in another Shakes-
pearean metaphor, 'for those milk paps/That through the window bars bore at men's eyes'.[9]

I think of a striking metaphor which occurs in one of the
poems of Gerard Manley Hopkins, where he speaks about the
horror of being an isolated ego: 'Selfyeast of spirit a dull dough
sours.'[10] The religious tragedy of being an egotistical self resist-
ing God is powerfully illustrated by this extremely homely metaphor of yeast in bread.

Here is a beautiful metaphor from *Julius Caesar:* Portia says
to Brutus, 'Dwell I but in the suburbs/Of your good pleasure?'[11]

I want to read the whole of this extraordinary sonnet,
'Prayer', by George Herbert. The poem is a series of rather
extravagant but very beautiful metaphors which illustrate very
clearly the imaginative power of bringing disparate elements
together to illustrate the point at issue:

> Prayer the Churches banquet, Angels age,
>   Gods breath in man returning to his birth,
>   The soul in paraphrase, heart in pilgrimage,
> The Christian plummet sounding heav'n and earth;
> Engine against th' Almightie, sinners towre,
>   Reversed thunder, Christ-side-piercing spear,
>   The six-daies world transposing in an houre,
> A kinde of tune, which all things heare and fear;
> Softnesse, and peace, and joy, and love, and blisse,
>   Exalted Manna, gladnesse of the best,
>   Heaven in ordinarie, man well drest,
> The milkie way, the bird of Paradise,
>   Church-bels beyond the starres heard, the souls bloud,
>   The land of spices; something understood.

The end is extraordinary: this whole series of extravagant
metaphors ends with 'something understood.' And it is per-

9. William Shakespeare, *Timon of Athens,* IV. iii. 115–16.
10. Gerard Manley Hopkins, 'Sonnet 67' in *The Poems of Gerard Manley
Hopkins,* ed. W. H. Gardner and N. H. Mackenzie (London: Oxford University
Press, 1967), 12.
11. William Shakespeare, *Julius Caesar,* II. i. 285–286.

fectly true that these metaphors, where the imagination has brought in elements from all over the place, do permit us to understand the mysterious process of prayer which Herbert, the passionate, ecstatic Christian, is talking about.

An interesting sidelight on metaphors is cast by the Chinese system of writing. The Chinese use ideographs which are, in many cases, crystallized metaphors. They bring together disparate elements which are symbolized in a single character and which stand for certain ideas. The character which stands for 'good' contains the two characters of a woman and a child—a touching and beautiful symbol. But the Chinese were very realistic people, and they knew, as Bacon said, that women and children were hostages to fortune and a man who has given hostages to fortune is impeded in many ways. Consequently the symbol for woman in conjunction with another symbol which, in its literal sense, stands for 'square', means 'hinder'. The Chinese person who sees these symbols is stimulated to think about what the symbols stand for and the significance of them in a way in which our alphabetical writing, although far more efficient and utilitarian than the Chinese, never does.

On a large scale, the imagination harmonizes these small elementary elements of art and much larger patterns into the great whole of the complete work of art. Here I must emphasize something which I feel very strongly, although I think there are a number of contemporary critics who disagree. I feel strongly that there is a hierarchy in perfections. You can have artistic perfection on a very small scale, but it is perfection of a lower order than perfection on a large scale, which involves the harmonization of very many aspects of experience. The song 'Full fathom five thy father lies'[12] is a perfection. There is no question about this. It is an incredibly beautiful small piece of poetry. But I would certainly say that this perfection is of a lower order than the perfection of *Macbeth* or *Hamlet*, which combines an immense mass of material into an artistically satisfying whole.

12. William Shakespeare, *The Tempest*, I. ii. 394.

I would say, for example, in the sphere of the visual arts, that a piece of Sung pottery is perfect, but its perfection is of a lower order than, say, one of the best of the Sung landscapes, which harmonizes a great number of elements. A piece of weaving or a carpet may be perfect, but it is a perfection of a lower order than the *Assumption* of El Greco, the *Nativity* of Piero, or the *Dos de Mayo* of Goya. And if I may venture to criticize a contemporary manifestation of art, I would think that a great many non-representational works, although extremely beautiful, are works of a perfection whose order is of a lower order than the perfection of any of the great compositions which I have mentioned before, simply because they harmonize far fewer elements. A work like the *Nativity* or the *Dos de Mayo* harmonizes not only extraordinarily complicated systems of form and color but also every kind of human feeling and ethical value judgements.

There is a kind of modern Puritanism which thinks that these so-called literary judgements should be omitted entirely from works of art. Why this should be, considering that human beings have been using art to express them for the last five thousand years, I don't know. But my own view is that if you can have a work of art which does harmonize all these elements, other things being equal, its perfection will be superior to one which harmonizes only a few elements.

Let us go into the question of the different kinds of art. A hundred and fifty years ago it was assumed that there was only one satisfactory kind of visual art, the Greek or Roman renaissance type. We have got past this simply because we know a great deal more than our parents knew. Photography and anthropology have put at our disposal the entire range of art for the last one hundred thousand years. We have now seen the works done by Palæolithic man; entire new cultures which were simply not known when I was a boy have come to our ken. We now know there are very many different kinds of art and that, as Whitman says, there are many forms of the Supreme, all of which have a perfect right to their own existence.

We see from the very beginning wide differences in the styles of visual works. In the caves at Lascaux in France one can see that twenty thousand years ago man painted animal figures in a fantastically naturalistic way. He used what Erich Jaensch and his fellow psychologists call 'eidetic imagery'; he had the capacity somehow to project what he had seen with absolute fidelity upon the wall of the cave. But ten thousand years later, when we come to Neolithic art, we find a totally different approach: Everything is represented in an entirely symbolic form. The human figure and animal figures have been reduced to the most abstract kind of expressionism.

We find the intense and violent expressionism of many types of so-called primitive art—African art, Polynesian art, pre-Columbian art—projecting internal feelings in the strongest possible way into external forms, which are then distorted by the extraordinary power of the emotion which is being poured into them. We have art involving what may be called empathy, which is illustrated very clearly in Chinese landscape paintings and in impressionism. We have purely decorative art, the art of the arabesque, which the Moslems were condemned to practice because they were not allowed to represent human forms. And we have a sort of architectonic art—building on geometric forms, such as we see in cubism, and the art of pure fantasy, the art of surrealism. All these have been illustrated at one time or another in different places, in different parts of the world, and all are obviously perfectly legitimate methods of giving order and meaning to the world. The one does not disvalue the other. They are all supremes of equal value, and a perfection can be achieved in each one of them.

I want to end with a very few words about the most difficult of all the arts, music. Music is a very mysterious field of art simply because the symbols of which it makes use are remote from our immediate experience. In literature we are using words which have a meaning fixed in advance, and in painting we are using forms from the external world with which we are fairly familiar. But in music we are using tones which seem to have a life of their own, apart from the external world, and rhythms which, though they have analogies with natural rhythms, are strangely independent of them. And yet, as all great musicians have insisted, and as anybody who has listened to music with understanding agrees, music has some kind of cognitive meaning. It does say something about the nature of the universe. Beethoven insisted on this very strongly, and we find similar statements by almost every great composer. They have this intense feeling that what they are saying is not just a mere pattern of sound.

On a strictly individual basis, these complicated rhythms tell us something about the equally complicated rhythms in the inner life of man. These are probably quite inexpressible in words, but then a great many things are inexpressible in words. We see the inexpressibility of music in words when we read an 'explanation' saying, 'At this point Beethoven was expressing his agony, having parted from his lady love' or something of the kind. The next programme will read, 'Beethoven at this point was laughing uproariously over the comedy of human life.'

All this proves that words are extremely unsatisfactory means for saying what music is about—it is certainly about the very subtle and obscure kinds of movements within the mind-body and the spirit. And maybe at the same time music is about the universe at large. It seems to express a kind of pure non-physical dynamism in the external world. It seems even to express something which Bergson described when he spoke of William James:

> The powerful feelings which stir the soul at special moments are forces as real as those that interest the physicist; man does not create them any more than he creates light or heat. According to James, we bathe in an atmosphere traversed by great spiritual currents.[13]

13. Henri Bergson, preface to William James, *Le pragmatisme* (Paris: Flammarion, 1911).

This may sound rather like a mystical view of what music stands for and what indeed all the arts stand for; but my own feeling is that there is a profound truth in this.

All the arts, though they speak about us in our relationship to the immediate experience, at the same time tell us something about the nature of the world, about the mysterious forces which we feel to be around us, and about the cosmic order of which we seem to have glimpses.

MAN AND RELIGION

I WOULD like to start by reading two or three lines from the twenty-first chapter of the Book of Revelation. This chapter contains a description of the New Jerusalem, and it ends like this: 'and the street of the city was pure gold as it were transparent glass. And I saw no temple therein: for the Lord God Almighty and the Lamb are the temple of it' (Revelation 21:21–22).

In the same way there was no temple—no religion, in the ordinary sense of the word—in Eden. Adam and Eve didn't require the ordinary apparatus of religion because they were in a position to hear the voice of the Lord as he walked 'in the garden in the cool of the day' (Genesis 3:8).

When we read the Book of Genesis, we find that religion, in the conventional sense of the word, began only after the expulsion of Adam and Eve from the garden, and that the first record of it is the building of the two altars by Cain and Abel. This was also the beginning of the first religious war. Cain was a husbandman—a vegetarian, like Hitler—and Abel was a herdsman and a meat eater. They were divided passionately on their different occupations, and this gave them a kind of religious absoluteness, with the sad result which we all know.

Delivered on November 23, 1959

198

In the third chapter of Genesis, after the birth of Seth, who was Adam's third son, there is mention of a new phase in religion. The verse reads: 'And to Seth, to him also was born a son; and he called his name Enos: then began men to call upon the name of the Lord' (Genesis 4:26). This evidently represents the beginning of what may be called the conceptual, verbalized side of religion.

These two sets of references illustrate very clearly that there are two main kinds of religion. There is the religion of immediate experience—the religion, in the words of Genesis, of hearing the voice of God walking in the garden in the cool of the day, the religion of direct acquaintance with the divine in the world. And then there is the religion of symbols, the religion of the imposition of order and meaning upon the world through verbal or non-verbal symbols and their manipulation, the religion of knowledge about the divine rather than direct acquaintance with it. These two types of religions have always existed, and we shall discuss them both.

Let us begin with religion as the manipulation of symbols to impose order and meaning upon the flux of experience. In practice we find that there are two types of symbol-manipulating religions: the religion of myth and the religion of creed and theology. Myth is obviously a kind of non-logical philosophy; it expresses in the form of a story or, very often, in the form of some visual image, or even in the form of a dance or a complicated ritual, some generalized feeling about the nature of the world and of man's experience in regard to it. Myth is unpretentious, in the sense that it doesn't claim to be strictly true. It is merely expressive of our feelings about experience. But although it is non-logical philosophy, it is often very profound philosophy, precisely because it is non-logical and non-discursive. It permits the bringing together in the story, the image, the picture, the statue, or the dance of a number of the disparate and even apparently incommensurable or incompatible parts of our experience. It brings them together and shows them to be an indissoluble whole, exactly as we experience them. In this sense it is the most profound kind of symbolism. For example, the myth of the great Mother, which runs through all of the earlier religions, shows the mother as the principle of life, of fecundity, of fertility, of kindness and nourishing compassion; but at the same time she is the principle of death and destruction. In Hinduism, Kali is at once the infinitely kind and loving mother and the terrifying Goddess of destruction, who has a necklace of skulls and drinks the blood of human beings from a skull. This picture is profoundly realistic; if you give life, you must necessarily give death, because life always ends in death and must be renewed through death. Whether such myths are true or not is quite an irrelevant question; they are simply expressive of our reactions to the mystery of the world in which we live.

We find earlier non-logical mythical religions very frequently associated with what have been called spiritual exercises, but which are in fact psychophysical exercises. By use of chant and dance and gesture, they get a genuine kind of revelation. The physical tensions which are built up by our anxious and ego-centered life are released. This release through physical gestures constitutes what the Quakers called an 'opening' through which the profounder forces of life without and within us can flow more freely. It is very interesting to see even within our own tradition how this occasional letting go for religious purposes has had profound and very salutary influences. The Quakers were called 'Quakers' for the simple reason that they quaked. The meetings of the early Quakers very frequently ended with the greater part of the assembly indulging in the strangest kind of violent bodily movements, which were profoundly releasing and which permitted, so to speak, the influx of the spirit.

As a matter of history the Quakers, as long as they quaked, had the greatest degree of inspiration and were at the height of their spiritual power. We have the same phenomenon in the

Shakers, and we see it in the contemporary religious movement called Subud—the coming upon the assembled people of curiously violent and involuntary physical movements, which produce a release and permit for many people the influx and the flowing through of deeply powerful spiritual forces. Here I would like to cite the eminent French Islamic scholar Emil Dermenghem, who says that modern Europe—of course modern Europe includes modern America—is almost alone in having renounced out of bourgeois respectability and Gallic Puritanism the participation of the body in the pursuit of the spirit.[1] In India as in Islam, chants, rhythms, and dance are spiritual exercises. But only small corners of our tradition have illustrated, through this permission to use the body, that the spirit may be left more free, a fact which is so manifestly clear when we study the history of the Oriental religions.

Religion as a system of beliefs is a profoundly different kind of religion, and it is the one which has been the most important in the West. The two types of religion—the religion of direct acquaintance with the divine and the religion of a system of beliefs—*have* co-existed in the West, but the mystics have always formed a minority in the midst of the official symbol-manipulating religions, and the relationship has been a rather uneasy symbiosis. The members of the official religion have tended to look upon the mystics as difficult, trouble-making people. They have even made puns about the name, calling mysticism 'mysti-schism'—a foggy, antinomian doctrine, which doesn't conform easily to authority. On their side the mystics have spoken not exactly with contempt—they don't feel contempt—but with sadness and compassion about those who are devoted to the symbolic religion, because they feel that the pursuit and the manipulation of symbols is simply incapable in the nature of things of achieving what they regard as the highest end, the union with God. William Blake, who was essentially

1. Emile Dermenghem, *Vies des saints musulmains* (Alger: Editions Baconnier), p. 285.

a mystic, was apt to express himself in rather violent terms about those he disagreed with. He has a little couplet where he says, 'Come hither, my boy, tell me what thou seest there'—and the boy answers, 'A fool tangled in a religious snare.'[2]

Within the tradition of Western Christianity, the Mystics have been assured of a tolerated position by the perpetuation at an early stage in Christian development of what is called a pious fraud. About the sixth century there appeared a series of Christian Neoplatonic volumes under the name of Dionysius the Areopagite, who was the first disciple of St. Paul in Athens. These volumes were taken to be almost of apostolic value, inasmuch as Dionysius was the first disciple of St. Paul. In point of fact the books were written either at the end of the fifth or at the beginning of the sixth century in Syria. The unknown author merely signed the name of Dionysius the Areopagite to them in order to give them a better hearing among his fellows. He was a Neoplatonist who had adopted Christianity and who combined the doctrine of Neoplatonic philosophy and the practices of ecstasy with Christian doctrines. The pious fraud was extremely successful. The book was translated into Latin in the ninth century by the philosopher Scotus Erigena, and thereafter it entered into the tradition of the Western Church and acted as a kind of bulwark and guarantee for the mystical minority within the Church. It was not until recent times that the fraud was recognized for what it was. Meanwhile, in one of the odd, ironical quirks of history, this curious bit of forgery played a very important and very beneficent part in the Western Christian tradition.

We have to consider now the relationship between the religion of immediate experience and the religion primarily concerned with symbols. In this context there is a very illuminating remark by Abbot John Chapman, a Benedictine who was one of the great spiritual directors of the twentieth century. His spiritual letters are works of great interest; he was obviously a

2. William Blake, 'Lacedæmonian Instruction'.

man who had had a profound mystical experience himself and
was able to help others along this same path. He remarks in one
of his letters on the great difficulty of reconciling—not merely
uniting—mysticism and Christianity:

> St. John of the Cross is like a sponge full of Christianity: you can
> squeeze it all out and the full mystical theory remains. Conse-
> quently, for fifteen years or so I hated St. John of the Cross and
> called him a Buddhist. I loved St. Theresa and read her again and
> again. She is first a Christian, only secondarily a mystic. Then I
> found that I had wasted fifteen years so far as prayer was con-
> cerned.[3]

By 'prayer' in this context Abbot Chapman did not of course
mean petitionary prayer. He was speaking about what is called
the prayer of quiet, the prayer of waiting upon the Lord in a
state of alert passivity and permitting the deepest elements
within the mind to come to the surface. Dionysius the Areopagite, in *Mystical Theology* and his other books, had constantly
insisted upon the fact that in order to become directly acquainted *with* God, rather than merely to know *about* God, one
must go beyond symbols and concepts. These are actually obstacles, according to Dionysius, to the immediate experience of
the divine. Empirically this has been found to be true by all the
spiritual masters, of both the Western and the Oriental worlds.
A striking example comes from the writings of Jean Jacques
Olier, who was a very well-known spiritual director of the
seventeenth century, a product of the Counter Reformation
and of the revival of mystical theology in France at the time of
Louis XIII. He wrote: 'The holy light of faith is so pure that
special illuminations are impure compared with it, even
thoughts of the saints or of the Blessed Virgin or of Jesus Christ
in His Humanity are alike hindrances to the sight of the pure
God.'[4] This seems, particularly from a Counter Reformation

3. Abbot John Chapman, *Spiritual Letters* (London, 1935).
4. Jean Jacques Olier. The phrase is found in M. H. I. Icard, *Doctrine de M.
Olier expliquée par sa vie et par ses écrits* (Paris: Seminary of Saint Sulpice,
1889), and quoted in Henri Bremond, *A Literary History of Religious Thought*

theologian, a very strange and daring statement, and yet it does represent a perfectly clear restatement of what had been said again and again by the mystics of the past. What Olier calls 'the sight of the pure God' is, psychologically speaking, the mystical experience. This is one thing, and belief in propositions about God, belief in dogmas and theological statements and liturgies inspired by these statements, is something entirely different.

In this context I would like to quote the words of an eminent contemporary Dominican theologian, Father Victor White, who is a particularly interesting writer, as he is both a theologian and a psychotherapist who worked a great deal with Jung, and as he is very well acquainted with modern psychological theories and practice. He says:

> Freud's conception of religion as a universal neurosis [is not] entirely without truth and value—once we have understood his terminology. We must remember that for him, not only religion, but dreams, unbidden phantasies, slips of the tongue and pen—everything short of an unrealizable idea of complete consciousness is somehow abnormal and pathological (cf. Freud's *Psychopathology of Everyday Life,* passim). But theology will also confirm that religion, in the sense of creeds and external cults, arises from man's relative unconsciousness, from his incomprehension of—and disharmony with—the creative mind behind the universe, and from his own inner conflicts and divisions. Such religion, in theological language, is the result of man's fall from original innocence and integrity, his remoteness on this earth from Divine vision.[5]

The religion of direct experience of the divine has been regarded as the privilege of a very few people. I personally don't think this is necessarily true at all. I think that practically everyone is capable of this immediate experience, provided he sets

---

in France (London: Society for Promoting Christian Knowledge, 1936), vol. 3, p. 428.

5. Victor White, *God and the Unconscious* (London: Harvill Press, 1952), pp. 45–46.

about it in the right way and is prepared to do what is necessary. We have simply taken for granted that the mystics represent a very small minority among a huge majority who must be content with the religion of creeds and symbols and sacred books and liturgies and organizations.

Belief is a matter of very great importance. One of the great best sellers of recent years is called *The Power of Belief*. This is a very good title, because belief is a very great source of power. It has power for the believer himself and permits the believing person to exercise power over others. It does in a sense move mountains. Belief, like any other source of power, can be used for both evil and good, and just as well for evil as for good. We have seen in our very own time the terrifying spectacle of Hitler very nearly conquering the entire world through the power of belief in something which was not only manifestly untrue but profoundly evil.

This tremendous fact of belief, which is so constantly cultivated within the symbol-manipulating religions, is essentially ambivalent. The consequence is that religion as a system of beliefs has always been an ambivalent force. It gives birth simultaneously to humility and to what the medieval poets call the 'proud prelate', the ecclesiastical tyrant. It gives birth to the highest form of art and to the lowest form of superstition. It lights the fires of charity, and it also lights the fires of the Inquisition and the fire that burned Servetus in the Geneva of Calvin. It gives birth to St. Francis and Elizabeth Fry, but it also gives birth to Torquemada and Kramer and Springer, the authors of the *Malleus Maleficorum*, the great handbook of witch hunters published about the same year Columbus discovered America. It gives birth to George Fox, but it also gives birth to Archbishop Laud. This tremendous force of religion as a theological system has always been ambivalent precisely because of the strange nature of belief itself and because of the strange capacity of man, when he embarks on his philosophical speculations, for coming up with extremely strange and fantastic answers.

Myths, on the whole, have been much less dangerous than theological systems because they are less precise and have fewer pretensions. Where you have theological systems it is claimed that these propositions about events in the past and events in the future and the structure of the universe are absolutely true; consequently reluctance to accept them is regarded as a rebellion against God, worthy of the most undying punishment. And we see that in fact these systems have, as a matter of historical record, been used as justification for almost every act of aggression and imperialistic expansion. There is hardly a single large-scale crime in history which has not been committed in the name of God. This was summed up many centuries ago in the hexameter of Lucretius: *'Tantum religio potuit suadere malorum'*[6] (such great evils was religion able to persuade men to commit). He should have added, *'Tantum religio potuit suadere bonorum'* (such great goods also could it persuade men to commit). Nevertheless, the good has had to be paid for by a great deal of evil.

This strife-producing quality of religion as a system of theological symbols has brought about not only the jihads and crusades of one religion against another, it has produced an enormous amount of internal friction within the same religion. The *odium theologicum,* the theological hatred, is notorious for its virulence, and the religious wars of the sixteenth and seventeenth centuries were of a degree of ferocity which passes all belief. In this context I think we should remember that we are accustomed now to say, 'O, what great evils Naturalism as a philosophy has brought upon the world!'—but in point of historical fact, supernaturalism has brought about just as great evils and perhaps even greater ones. We must not allow ourselves to be carried away by this kind of rhetoric.

I mentioned before the extraordinary capacity of philosophers and theologians to produce fantastic ideas which they

6. Lucretius, *De Rerum Natura,* I, 101.

then dignify with the name of dogma or revelation. As an example of this I would like to cite a few facts about one of the fundamental ideas in Christianity, the idea of the atonement. Such information as I have here is based upon the excellent article, a long essay on the subject, in Hastings's *Encyclopedia of Religion and Ethics*. The essay is by Dr. Adams Brown, who at one time was professor of theology at the Union Theological Seminary in New York. He has set forth the history of this doctrine very lucidly and summed it up very cogently at the end. Let me quickly go through it, because it illustrates clearly the dangers of symbol-manipulating religion.

In the earliest period of Christianity, Christ's death was regarded either as a covenant sacrifice comparable to the sacrifice of the pascal lamb in the Jewish religion or as a ransom, exactly comparable to the price paid by a slave to obtain his freedom or to the price paid by a war prisoner for his release. Both of these ideas are hinted at in the Gospels. Later on, in post-Gospel theology, there came the notion that Christ's death was the bloody expiation for original sin. This was based on the very ancient idea that any wrongdoing required expiation by suffering on the part of the sinner himself or on the part of a substitute for the sinner. In the Old Testament we read that David's sin in making a census of his people was punished by a plague which killed seventy thousand of his subjects but didn't kill David.

In Patristic times we find a profound difference on this subject between the Greek theologians and the Latin theologians. The Greek theologians were not primarily concerned with the death of Christ; they were concerned with life, and the death was so to speak a mere incident in the life. Their view of the atonement was that it existed not to save man from guilt but to save him from the corruption into which he had fallen after the fall of Adam and Eve. Consequently the life was more important than the death. Ireneus says that Christ came and lived the life of man in order that man might live a life comparable to his

—and that this was the saving quality of the atonement.

Among the Latin fathers the stress was entirely different. Here the idea was that man was being redeemed, not from corruption primarily, but from guilt. He was redeemed from the punishment which had to be inflicted upon him for the sin of Adam. Whereas the Greek theologians regarded God as primarily Absolute Spirit, the Latin theologians regarded God as Governor and Lawgiver, with the mind of a Roman lawyer (their theology tends to be in legalistic terms). The doctrine was developed slowly, but we get in St. Augustine a continual stress on the horror of original sin and on the idea that guilt is fully inherited by all members of the human race, so that an unbaptised child must necessarily go directly to hell.

This view was developed over the centuries, and there was a long period of discussion about the question of the ransom. To whom was the ransom of the death of Christ paid? There were many theologians who insisted that the ransom was paid to Satan, that God had handed the world over to Satan but wished to take it back again and had to pay this enormous price to Satan for the privilege. On the other hand, there were theologians who insisted that the ransom was paid to satisfy the honour of God. God had been infinitely offended, and the only reparation for an infinite offense was an infinite satisfaction, the death of the God-man, Christ.

It was the latter view which prevailed in the more or less official doctrine formulated by St. Anselm in the twelfth century. Anselm said that the death of this infinite Person produced a surplus of satisfaction, which constituted a kind of fund of merit that could be used for the absolution of sins. It was on the basis of this doctrine that the medieval church enlarged the practice of selling indulgences, which led in due course to the Reformation.

In the Reformation we find Calvin, who felt that retributive justice was an essential part of the character of God and that Christ was actually bearing the punishment which was due to man. 'The Christ'—these are the words he used—'bore the weight of the Divine anger . . . and experienced all the signs of an angry and avenging God.'[7] These views were modified by the Arminians and the Socinians and by Hugo Grotius in the sixteenth and seventeenth centuries and have given place gradually to a more ethical and spiritual view in modern Protestantism.

Now I would like to quote the passage in which Professor Adams Brown sums up the whole of this very strange history:

> The atoning character of Christ's death is found now in its penal quality as suffering, now in its ethical character as obedience. It is represented now as a ransom to redeem man from Satan, now as a satisfaction due to the honour of God, now as a penalty demanded by His justice. Its necessity is grounded now in the nature of things, and, again, is explained as a result of an arrangement due to God's mere good pleasure or answering his sense of fitness. The means by which its benefits are mediated to men are sometimes mystically conceived as in the Greek theology of the Sacrament; sometimes legally, as in the Protestant formula of imputation; and, still again, morally and spiritually, as in the more personal theories of recent Protestantism. Surveying differences so extreme, one might well be tempted to ask, with some recent critics, whether indeed we have here to do with an essential element in Christian doctrine, or simply with a survival of primitive ideas whose presence in the Christian system can constitute a perplexity rather than aid to faith. But the differences we have discussed are not greater than may be paralleled in the case of every other Christian doctrine.[8]

The reasons for these differences even in particular doctrines are to be sought in fundamental differences in man's conception of God and of His relation to the world. Where God is thought to be Absolute Spirit the atonement is conceived as the

---

7. Calvin, *Institutiones Romanæ Religionis*, II, xvi, 11.
8. Adams Brown, 'Expiation and Atonement' in the summary in *Encyclopedia of Religion and Ethics*, ed. James Hastings (New York: Scribner, 1925), vol. 5, p. 650.

Greek theologians conceived it; in the theology of Roman Catholicism and earlier Protestantism, God is conceived primarily
as governor and judge and legal phraseology seems a natural
expression of religious faith; where ethical doctrines come to
the fore, as in modern views of the atonement, a kind of ethical
and spiritual language is used. This confusion indicates very
clearly the extraordinary difficulties we are up against when we
embark upon a systematic theologization of experience into
conceptual and symbolic terms. The advantages which certainly accrue from accurate theological expression seem to me
offset by the very great disadvantages which the history of organized religion makes evident.

What has been the attitude of the proponent of religion as
immediate experience toward the religion expressed in terms
of symbols? Meister Eckhart, one of the great mystics of the
Middle Ages, expresses it in an extreme form: 'Why dost thou
prate of God? Whatever thou sayest of Him is untrue.'[9] Here
we have to make a short digression on the use of the word
'truth' in religious literature. The word 'truth' is used in at least
three common senses. It is used synonymously with Reality
when we say 'God is Truth', which means that God is the Pri-
mordial Fact. It is used in the sense of immediate experience,
as in the fourth Gospel, where it is said that God must be wor-
shipped 'in Spirit and in Truth' (John 4:24), meaning with an
immediate apprehension of Divine Reality. Finally, it is used in
the common sense of the word, as correspondence between
symbolic propositions and the fact to which they refer. Eckhart
was a theologian as well as a mystic and he would not have
denied that truth in the third sense was to some degree possible
in theology. He would have said that some theological propositions were certainly truer than others. But he would have denied that there was any possibility of the final end of man, the
union with God—truth in the second sense—being achieved by

9. Meister Eckhart, *Die lateinischen Werke* (Stuttgart, 1938), p. 92

means of manipulating theological symbols.

This insistence on the inefficacy of symbolic religion for the ultimate purpose of union with God has been stressed by all the Oriental religions. We find it in the literature of Hinduism, in the literature of Mahayana Buddhism, of Taoism, and so on. Hui-neng says that the truth has never been preached by the Buddha, seeing that one has to realize it within oneself, and that what is known of the teaching of Buddha is not the teaching of Buddha, which has to be an interior experience. Then we get a paradoxical phrase: 'What is the ultimate teaching of the Buddha? You won't understand it unless you have it.' The author goes on to say, 'Don't be so ignorant as to mistake the pointing finger for the moon at which you are pointing,' and he says that the habit of imagining that the pointing finger is the moon condemns all efforts to realize oneness with Reality to total failure. There were even Zen masters who prescribed that anybody who used the word 'Buddha' should have his mouth washed out with soap because it was so remote from the goal of immediate experience.

This has been the usual attitude of mystics at all times, but above all in the Orient, where philosophy has been in one respect profoundly different from Western philosophy. Oriental philosophy has always been what I may call a kind of transcendental operationalism; it starts with somebody doing something about the self and then, from the experience attained, going on to speculate and theorize about the significance of the experience. In contrast, all too frequently Western philosophy, above all modern Western philosophy, is pure speculation based on theoretical knowledge that ends only in theoretical conclusions. However, there have been many exceptions to this rule in the West, above all among the mystics, who have insisted just as strongly as their Oriental counterparts on the necessity for direct experience and on the inefficacy of symbols and of ordinary discursive thought. St. John of the Cross says categorically, 'Nothing that the imagination may conceive or the understanding comprehend, in this life, is or can be a proximate means of union with God.'[10]

The same idea is expressed by the great Anglican Mystic of the eighteenth century, William Law:

> To find or know God in reality by any outward proofs, or by anything but by God Himself made manifest and self-evident to you, will never be your case either here or hereafter. For neither God, nor heaven, nor hell, nor the devil, nor the flesh, can be any otherwise knowable in you or by you but their own existence and manifestation in you. And all pretended knowledge of any of these things, beyond and without this self-evident sensibility of their birth within you, is only such knowledge of them as the blind man hath of the light that hath never entered into him.[11]

What is the mystical experience? I take it that the mystical experience is essentially the being aware of and, while the experience lasts, being identified with a form of pure consciousness, of unstructured transpersonal consciousness which lies, so to speak, upstream from the ordinary discursive consciousness of everyday. It is a non-egotistic consciousness, a kind of formless and timeless consciousness, which seems to underlie the consciousness of the separate ego in time.

Why should this sort of consciousness be regarded as valuable? I think for two reasons. First, it is regarded as valuable because of the self-evident sensibility of values. As William Law would say, it is intrinsically valuable, just as the experience of beauty is intrinsically valuable, but much more so. Second, it is valuable because as a matter of empirical experience it does bring about changes in thought and character and feeling which the experiencer and those about him regard as manifestly desirable. It makes possible a sense of unity and solidarity with the world. It brings about the possibility of that kind of unjudging love and compassion which is stressed so much in the

10. St. John of the Cross, *The Ascent of Mount Carmel*, II.
11. William Law, quoted in Aldous Huxley, *The Perennial Philosophy* (London: Chatto & Windus, 1957), p.150.

Gospel, where Christ says, 'Judge not that ye be not judged' (Matthew 7:1). St. Catherine of Siena, on her death-bed, stressed this point with great force: 'For *no* reason whatsoever ought we to judge the action of creatures or their motives. Even when we see that it is actual sin we ought not to pass judgment on it, but have holy and sincere compassion and offer it up to God with humble and devout prayer.'[12]

The mystic is made capable of this kind of life. He is able to understand organically such portentous phrases, which for the ordinary person are extremely difficult to understand—phrases such as 'God is Love' (1 John 4:8) and 'Though he slay me, yet will I trust him' (Job 13:15).

There are other fruits of the mystical experience. There is certainly an overcoming of the fear of death, a conviction that the soul has become identical with the Absolute Principle which expresses itself in every moment in its totality. There is an acceptance of suffering and a passionate desire to alleviate suffering in others. There is a combination of what Buddhists call Prajnaparamita, which is the wisdom of the other shore, with Mahakaruna, which is universal compassion. As Eckhart says, what is taken in by contemplation is given out in love. This is the value of the experience. As for the theology of it, this is profoundly simple and is summed up in the three words which are at the base of virtually all Indian religion and philosophy: 'Tat Twam asi' (Thou art that), the sense being that the deepest part of the soul is identical with the Divine nature, that the Atman, the deep soul, is the same as Brahman, the Universal Principle, or, in Eckhart's words, that the ground of the soul is the same as the ground of the Godhead. It is the idea of the inner light, the *scintilla animae* (spark of the soul); the scholastics had a technical phrase for it, the 'synderesis'.

Now, very briefly, I must touch on the means for reaching this

12. Account of St. Catherine of Siena's spiritual testament, written down by Tommaso di Petra and quoted in Johannes Jorgensen, *Saint Catherine of Siena*, (New York: Longmans, 1939).

state. It has been constantly stressed that the means do not consist in mental activity and discursive reasoning; they consist in what Roger Fry, speaking about art, used to call 'alert passivity', or what the modern American mystic, the great teacher of reading to the world, Frank Laubach, has called 'determined sensitiveness'. You don't do anything, but you are determinedly sensitive to letting something be done within you. This has been expressed by some of the great masters of the spiritual life in the West. St. Francis de Sales, writing to his pupil St. Jeanne Chantal, says, 'You tell me you do nothing in prayer. But what do you want to do in prayer, except presenting your nothingness to God?'[13] And St. Jeanne Chantal writes in one of her letters:

> His [God's] goodness bestowed upon me this method of devotion consisting in a simple beholding and realizing of His divine presence, in which I felt utterly lost, absorbed, and at rest in Him. And this grace has been continued to me, although by my unfaithfulness I have opposed it much; permitting entrance into my mind of fears of being useless in this condition, so that desiring to do somewhat on my part, I spoiled all.[14]

This attitude of the masters of prayer is in its final analysis exactly the same as that recommended by the teacher of any psychophysical skill. The man who teaches you how to play golf or tennis, your singing teacher or piano teacher, will tell you the same thing: you must somehow combine activity with relaxation, you must let go of the clutching personal self, in order to let this deeper self within you, which you interfere with, come through and perform its miracles.

In a certain sense one can say that what we are doing all the time is trying to get into our own light. Our superficial selves eclipse our deeper selves and so don't permit this light force, which is an impartial fact within us, to come through. In effect

13. St. François de Sales, *Oeuvres Choisies* (Paris: Royer, 1843), p. 299.
14. St. Jeanne Chantal, *Oeuvres*, I, 21, quoted in Henri Bremond, *A Literary History of Religious Thought in France* (London: Society for Promoting Christian Knowledge, 1936), vol. 2, p. 406.

the whole of the technique of proficiency in every field, including this highest form of spiritual proficiency, is a dis-eclipsing process, a process of getting out of our own light. Of course, one doesn't have to formulate this process in theological terms. I myself happen to believe that the deeper self within us is in some way continuous with the mind of the universe or whatever you like to call it. But as I say, you don't necessarily have to accept this.

We see that there is no conflict between the mystical approach to religion and the scientific approach, because one is not committed by mysticism to any cut-and-dried statement about the structure of the universe. You can practice mysticism entirely in psychological terms, and on the basis of a complete agnosticism in regard to the conceptual ideas of orthodox religion, and yet come to knowledge—gnosis—and the fruits of knowledge will be the fruits of the spirit: love, joy, peace, and the capacity to help other people. And as Christ said in the Gospel, 'The tree is known by his fruit' (Matthew 12:33).

NATURAL HISTORY

OF VISIONS

I SHALL begin this lecture with
a question. It is one of those seemingly innocent but extremely
searching and profound questions which inquisitive children
pose to their parents and their parents simply don't know how
to answer and so just say, Well, now, don't be silly, run along and
play. It is a question like, Why is grass green? To answer that
question you have to go into botany, biochemistry, physics,
astronomy, and even metaphysics or theology. Similarly, this
question which I am going to start with, though perhaps not so
searching as Why is grass green? is one which takes us very far
afield. The question is, Why are precious stones precious? And
we shall find that in the course of trying to answer this question
we shall go a long way into the whole problem of the structure
of the mind and the relation of what I may call the stranger and
more remote areas of the mind with all kinds of cultural and
religious and philosophical aspects of our life.

Why are precious stones precious? The moment one starts to
think about this question, it seems unutterably queer that
human beings in the course of history should have spent such
an enormous amount of time, energy, and money on collecting
transparent or variously colored pebbles and hoarding them up

Delivered on December 7, 1959

216

and cutting them and setting them in the most elaborate forms
and fighting battles over them. There is quite obviously no
economic justification. Of course, if one does have a lot of precious stones, given the fact that they are by convention precious, it does help one economically. But precious stones in
themselves don't help us in any basic way. You can't eat precious stones, you can't till the soil with precious stones; there is
nothing they can do for you.

Even from a purely æsthetic point of view, the preciousness
of precious stones is very strange. One wonders exactly why
they have such great charm. They can't be said to be beautiful
in the sense that works of art are beautiful. A work of art is
beautiful in the sense that it has parts which are beautifully
harmonized. A work of art, whether it is musical art or visual
art or poetic art, is always a system, but a precious stone is
simply a single object; it is like a single note out of a piece of
music. Now, if you play a single note, although it may have a
great deal of charm, it is not something that you feel to be
intrinsically very beautiful; but in regard to precious stones,
people will spend tremendous energies and time and money in
trying to get hold of them. So we see that there must be something in the precious stone to which the human mind responds
in a very obscure and, on the face of it, rather unaccountable
way.

One of the reasons for our interest in precious stones is given,
curiously enough, in the *Phaedo*, where Socrates is speaking
about the ideal world, a basic metaphysical idea of Plato. Socrates says that there is an ideal world, of which our world is in a
sense a rather bad copy, beyond and above the material world.

> In this other earth the colors are much purer and more brilliant
> than they are down here. The mountains and stones have a richer
> gloss, a livelier transparency and intensity of hue. The precious
> stones of this lower world, our highly prized cornelians, topazes,
> emeralds, jaspers and all the rest of them are but tiny fragments

of these stones above. In the other earth there is no stone but that is precious and equals in beauty every gem of ours.[1]

Plato adds that the view of this earth is 'a sight to gladden the beholder's eye.'[2] This is a very curious remark because it makes quite clear that when Plato speaks about the ideal world, he isn't speaking merely of a metaphysical idea. This other world has a landscape with stones and mountains in it, and these stones and mountains have the quality precisely of precious stones in our world. More than a mere philosophic abstraction, it is something which *exists* in the human mind, which is part of our inner world of thought and feeling and insight, and which, in a certain sense, we can actually see. This inner world is what I call the world of visions, and it has something very closely to do with the preciousness of precious stones. But before we get into this, let me talk a little in general about the different regions of man's inner world.

We carry about inside our skulls a large and very variegated universe, with regions in it exceedingly strange, regions which most of us at most times don't penetrate at all, but which are always there. There is the world of memory, of fantasy and imagination, and of dreams closely connected with what the Freudians and the Jungians call the personal unconscious. There is the world of what Jung calls the collective unconscious, with archetypal forms and symbols which seem to be common to all human beings. And there is, finally, the most remote of all our inner worlds, which I call the world of visions. It is literally another world, very different from the personal worlds of our experience.

Now let me elaborate a little on these classifications, first of all on the world of memory. Memory is something unutterably strange, as anybody who has ever thought about it must have discovered, and one of the strangest facts about memory is that

1. Plato, *Phædo*, 110.
2. Ibid., 111.

it can be clearly divided into two quite distinct and separate types. There is the memory which may be called complete recall, the actual re-living in present time of past experience; and there is what we normally call memory, which is a much vaguer and more concentrated form.

Complete recall is something which a few people seem to be capable of all the time. It was said of the great American novelist Thomas Wolfe that he had the capacity for complete recall. As a novelist myself I can see that this would be in some ways a great advantage, but in other ways it must be extremely difficult to deal with because it must be very hard to know when to stop. If one has absolutely complete recall of everything that has happened to one, one can obviously go on writing for just as long as one's life has lasted without ever coming to an end, and this we do see in Wolfe's books. But one can also see in his books an extraordinary vividness in everything that he visualized.

Most of us do not have this capacity at will, but in certain circumstances it can be evoked in a great number of people. It can be evoked, for example, by means of hypnosis. The hypnotized person can bring to the surface all kinds of material which he has consciously forgotten—and in the utmost detail. Something like complete recall can also be evoked in a state of reverie, particularly if the person in reverie is prompted and helped by a capable psychiatrist or psychologist. And there are certain drugs which will help evoke recall. During the Second World War battle fatigue resulting in breakdowns, very often with hysterical blindness or deafness or paralysis, was treated either by hypnosis or, when there was no time to administer hypnosis, by giving such drugs as sodium amytal or ether, which somehow lowered the threshold between the conscious and the unconscious and permitted the recall of the traumatic material which was causing the trouble. The psychiatrists were then able to produce an abreaction to this material and were able to get these unfortunate soldiers out of their traumatic condition.

There seems to be no doubt at all, from the evidence of hypnosis and of drugs, that all of our experiences are stored in the mind and, under certain favourable circumstances, may be completely recalled. In recent years the eminent Canadian surgeon Wilder Penfield has done some very interesting experiments during his brain operations on people who had epilepsy of a kind which is due to brain damage. As you know, the brain feels no pain at all; consequently the operations are performed under a local anæsthetic just sufficient to permit the skull to be opened. While the patients were on the table, Penfield would touch certain areas of the temporal lobe with a tiny electrode, and this would evoke a complete recall of incidents which had happened many years before. So there was this very strange phenomenon of the patient existing in two worlds simultaneously, in the operating room and in some place, possibly thousands of miles away and many years earlier, which the touch of the electrode had caused him suddenly to recall in its full intensity and with all the emotions which he had at the time. When a particular spot was touched again, exactly the same recall would be produced, as though a record had been put on and were being replayed. Whether or not this peculiarity of localized recall in the brain is confined to epileptic patients, I don't think anybody knows, and I rather hope nobody will try experiments on normal people, cutting holes in their skulls, to find the answer. Meanwhile, we see that there are these possibilities of physically inducing complete recall.

On the rare occasions when total recall happens, it is obviously of extraordinary interest. A total recall has never happened to me, but people who have had them find them very exciting and also very therapeutic. They can get rid of all kinds of material which is, so to speak, festering in the lower areas of their mind.

Over and against the complete recall of total memory we have to place our ordinary memories, which are of a quite different order (although total recall presumably makes the limited recall of ordinary memory possible). Ordinary memory is a kind of summary or digest of past events which some area of our mind—what some psychologists call the preconscious—prepares for us out of total recall. This digest has a sort of utilitarian value for us—it helps us in our ordinary life and obviously has biological value as well as social value. The selection made by the preconscious mind out of our total memory is made also in the light of our general philosophy of life; it has to conform with our general feeling of what happiness is. Many aspects which in the total recall we should regard as traumatic or as irrelevant are left out in ordinary memory, and only those aspects which are biologically or socially useful to us remain.

Now let us turn to the world of fantasy and imagination. Here we see something which varies over an enormous range among different people and in the same people at different times. We can have fantasies and daydreams and imaginations of the vaguest kind or of the most elaborate and detailed variety. They can run the entire gamut from almost complete incoherence, such as we get in the state of delirium, to the most elaborate and highly organized kind of dramatic or narrative story. In its more elaborate form we have a real story-telling faculty, which exists in all human beings in a rather inchoate and undeveloped form, but which is highly developed in a few.

Before I go into the question of those people in whom the story-telling faculty is very highly developed, let me say that it is possible to induce it by means of hypnosis or reverie (which is, after all, very much like hypnosis) in people who normally don't exhibit it very strongly. Very frequently these elaborate stories are interpreted by those who hear them as accounts of previous lives in Atlantis or Lemuria, but I don't think we have necessarily to believe that this is so, because it is quite clear that we all potentially have the story-telling faculty and that certain people have it most powerfully; they can, so to speak, get at this area of the preconscious mind very easily and bring it up to the surface. I remember when I was a small boy at boarding school and we used to tell stories when lights were out. Most of the stories, needless to say, were pretty dull, but there was one boy I shall never forget. He was not a particularly bright boy, but he had this quite exceptional gift and would go on pouring forth extraordinary adventures without any difficulty night after night in a kind of endless serial which kept us all awake for hours.

We get great story-tellers in the world of novels. Alexandre Dumas had no difficulty in pouring forth the *Count of Monte Cristo* and *The Three Musketeers* without even pausing for breath—they just came rushing out. On a higher level of art we have a very interesting example of this story-telling faculty existing definitely on the unconscious or preconscious level in the case of Robert Louis Stevenson, who tells us in his book *Across the Plains* that all his short stories were provided for him by his unconscious, either in reverie or in actual dreams while he was asleep. He referred to this other part of his mind as 'the brownies'—little fairy people who inhabited his skull and would bring forth material which in his conscious state he simply wrote down and elaborated. He says that when he was a boy the brownies used to produce material in a rather haphazard way, but when he had to make his living as a writer they collaborated with him and produced good saleable material.

We next come to the world of dreams, which is a kind of incoherent form of the story-telling world. There are the ordinary dreams which obviously have to deal with the affairs which preoccupy our personal unconscious, and then there are what Jung calls the great dreams which have to do with what he calls the collective unconscious—the great permanent human symbols which run through the whole of human history and which seem to be common to almost all mankind.

Finally, beyond all these, there is the world of visionary experience, which is in some sense a real other world, profoundly different from the world of the personal unconscious and even that of the collective unconscious. It has something deeply strange about it. Before we go into a description of what goes on in this remote area of the mind, let me say a little about the degree to which this distant region is accessible to the conscious side of human beings. If we look at the biographies of eminent poets and painters and musicians, we find that certain of them were able spontaneously to enter this visionary world. They could pass almost at will from the ordinary world of experience into the world of visionary experience. William Blake was able to go at almost any time into this other world of visions. It is true that for a good many years in the middle of his life he was unable to enter this world, but he recovered the faculty later on and went through to the end of his days going back and forth from the ordinary world of tables and chairs to something quite different, to the world which he describes in his poems and his prophetic books, and which he illustrates less successfully— because he was a much less great painter than he was a poet— in his various prints and paintings.

Over and above these poets—and I can't go into the list of them—we can say without doubt that there are many quite ordinary people—ordinary from the point of view of their pow- ers of expression—who have this power to go from our every- day world into the visionary world and back. They do not have the power, as inspired poets and painters have had, of express- ing what they have seen, but they nevertheless do have this capacity for entering a very, very strange world of the mind.

In the past the capacity to have visions was regarded as ex- tremely creditable, and anybody who had them was apt to boast about them. Those who have visions now are apt to keep their mouths shut for fear of being sent to the asylum, but there is nothing intrinsically unhealthy about having visions. It is per- fectly true that many insane people do have visions, but many sane people also have visions and know perfectly well that they are having them. A person who has visions reaches the point of insanity only when he doesn't know he is having visions and mixes them up with real life—or is so obsessed by his visions that he can't get back into real life. Those people who have the power to enter the world of visions and to go back enjoy both worlds to the utmost degree.

How do people get into this visionary world? So far we have been talking about those who, for whatever reason, are so constituted that they can go and come between the ordinary world and the visionary world. They don't know how; it just happens to them. But there are methods of transporting into this visionary world people who normally can't get into it. Some of these methods are psychological; others involve making changes in body chemistry which, for some reason that we don't understand, permit these distant areas of the mind to come through into consciousness. We find that under hypnosis certain people can go through not merely into the story-telling world, but far beyond, into the world of visions. This is rather uncommon but it quite definitely happens in some cases.

One method of inducing visions by psychological means is the method of complete isolation, which was discovered empirically in many of the religious traditions of the world. The Christian monks of the Thebaide in Egypt in the third and fourth centuries of our era discovered that by going into complete isolation in the desert they were able to induce visions, some of which were of a celestial nature, but very many of which were infernal in quality. Anybody who has frequented picture galleries all over the world will have noticed a great many pictures of the temptations of St. Anthony—one of the favourite subjects of medieval and early Renaissance painters—in which one sees the hermit being plagued by the most hideous visions.

The technique of complete isolation has been followed from time immemorial in India. In the old Hindu traditions and in the Tibetan tradition we get accounts of forest dwellers who lived in caves high up in the Himalayas and who, by dint of completely isolating themselves, lay themselves open to this visionary world. The interesting thing is that within recent years these procedures have been exactly imitated and in a sense perfected in various psychological laboratories, especially in the 'limited environment' studies of D. O. Hebb at McGill University and John Lilly at the National Institute of Health. People are put where they can neither see nor hear anything, and in extreme cases they are immersed in a tepid bath so there is virtually no change in any of the feelings on the skin. In a few hours extraordinary visionary experiences will begin.

Evidently the thing which prevents all of us from having continuous visionary experiences is the fact that we are having continuous experiences of the external world. When the stimuli from the outside are cut off, the brain and the mind, however these two are associated, come up with remarkable visions, some of which are evidently extremely terrifying—many of the experimenters have simply cut short their experiments because the visions were so very unpleasant—but some of which are of a very positive and beautiful character.

These are the two main psychological methods of gaining access to the realm of visions. Then there are the methods which consist in causing changes in body chemistry. These changes are of two kinds: changes produced indirectly and changes produced directly. Indirect changes have been produced in every culture from time immemorial by means of fasting, which, if prolonged for some time, causes profound changes in body chemistry, which in their turn undoubtedly facilitate entry to the visionary world. As the anthropologists have shown, fasting for the specific purpose of obtaining visions was practiced all over this continent among the American Indians. And in the great religious traditions of the rest of the world fasting has been practiced partly for purposes of mortification —the idea being that if you punish the body in this world you will not be punished in the next—but also because the fasting empirically was found to facilitate entry into the visionary world and even into the mystical world beyond the visionary.

Another method of changing body chemistry, which is extensively practiced in India, is breathing exercises, all of which are intended to lead in the long run to prolonged suspensions of breath; when the breath is suspended for a very long period you get a high concentration of carbon dioxide in the blood, and empirically we know that a high concentration of carbon dioxide leads to visionary experiences. The inhalation of a mixture of carbon dioxide and oxygen will rapidly produce very peculiar mental conditions and, in some people, either recall of buried material or visions.

Then there are the direct methods of changing body chemistry which, as the historians of religion have shown, have been used at one time or another in almost all the religious traditions of the world: inducing visionary experiences by means of drugs. In the Middle East and in Greece, alcohol was freely used for this purpose—there are even references to it in the Old Testament. Many of the minor schools of the prophets, who are very much disapproved of by the other schools, were trying to use alcohol for the purpose of entering the visionary world. A great many other drugs have been used—hashish, opium, and what not—most of them extremely harmful but some of them naturally occurring drugs which open up the consciousness to the visionary experience and which appear to be relatively harmless to the physiology and not to be addictive in any way. The best known of the relatively harmless vision-inducers is the sacred mushroom of Mexico, which was described by my friend Gordon Wasson a couple of years ago in *Life*.[3] The active principle of these mushrooms, which is called psilocybin, was synthesized last year by Doctor Albert Hoffman of Switzerland, who also synthesized the extraordinary drug called lysergic acid (LSD-25). The other naturally occurring vision-inducer which has been used from time immemorial in the Southwest in this country, and whose use has now spread right up into Canada, is the peyote cactus, whose active principle, mescaline, was synthesized about thirty or forty years ago. At the present time,

3. *Life*, 42:19 (13 May 1957), p. 100.

most experimenters in the field of exploring the remoter areas of the mind are using LSD, which can be used in incredibly small doses of as little as 0.0001 grams and will produce extraordinary visionary effects.

These are the main methods of getting at the visionary world. Now let us examine the nature of that world and see in what way it has relevance to our original question, Why are precious stones precious? When we examine the visionary world, we discover some very interesting facts. For example, visions are extremely strange, but they are not random; they obey certain laws. Every person's vision is unique, as every person is unique, but all these unique visions seem to belong roughly to one family; they are, so to speak, members of a single species. This is brought home quite clearly by such collections of case histories as those brought together by Heinrich Klüver in his monograph on peyote, published more than twenty years ago, and by the work done by experimenters with LSD and mescaline in more recent years.

The highest common factor in the visionary experience is the experience of subjective light. This occurs in the most transcendent form of vision, the form of vision which seems to modulate, so to speak, in the full-blown mystical experience. In these highest forms of vision, the light is undifferentiated; it is what in Buddhist literature is called the 'pure light of the void'. It is an immense white light of extraordinary power. The example with which we are all most familiar is that of St. Paul on the road to Damascus, when he suddenly saw this overwhelming light and at the same time heard a voice saying, 'Saul, Saul, why persecutest thou me?' (Acts 9:4). The effect of this subjective light was so prodigious as to leave him blinded for several days. And St. Paul's was by no means a unique case. The Neoplatonist philosopher Plotinus had several of these profound mystical experiences in the course of his life. He tells us that they were all associated with the same tremendous light, and he uses a phrase which sums up from his own experience much of what

Plato had said five hundred years earlier in regard to the ideal world. Plotinus says that everything shines in the world of pure intelligence, and in the world of sense the most beautiful thing is fire.[4] This statement begins to throw some light on why precious stones are precious: the brilliant and luminous quality of the world of visions is somehow reflected in our world in luminous things such as fire.

Another well-known case of the experience of overpowering light is that of Mohammed. The revelation which came to him and which made him a prophet was accompanied by a light so tremendous—he was awakened out of his sleep by it—that he fell down in a faint. Nearer our own times, in the sixteenth century, we have the example of the great Catholic mystic St. John of the Cross. He had attempted to reform his Order, but his fellow monks didn't want to be reformed, and he was put in prison. While there, he had several experiences of overpowering light. In one the light was said to have been seen by his jailer, another friar of the Order. When he finally made his escape from his cell, it was by following a light which came to him and showed him the way out. A little later we find the great Protestant mystic Jacob Boehme describing experiences of the same kind, in which he was surrounded by and swallowed up in a tremendous light.

This experience of the pure light of the void is a visionary experience of what may be called the highest, the most mystical, kind. On a rather lower level the lights seem to be broken up and become, so to speak, incorporated in different objects and persons and figures. It is as though this tremendous white light were somehow refracted through a prism and broken up into different coloured lights. In this lower form of vision we have the intensification of light in some way associated with the story-telling faculty, so that there are visions of great complexity and elaboration in which light plays a tremendous part, but

4. Plotinus, *Enneads*, III, viii, 30.

it is not the pure white light of the great theophanies.

As an example of how this coloured light of the lower kind of vision operates, let me cite the case of Weir Mitchell, a well-known psychologist of the end of the last century who described his experiences with peyote. What he described was first of all a vision of coloured, three-dimensional geometric forms, which became concretized in carvings and mosaics and carpets; then an enormous architectural form appeared, a great Gothic tower encrusted with what appeared to be gems of such enormous size that they looked like transparent fruits; then there were immense and magnificent landscapes, also with self-luminous objects like gems in them; and the experience ended with a vision of the ocean with the waves marvellously coloured and sparkling like jewels rolling in.

Many other people have had similar visions—the spontaneous visions of Blake, for example, were essentially of the same nature. One of the interesting facts about these visions is that when figures are seen, as they often are, they are not only extraordinarily majestic—Blake describes them as Seraphim and says they were one hundred twenty feet high—but, when their faces are seen, they are not the faces of anybody that the subject knows or has ever known; they are presented to him by his own mind as a completely strange form.

This is, from a theological point of view, very interesting, inasmuch as the whole theology of angels is not, as many people now suppose, based on the idea that angels are the souls of the departed. Angels are a totally different species; they don't belong to the human species at all. I think there is a real psychological basis for this theological view of the nature of angels, inasmuch as when figures are seen in visions, they are not people that we know. Whatever it is in our mind which creates these visions, it presents us with something totally novel which appears to have absolutely nothing to do with our private life, nor even with the archetypal life of humanity as a whole. It is literally another world.

There is good reason to suppose that many children have this kind of visionary experience and that they not only see visions with their eyes closed but also see the preternatural luminosity of the visionary world in the external world. This is another common feature of those who have had visionary experiences. It is as though some of the brightness of what Plato calls the ideal world spills over into the normal world so that it is seen as being in some way transfigured and of an incredible beauty. I think that probably quite a number of children do perceive the world in this way and then in course of time they lose the capacity. This loss has been described very vividly in Wordsworth's ode on the 'Intimations of Immortality', which begins,

> There was a time when meadow, grove, and stream,
> The earth, and every common sight,
>   To me did seem
>   Apparelled in celestial light,
> The glory and the freshness of a dream.[5]

And then this gradually disappeared. As time went on, what Wordsworth calls 'shades of the prison-house'[6] closed around him, and the world, far from being transfigured, came to seem as we ordinarily see it, rather dull and dreary.

I would also like to read an extremely beautiful passage from the *Centuries of Meditations* of Thomas Traherne, who lived one hundred fifty years before Wordsworth, and who describes in prose his own experiences of childhood.

> The dust and stones of the street were as precious as gold ... The green trees when I saw them first through one of the gates transported and ravished me, their sweetness and unusual beauty made my heart to leap and almost mad with ecstasy, they were such strange and wonderful things. The Men! O what venerable and reverend creatures did the aged seem! Immortal Cherubims!

5. William Wordsworth, 'Ode. Intimations of Immortality from Recollections of Early Childhood', 1–5.
6. Ibid., 67.

And young men glittering and sparkling Angels, and maids strange seraphic pieces of life and beauty! Boys and girls tumbling in the streets, and playing, were moving jewels . . . Eternity was manifest in the Light of the Day, and something infinite behind everything appeared. . . . with much ado I was corrupted, and made to learn the dirty devices of this world. Which now I unlearn, and become, as it were, a little child again that I may enter into the Kingdom of God.[7]

In another passage he speaks of the Kingdom of God as being the external world seen in this visionary way.

The world is a mirror of infinite beauty, yet no man sees it. It is a Temple of Majesty, yet no man regards it. It is a region of Light and Peace, did not men disquiet it. It is the Paradise of God. . . . It is the place of Angels and the Gate of Heaven.[8]

This is the world transfigured by the visionary experience, a world which many poets, and many people who are not poets, have seen. It is an experience which people have after convalescence, when they are, as it were, reborn into the world and suddenly, with this kind of visionary sight, they perceive its miraculous beauty.

There are certain aspects of ordinary sunlight which can produce this visionary view of the world. I would like to read another very beautiful poem by Wordsworth, where he describes the effect of sunset:

No sound is uttered, but a deep
And solemn harmony pervades
The hollow vale from steep to steep,
And penetrates the glades.
Far-distant images draw nigh,
Called forth by wondrous potency
Of beamy radiance, that imbues
Whate'er it strikes, with gem-like hues!

7. Thomas Traherne, *Centuries of Meditations,* the third century, 3.
8. Ibid., the first century, 31.

In vision exquisitely clear,
Herds range along the mountain-side;
And glistening antlers are descried;
And gilded flocks appear.
Thine is the tranquil hour, purpureal Eve!
But long as god-like wish, or hope divine,
Informs my spirit, ne'er can I believe
That this magnificence is wholly thine!
From worlds not quickened by the sun
A portion of the gift is won;
An intermingling of Heaven's pomp is spread
On ground which British shepherds tread![9]

This is very beautiful and indicates the spontaneous way in which the poet interprets the natural phenomenon of sunset in supernatural terms. It seems to be profoundly inevitable.

Now, finally, we can begin to see why precious stones are precious. I think they are precious because they are the objects in the external world which most nearly resemble the things which people see in the visionary world. The ruby or the emerald is like the transparent fruit which the Mystic sees encrusting the rocks and the architecture of the visionary world. They have this gem-like quality which can be perceived in certain circumstances in the external world by an eye which has lost its natural dimness. Not only are gems valuable to us because they remind us of what goes on in the visionary world, they also, by themselves, induce a kind of vision. Most of us rather seldom have visionary experiences, but we all potentially have them, and I think that objects such as gems somehow remind us of what is going on in the back of our head and take us a certain way toward this other world. There is a phrase which is constantly used in older literature: it is said that a vision is 'transporting'—we are transported by visionary objects in the external world towards the visionary world which lies within us and

9. William Wordsworth, 'Composed upon an Evening of Extraordinary Splendour and Beauty', ii.

of which a part of our mind is somehow always conscious. It is precisely this double function which makes the precious stone precious: it reminds us of what is going on in the visionary world and it transports us toward that world.

There are many aspects of art which are really understandable only when we take into account this strange aspect of our mind which is capable of visionary experience. There are various ways of producing visionary works of art, the most obvious of which is to make the work of art out of materials which are themselves intrinsically vision-inducing, such as gems and precious metals. We find that the furniture of the altar in virtually every religion concentrates on these vision-inducing materials. These chalices set with gems and these shining surfaces have a double influence upon us: they remind us of the extraordinary world we carry about with us and they transport us at least part of the way toward it.

There are numerous other ways of producing visionary works of art which I cannot go into in detail, but I will end up by pointing out the very curious and interesting fact that most of the popular arts of history have had a great deal to do with visionary experience. Take an art which was profoundly popular during the Middle Ages—the art of stained glass, which is one of the most magnificent of all the arts.

Because gems were not particularly common in Western Europe there are frequent references to glass in accounts of visionary experiences. In the Welsh tradition, the islands of the blessed were called Ynisvitrin, the Isles of Glass; similarly, there was a glass fair in the Teutonic tradition, a mountain of glass where the souls of the departed lived. In the Apocalypse the author speaks of the sea of glass and the gold of the streets of Jerusalem, which was transparent like glass. We find this in Hindu literature, in Japanese literature, in Chinese literature. It is always this same picture, almost word for word the kind of vision which Weir Mitchell had under the influence of peyote.

The popularity of stained glass as an art form is very clearly indicated by the fact that in the twelfth and thirteenth centuries, when the great stained glasses of Western Europe were being made, collection boxes were placed in all the churches for money contributions for setting up stained glass windows, and we are told by contemporaries that these boxes were always full. People evidently had a passion for these extraordinary works which could convert an entire cathedral into a single huge gem. Anyone who has visited Chartres or the Sainte Chapelle in Paris knows what it is like to enter a building which is one vast jewel. The experience is profoundly vision-inducing.

There are other popular arts which have lasted from time immemorial and which are specifically vision-inducing. Fireworks were immensely popular in the days of the Roman Empire—they were almost as popular as gladiatorial games—and they were of an extraordinary elaboration. With the advances in the technology of chemistry they reached a kind of apogee in the nineteenth century, when great fireworks displays on the Fourth of July here and on the Fourteenth of July in France, and at coronations and canonizations and so on, played a great part in popular entertainment and were highly valued by the masses of the people.

Another popular art is the art of pageantry, which has been used by kings and ecclesiastics to increase their own prestige. The immensely elaborate fancy dress of ecclesiastical and royal personages does greatly enhance the prestige of the person who wears it, but at the same time there is no question at all that it has given immense pleasure to great masses of people, who will travel for miles to see great state or religious pageantries. The most remarkable of these in recent times was one which, unlike the great pageants of the past, has actually been preserved for posterity. I refer to the coronation of Queen Elizabeth II, which, thanks to floodlights and movie cameras and colour films, has been preserved in its fantastically rich and beautiful elaboration and will go down as a remarkable example to posterity.

Closely associated with pageantry is theatrical spectacle. This has always gone hand in hand with the drama. The drama is human life in action, and spectacle is the visionary world shown upon the stage. The highest manifestations of this were seen in the Elizabethan and Jacobean masques of the sixteenth and seventeenth centuries. Spectacle has become much more visionary in recent years as a result of advances in technology. Thanks to the invention in the late eighteenth century of the parabolic mirror, which permits the projection of a narrow beam of light, the invention of limelight, which came in 1824, and the discovery of electricity in the 1880s, we are now able to cast a light such as never was on land or sea upon figures on the stage and to produce the visionary effect of an intense preternatural colour and light. The apotheosis of this comes in the great coloured movies, the big spectaculars and the big coloured documentaries, which really do produce a visionary effect.

On a humbler scale, we can see this now as we walk out on the streets with their Christmas decorations—which are essentially a kind of popular visionary art. These little twinkling lights do remind us of this other world; they seem in some way magical. We give them names like fairy lamps, as we have given the name of magic lantern to the projector of luminous images. So we see that there has been always in the popular mind a curious awareness of the visionary world and a response to even the crudest kind of visionary art. There is something I find extremely touching about these Christmas decorations. They are slightly commercialized, unfortunately, and slightly absurd, but nonetheless they are a symptom of the strange fact that all of us carry around at the back of our head this mysterious other world which I have called the world of visions.

LATENT HUMAN

POTENTIALITIES

I WANT to talk in this lecture about a subject which is of profound importance to everyone: the possibility of realizing latent human potentialities. I think we don't have to flatter ourselves by imagining that we have already realized all the potentialities with which we are born. There are many, in almost all of us, which might be released and made effective. As a matter of historical fact, human beings have actualized faculties and powers which in the past had been completely latent and unimaginable. Our biological make-up has not really changed since the upper Palæolithic, and we are now using much more effectively exactly the same natural equipment we had fifteen or twenty thousand years ago. This is a very encouraging fact. It shows that man can get more out of himself without necessarily changing himself biologically.

Before we start discussing the problem of how these latent potentialities are to be actualized, it is necessary to talk about human needs. For it is only in relation to needs that we can discuss potentialities. We can start with the basic biological needs of man, which are the need for food and the need for preservation of life from the elements and from natural or human enemies. These two fundamental biological needs must

Delivered on December 14, 1959

be fulfilled in order for man to survive at all. Then, going up the scale, we find strictly psychological needs such as the apparently universal need to give and to receive love. This need has been stressed very strongly in recent years by anthropologists and psychologists who have pointed out that if it is not satisfied in infancy and childhood the child is apt to grow up into a psychopath or even into a moral imbecile.

Closely related to the need for love is the need for belongingness, the need to satisfy what Adler called the *Gemeinschaftgefühl*, the feeling of community with people. Then there is the need for respect and recognition from other people, which is a very powerful need, and the need—a little more rarefied—for self-respect: we have to be able to think of ourselves with some kind of esteem.

Next we come to still more rarefied but nevertheless (in certain people and under favourable conditions) very strong needs: the need for satisfying curiosity; the need to satisfy the hunger for knowledge—knowledge for its own sake, not necessarily for utilitarian purposes; the need for order and for meaning in life; and the need for expression—we are symbol-making animals and we have evidently a real desire to express what we feel and think about in terms of symbols. Finally, there is the need to grow to the limits of our capacities, to actualize our potentialities—which is a basic need when the conditions are favourable for its appearance. I think of the first line of Mallarmé's sonnet about Edgar Allan Poe, *'Tel qu'en Lui-même enfin l'éternité le change'* (as eternity changes him into himself).[1] But we don't have to wait for eternity, necessarily; it is possible, I believe, to become ourselves in the fullest ego-transcending form even in this life. It certainly is worth trying.

We see from this list that these needs are arranged in a kind of hierarchy. If the primary biological needs are not fulfilled, then the other needs will simply not be felt. Not only will they

1. Stéphane Mallarmé, 'Le Tombeau d'Edgar Poe', in *Poésies* (Paris: Gallimard, 1942).

not be realized and satisfied, but they won't even enter our consciousness. A man who is hungry is preoccupied with only one thought, which is food. He is reduced to something subhuman—an empty stomach and an emaciated frame—and nothing more. It is the same with safety. If one is continually menaced, it is extraordinarily difficult to feel any of the higher needs. It may be possible, if hunger is satisfied, to feel and even satisfy the needs for love and for belongingness while living in a state of chronic insecurity, but it certainly will not be possible to feel the higher needs for knowledge and for growth and the various other purely human needs.

Then we come to the primary psychological needs. Unless the needs for love and belongingness and respect and self-respect are satisfied, it is very difficult for the intrinsically human needs for knowledge, for order and meaning, for expression and growth, even to be felt—and much more difficult for them to be actualized in practice and to come to fulfillment. These needs are definitely born with us; they are quasi-instincts. I know the word 'instinct' is now a bad word. It is one which psychologists don't like at all, but I would be inclined to agree with the great German ethologist Konrad Lorenz when he says that the time has come to take the stink out of instinct, because it does seem to me that whatever you may call these things, they are inborn tendencies. In this context I find extremely helpful A. H. Maslow's idea that these basic needs can be described as weak instincts. They are not the kind of all-or-nothing instinct which compels a bird to build its nest; they are conditional instincts, tendencies which will arise provided the 'lower' biological and psychological needs have been fulfilled. When these higher needs present themselves we are in a position to attempt, at least, to fulfil them and thereby to realize the latent potentialities which lie within us.

It seems to me that, in the light of what we have been saying, we can speak realistically about the whole nature-nurture controversy. Obviously neither nature nor nurture exists independently. We come into the world as a specific body with inborn needs, and we come into contact with a specific environment. Conversely, the specific environment has to work upon a specific hereditary parcel, a bundle which is delivered to it. The two are always synergic, working together in a continuous way. The point is that it is only when the environmental conditions are most favourable that the hereditary factors can express themselves fully. In a bad environment even the best hereditary factors may be masked or smothered; it requires the best kind of environment for us to be able to realize our latent inborn capacities. So, if we want to be eugenists, we also have to be social reformers, because it is no good breeding a magnificent race of human beings if the conditions under which they live are so bad that the excellencies which we have bred into the race cannot be fulfilled. Conversely, it is no good having a magnificent environment if the hereditary material on which the environment has to work is of poor quality. We have always to think of these two factors, nurture and nature, heredity and environment, as absolutely inseparable terms, both of which must be developed to the highest possible limit.

What are the circumstances in which human beings are most capable of realizing their potentialities and expressing their latent powers effectively? Observation shows that there seem to be two classes of circumstances which allow for a maximum expression of human power. One is the moment of crisis. We have all seen the extraordinary fact that in a crisis most people will not merely behave very well, they will show capacities which they simply have never shown before. The other circumstance in which there will be an exceptional display of human power occurs when there is some kind of upsurge of joy and creativity—what Homer called *menos*—when some kind of divine influx comes rushing in and raises us, so to speak, to a higher level, where we are capable of being more than our ordinary selves.

But a crisis, to be a crisis, must be short; a crisis which

becomes chronic, which goes on for too long, leads inevitably
to breakdown. The weaker members of a society in crisis break
down rather soon; the strongest members can hold out longer,
but they too, in the long run, disintegrate under prolonged
pressure. The moral is that we simply have to avoid such prolon-
gation of pressure, all the more so because long before human
beings actually break down, life in general becomes so limited
and narrowed and finally subhuman that it is quite impossible
for the higher needs of individuals and the higher needs of
society at large to be met. In the same way, we cannot rely upon
uprushes of joy and creativity. The spirit bloweth where it
listeth, and we don't know when these things are coming. It is
possible, as I shall hint later on, that we may in future learn to
control these uprushes and to produce them at will to some
extent; at present we certainly cannot. Thus we cannot rely
either upon crisis or upon these upsurges of power to help us.
What we can rely upon is the pretty good performance of
human beings in a society which satisfies their basic needs and
at least gives them the opportunity of satisfying their higher
ones. In fact, a reasonably good society where people are properly fed and are not subject to too terrible frustrations is the one
in which we can expect potentialities best to be fulfilled in the
best way.

Ideally, in order that individual potentialities may be completely developed in all individuals, we should have a perfect
society. This is a consummation devoutly to be wished, but it is
one which is not likely to be fulfilled within any foreseeable
span of time. Therefore I shall not spend any time in this lecture
discussing the social reforms which are desirable for the purpose of helping individuals to fulfill their potentialities. This
would take us much too far afield. What I shall do is talk about
certain obvious deficiencies and consider the ways in which
these might be made good for individuals and, indirectly, for
society, within a social set-up not too different from our own.

How are we then going to improve the circumstances of
individual life in such a way that our higher needs may be

satisfied? What methods are we going to use to make our potentialities realizable? Very briefly, let me touch on one possibility which is still largely a possibility and not a realized fact. This is what may be called the pharmacological approach to the problem. It was announced a year or so ago by Soviet scientists that they were engaged upon a five-year plan to find pharmacological methods for increasing mental efficiency and endurance in individuals without doing any appreciable harm to the body. Pharmacologists tell me that this is probably not an impossible dream; rather it is quite in the cards that chemicals which do not seriously, or even appreciably, harm the body may be found to help the mind in its task of realizing latent potentialities.

One can imagine a chemical similar but greatly superior to the so-called psychic energizers which have already done such remarkable work in psychotherapy in cases of depression. It is possible to imagine substances which would produce a profound euphoria—the uprush of joy which is one of the conditions of human effectiveness—and which also might produce a lowering of the barrier which normally separates the conscious from the preconscious mind. This would permit what Lawrence Kubie calls the preconscious or creative mind to come more easily to the surface and provide us with the kind of inspiration to artistic creation and to effectiveness in life which is essential to the fully developed human being.

There might also be chemicals which could permit us to be more alert, more capable of sustained tension, or which might make us more patient and more friendly. We all know that it is much wiser to approach the boss after lunch than before lunch—he probably feels a good deal happier after lunch than he does when he is hungry. And we have all had the experience of how a cup of coffee or tea may make a profound difference in our mood. There seems to be no reason why substances should not be found that are as relatively harmless as tea or coffee and yet are considerably more powerful in their influences upon the mind.

It is quite clear, however, that pharmacology alone is not

likely to do the trick. We have to have, in conjunction with it, some kind of educational process. At present we teach our children to obtain a knowledge of useful things, to have an understanding of what's what and to behave like civilized human beings, if possible. But we do not train the mind-bodies which have to do the learning and which have to do the living. We give them the knowledge and we give them moral injunctions, but we don't then go on to train them in such a way that they can put these injunctions into effect. This is one of the grave weaknesses of our current ethical and educational systems.

Let us consider the fields in which such a specific training of the mind-body might be most useful. The basic and most important is obviously the field of perception. In order to survive, to realize our needs and wants and to actualize our latent potentialities, we need to have a really efficient perceptual apparatus. Yet training in perception is something whose importance we are only just beginning to realize. Consider the stultifying effects which poor seeing has upon human beings: it results in poor reading habits, retardation at school, and all kinds of neurotic and antisocial reactions to such retardation, which may then result in juvenile delinquency.

Seeing is, like talking and walking, a learned activity. We are not born seeing perfectly. We learn to see perfectly, and it is an act which is partly physiological and also very largely mental. There may then be much that will help in the realization of potentialities to be gained simply by teaching children what I have called, in a book which I wrote years ago, the 'art of seeing'. This art of seeing has recently attracted a good deal of attention in orthodox circles, and I have been rather amused in recent years to find many of the propositions which I set forth, following a remarkable pioneer in the field, Dr. W. H. Bates, who died in 1930—propositions for which we were both called fools and charlatans—being adopted by those who are professionally concerned with the problem of vision and its relation to education and to general social problems.

There is no time to go into the details of training in the art of seeing or in remedial reading. The evidence of what bad seeing may do to children and some account of the techniques being used, not merely in remedial reading, but, much more basically, in the art of seeing, are to be found in a short but very pithy and interesting article by Dr. James Curran, which appeared two years ago in the *Optometrical Weekly,* and which has an extant bibliography attached to it. It seems to be quite clear, however, that this kind of training can be used not merely therapeutically but also preventively. And it can be used as a concomitant to all systems of teaching from the earliest years.

I think we can generalize and say that the more discriminating and acute and precise our perceptions are, the better on the whole will be our general intelligence. I think most people would agree to this. It is perfectly true that certain kinds of intelligence, such as the intelligence which is required for logical analysis, can probably exist without a very highly developed perceptual apparatus; but I would also think it true that intelligence for life situations and for mental activities is a little less rarefied and specialized than logical analysis. For these kinds of intelligence, a highly developed perceptual capacity is really necessary. We have to learn to perceive clearly how it feels to be what we are where we are. We have to know what surrounds us; we have to know how we react to what surrounds us; we have to know what is happening within our bodies; and we have to have a clear idea of what it is that we are thinking and feeling and wishing and willing. In other words, we have to obey the old Socratic maxim—it was a very old maxim even in the time of Socrates—'Know Thyself'.

Before we go on to discuss positive ways of knowing ourselves, let us consider the obstacles to self-knowledge which are most common in our world. The greatest obstacle to awareness —generalized (or acute) discriminating awareness—is neurosis. Neurosis can be defined in one of its aspects as a fixation upon a single aspect of life, a looking at the world through one particular set of distorting lenses, and hence as the inability to see a wider angle of life and to perceive realistically what is going on around us. As we have seen, most neuroses are clearly due to events which took place in the past, often in early childhood, and what happens is that we are influenced *now* by events which took place *then*—we are reacting to the present in terms of the past. The cure of neurosis, however it is carried out, is some method by which a person may be brought out of his unconscious obsession to a full awareness of events taking place now and be given the capacity for responding appropriately and realistically to these present events.

Non-neurotic or relatively non-neurotic people also face obstacles in the way of awareness—obstacles which are described frequently in literature—for example, monomaniacal preoccupation with a single interest or domination by a single passion such as avarice or the love of power or sexual enjoyment for its own sake, apart from love. All that used to be called by old-fashioned moralists 'the passions' are essentially narrowings down of our awareness. They are all blinkers which confine our vision to a very small field and prevent us from becoming conscious of ourselves and of everything going on around us.

Another very common obstacle in the way of awareness is a kind of misplaced intellectualism. It is the kind of intellectualism that regards words and concepts as being somehow more real and more important than actual events and things. There is a very amusing account of an eminent man's succumbing to this kind of obstacle to awareness in the Goncourt journals. Ernest Renan, the great nineteenth century French scholar, who was very fond of talking about aesthetics, was holding forth at great length about the beautiful, the true, etc., when suddenly Edmond Goncourt interrupted him and asked, 'What is the colour of the wallpaper in your dining room?' Renan hadn't the faintest idea. Obviously he hadn't really got very much factual basis for discussing beauty; he was simply discussing a whole fabric of words rather than immediate experiences—

which in fact are the only experiences of beauty.

Another obstacle to awareness is habit and routine. Both habit and routine are extremely valuable. They permit us to save a great deal of time and to do unimportant things—inasmuch as anything is unimportant—rapidly and efficiently. But they are also extremely dangerous. If we become the victims of our habits and our routines we tend to react to present events without spontaneity. We tend to react to them in terms of something which we learned in the past instead of reacting to them as they are here and now.

Ideally we should somehow make the best of both worlds, and this is always the moral we get down to. We have to be sufficiently aware of the newness and uniqueness of every event here and now to be able to react appropriately and spontaneously to it. At the same time, we have to be sufficiently aware of the unique event's resemblance to past events to permit our past experience to help us be more efficient in coping with the immediate experience. But in all too many cases we find that our reliance on habit, on words and on concepts, tends to blind us to the immediate reality in front of us. It would be a very good thing if in all education children were trained to realize the importance both of habit and of non-habit, although how exactly this is to be done, I don't know.

Let us now consider some of the positive ways in which perceptual awareness can be increased. Here I shall mention a book which I think is well worth reading; its thesis is not novel, as I shall show in a few minutes (it goes back thousands of years), but it is rather novel in the present context where we have forgotten a great many important things. The book is *Gestalt Therapy* by Perls, Hefferline, and Goodman.[2] Their method of dealing with neurotic problems is essentially to teach people to be aware—this is the beginning of their therapy—and they prescribe courses in becoming aware of external events. They

2. Frederick S. Perls, Ralph F. Hefferline, and Paul Goodman, *Gestalt Therapy* (New York: Julian Press, 1951).

suggest for example that we should make up sentences which begin 'Here and now, I perceive' (whatever it may be) 'the light in my eyes, these shining objects in front of me, this red thing, this yellow paper, various aches and pains which I may have,' and so on. Such extraordinarily simple and apparently childish exercises in awareness are extremely helpful in bringing us out of our absurd preoccupation with the past and the future, with daydreaming, and with pleasant or unpleasant memories, which occupies so much of our time and energy—in short, in bringing us out of this morass of non-actuality into present time and into the possibility at least of reacting realistically and appropriately to what is happening. These authors specify a number of other exercises, such as shifting the focus of attention toward an awareness of objects in relation to their background (seeing how things in the background, which are relatively dim, come forward when you pay attention to them and how what was the foreground then becomes a side object or a background). They speak of the importance of becoming acutely aware of events within the body and events going on in the mind. In general the whole process is a thoroughgoing training in the basic perceptual awareness which we need in order to exercise all the other functions of the mind-body.

This work of the Gestalt therapists is by no means new in our century. A remarkable Swiss psychotherapist, Dr. Roger Vittoz, who died in 1925—I remember hearing of his methods at the time, I never saw him—was extremely successful in dealing with neurosis. As far as one can gather, he was a great deal more successful than the psychoanalysts; his method was essentially to train his patients to become aware of seemingly the most trivial actions (because no action is fully trivial). It was a process of becoming aware and learning how to use will and how to be conscious of whatever is being done. When Vittoz died, his method was completely neglected. This is one of the tragic things which is constantly happening in the history of ideas: excellent ideas are brought forth and acted upon, but for various sociological reasons they are often totally forgotten for a long period. Vittoz's ideas didn't happen to fit in with the psychological notions current at the time. People preferred the much more complicated and rarefied methods of psychoanalysis to his rather straightforward and simple approach, even though it apparently happened to be very successful, according to all accounts.

What is extremely interesting is that both Vittoz and the Gestalt therapists are actually reviving procedures which were current in various systems of Oriental philosophy and psychology one or two thousand years ago. This business of being acutely aware of everything within and without is a standard procedure in the Buddhist, Tantric, and Zen psychology. There is a text, for example, which is introduced by a dialogue between Shiva, the great god, and his wife, Parvati. Parvati asks Shiva the secret of her profound consciousness—the consciousness of *Tat twam asi,* of the Thou Art That, the consciousness that the Atman is identical with the Brahman. Shiva proceeds to give her a list of 118 exercises in awareness which he says are all extremely helpful toward achieving this ultimate consciousness. They are exercises in awareness in every life situation, from eating one's dinner to sneezing, from going to sleep to making love to having dreams to daydreaming. It is the most comprehensive series of exercises in consciousness that I know of, and it is very curious to find that this immensely valuable psychological discovery has been allowed to remain as some sort of vague Oriental superstition which we haven't bothered about. Now, after so many years, it is coming to the surface and will prove to be of very great value.[3]

Let me touch on another technique of awareness, one in which John Dewey was greatly interested. I refer to the technique developed by F. M. Alexander (who died at the age of 80) for becoming aware of the proper posture—the proper relation-

3. Paul Reps, comp., 'Centering,' in *Zen Flesh, Zen Bones* (Garden City, N.Y.: Anchor Books, 1961), p. 157

ship between the neck and the trunk above all—which permits
the best possible functioning of the psychophysical organism.
Dewey, who had studied the technique with Alexander, wrote
introductions to three of Alexander's books; in one of these
introductions he says quite definitely that he regards this technique as being to education what education is to life in general,
that it is the thing which gives education the possibility of really
doing some good. Yet among the hundreds of thousands of
educators who have followed Dewey, virtually none, so far as
I know, paid any attention to this method of training the mind-
body which Dewey regarded as of primary importance in education; it has been allowed simply to fall away, and so far as I
know, there is only one school in the United States where it is
applied to the education of children. This, then, is another example of what is quite clearly a very important idea, recognized
by a first-rank philosopher as being of immense practical and
theoretical significance, allowed to lapse because it just doesn't
happen to be in with the current academic views of the time.

Now let me go on with some of the other ways of training the
mind-body. A very important form of training is clearly the
training of the imagination. Here I recommend Herbert Read's
Education Through Art, in which he talks of the possibility of
training children's imagination in such a way that they may
retain the remarkable faculty of eidetic imagery, which most
children seem to have, in later life. Generally intense power of
visualization disappears about the time of puberty, but there
seems to be no reason why it shouldn't be preserved and remain
a source of enjoyment and of intellectual benefit to human
beings, even in their adult phase. In *Gestalt Therapy*, too, many
interesting exercises in the use of imagination are prescribed to
pry the mind loose from its old bad habits of thinking and
feeling. I can't go into them here, but they are well worth
looking at. They do help to pull us out of this illusion of a sort
of bogus personality, which we create by means of our bad
habits.

It seems now to be quite clear that any development of awareness must go hand in hand with the development of our knowledge of language and concepts. If we are going to be aware of our direct experience, we must also be aware of the relationship between direct experience and the world of symbols and language and concepts in which we live. We are like icebergs. We float in immediate reality, but we project into the winds of doctrine insofar as we rise out of immediate experience into the world of concepts. For it is quite certain that there is no such thing as absolute immediate experience, that all our experiences have a kind of linguistic tinge to them, just as there is no question at all that we are able to go much further in the direction of immediate experience than we generally do go. Thus it is extremely important that we should be aware of the relationship between the experiences that we are immediately presented with and the words in terms of which we think about them and express them and explain them. In other words, twentieth-century developments in linguistics in general and in semantics should find their way into education on every level. I would think that there should be simultaneously a training of the mind-body in perception, in imagination, and in the use of language. All of these seem to me to go together in an essential way.

Now, closely related to problems of awareness in general are problems in love. Love and knowledge go very closely together. Love without knowledge is largely impotent, and knowledge without love is frequently inhuman. In the world as we see it today, there is obviously a great deal of loveless knowledge and of knowledgeless love—not to mention a good deal of both knowledgeless and unfortunately very knowledgeable hate floating around. Our problem is to find some way in which we can make it more possible for more human beings to love in an aware and knowledgeably directed way.

Oddly enough, we can learn quite a lot in the field of love from some of the primitive peoples. Anthropologists in recent years have been investigating all kinds of psychological and social arrangements which we will never be able to observe under laboratory conditions. (This is why it is so extremely important that these primitive peoples should be carefully and sympathetically observed before they all disappear and are completely homogenized by the rising tide of technology and propaganda.) In this question of love we find extraordinary examples of primitive intelligence. Margaret Mead has described the amazing practices of the Arapesh, which are a tiny tribe in New Guinea, an essentially non-violent and co-operative society. They have set the highest value upon love and friendliness and have developed methods which are used from the earliest years for encouraging and implementing the ideals of love. Dr. Mead tells how the Arapesh mother, when nursing her baby, will continuously murmur the words 'good, good', and while the baby is sucking the milk and the mother is murmuring this, she will rub the child against the family dog, or against the family pig, or against a human being in the family circle or even outside the family circle, so that the child is brought up with a kind of conditioned reflex for feeling confidence and love and the goodness of other people.

You may say that this is merely a conditioned reflex, but we are all influenced by conditioned reflexes all the time, so we may as well see that our conditioned reflexes are good rather than bad. I think that there is—as many sociologists have pointed out since the Arapesh findings were published some years ago—plenty of room for us to learn a lot from these very simple people, who have discovered methods for increasing the amount of love and intensifying its quality in society.

Another arrangement from primitive societies which might very well be borrowed, and which also tends to increase love and decrease frustration, is the arrangement of the multiple family which we find in many Polynesian societies. There a child has many potential homes. A whole group of people take responsibility for the child, who is free, as soon as it can walk, to go from one place to another. In all these places it will find rights and responsibilities. This scheme overcomes many of the grave disadvantages from which we suffer owing to the extremely restricted family set-up in which we are now condemned to live. In the past, the family arrangement in the West covered a much larger number of people because people lived in the same village and many generations were present always, as well as cousins and aunts, and so on. But the Polynesian method seems to be even better than what we had here, and far better than what we have at present. Perhaps this is a fanciful idea, but I don't see why, for example, we shouldn't develop a kind of mutual adoption club out of the baby-sitting co-operatives which are now becoming so common in the modern world. It seems to me that there would be an immense advantage in doing precisely this.

Finally, let us consider a very painful problem, the problem of prejudice and mutual dislike, both international and intranational. A great deal of work has been done on the problem of prejudice and how to diminish it, on how to increase the amount of good feeling between different racial and religious and class groups. The nature of the researches and the methods used and the results obtained have been summed up by Gordon Allport in his book, *The Nature of Prejudice*. Allport's conclusion is, I am sorry to say, one of tempered pessimism. He says that the evidence shows that probably four-fifths of all American adults are affected to some extent by prejudices and that there are weighty considerations which lead him to believe that it will be exceedingly difficult to change this 'ominous proportion'; we shall not do so, in spite of all the great efforts which are being used—legislative methods, propaganda methods, methods of group co-operation, methods of individual therapy, teaching in schools, and all the rest. Some of these methods are more effective than others, and it is possible that yet other methods may be discovered in the future. Allport's view is that although the outlook is not particularly bright, it is our duty to pursue the means by which an increase in good feeling and a decrease in prejudice can be brought about.

One of the basic problems here is expressed in an epigram of William Blake's: 'Damn braces. Bless relaxes.'[3] The meaning of this is, of course, that there is a higher psychological dividend to be obtained from negative emotions than there is from rather lukewarm positive emotions. The highest psychological dividend is undoubtedly paid by love, but hate pays a considerably higher dividend than mere tolerance or acceptance. It is a tragic fact that we get a bigger kick out of hate than we do out of these rather placid virtues; the question is, can we raise the lukewarmness of mere tolerance to something a little warmer and more powerful? Can we get good feelings—not merely an absence of bad feeling—to take the place of the bad feelings? I think one of the things which may help in the long run in minimizing the desire for negative emotion as a form of stimulus, as a kick, will be precisely better training in perception.

There is no doubt at all that a person with trained perceptions finds the world a great deal more interesting than does one whose perceptions are untrained, and therefore he may have less need of either the vicarious excitements provided by Westerns and murder stories or the much more dangerous excitements provided by racial antagonisms and nationalistic orgies. I think that if in everybody, again following a phrase of Blake's, the doors of perception were cleansed, everything would be seen as it is: infinite. And if we all had the doors of our perceptions cleansed, and if we habitually saw the world as infinite and holy, we should obviously find it a great deal less necessary to go in for bullfighting, attacking minorities or working up frenzies against foreign peoples. So all these things work in together. Let us hope that sooner or later we shall find some method by which, combining awareness with these various trainings in good feeling, we may increase the sum of human

3. William Blake, *The Marriage of Heaven and Hell*, 'Proverbs of Hell'.

decency and make the realization of many of our latent potentialities possible.

With this, I will draw to a close and end by thanking you for
much patience in listening to what I am afraid has been a very
rambling series of discourses. Everybody here has been extremely kind to me. The only criticism I have had has been in
reference to some of the people that I thought had made important contributions, such as W. H. Sheldon. I may be wrong, and
Sheldon may be wrong, but I happen to think he is right. In
regard to this I will just say what I have already said, that it is
not necessarily true that, because a particular doctrine at a
particular moment is orthodox, it is correct. There have been
too many examples in the past of orthodoxies proved to be
profoundly incorrect, for anybody to feel it necessary to accept
everything in the orthodox view.

I close with a remark which Oliver Cromwell made in his
letter of 3 August 1650 to the General Assembly of the Church
of Scotland: 'I beseech you, in the bowels of Christ, think it
possible you may be mistaken.' I feel that these words should be
written in gold over every rostrum and in front of every lecture
table and over every church door. It is, after all, an expression
of what is one of the great discoveries of modern times—the
working hypothesis, which has replaced the idea of the dogma
or the doctrine. We may form a hypothesis and be perfectly
prepared to alter it as new facts appear; we do not have to stick
to it through thick and thin and martyr other people because
of it. And with this last word—that I hope I can conceive I may
be mistaken—I will leave you.

INDEX

Acton, Lord, 80, 83
Adams, Sir Grantley, 47
Adler, Alfred, 66, 237
Aeschylus, 31
Age of Gold, 91, 92, 118
Age of Iron, 91
Agriculture and population, 43, 45,
    47–48, 50, 52
Albert, Prince Consort, 94
Alexander, F. M., 247–248
Allport, Gordon, 251–252
Ampère, André Marie, 162
Animal magnetism, 180
Animals: in balance of nature,
    34–35; destroyed by man, 15–17;
    developed by man, 14–15; fighting
    behaviour of, 74–76; intelligence
    of, 171–172; perceptions of,
    174–175
Anselm, St., 208
Anson, Barry Joseph, 63
Ants, harvester, 74
Aristotle, 8, 9, 59, 138, 141, 154, 179
Arnold, Matthew, 75, 185
Art, 182–197; Christ in, 149–150; as
    communication and therapy, 186;
    creative imagination in, 190–191,
    193; landscape painting, 19,
    39–40, 194, 195; in art, 38–41;
    non-representational, 40, 187–188;
    primitive, 195; spatial and
    temporal, 188–190; symmetry in,

188–189; sympathy in, 184–185;
    types and styles of, 194–195;
    visions in, 233–235
Atomic bombs, see Nuclear weapons
Augustine, St., 60–62, 92, 93, 208
Austen, Jane, 115
Automatic writing, 161
Aztecs, human sacrifice, 177–178

Baader, Franz Xavier von, 160
Bacon, Francis, 8–10, 193
Barbados, 47
Basho, 38
Bates, W. H., 242
Beethoven, Ludwig van, 196
Behaviourism, 9–10, 63, 187
Bell, Clive, 183
Bentham, Jeremy, 46
Bergson, Henri, 137, 167, 196
Bertalanffy, Ludwig von, 37
Bhagavad Gita, 69
Bible: Acts, 227; Colossians, 133;
    Corinthians, 170; Genesis, 133,
    198–199; Hebrews, 158; Job, 213;
    John, 210; I John, 213; Matthew,
    50, 213, 215; Philippians, 133–134;
    Psalms, 12, 134; Revelation, 198;
    Romans, 170; Song of Solomon, 12
Biochemistry, 103–104, 140
Birth control, 51–53, 57–58
Blake, William, 150, 153–154,

Blake *(Continued)*
201–202, 252; visions, 163–164,
223, 229
Blakeslee, Albert, 64
Blyth, Benjamin, calculating boy,
161–162
Body: biochemical variations, 140;
dysplasias, 143–144, 149; and ego,
138; and mind or soul, 133–136;
physical types and temperaments,
67–69, 141–151; physiological
intelligence, 138–140;
physiological variations, 63–65;
psychological factors, 65–68
Boehme, Jacob, 228
Boltzmann, Ludwig, 110
Bonner, James, 102
Boulez, Pierre, 187
Bovaryism, 72
Brain operations in epilepsy, 220
Brain-washing, 156
Braun, Werner von, 107
Breuer, Josef, 127
Brigid of Sweden, St., 164
Broad, C. D., 166
Brooke, Fulke Greville, Lord,
121–122
Brown, Adams, 207, 209
Brown, Harrison, 102, 103, 107
Brown, Norman, 147
Buddhism, 129–130, 135, 155, 157,
166, 211, 213, 247
Bury, J. B., 92

Calculating boys, 161–162
Calvin, John, 208–209
Carroll, Lewis, 49
Cartesian philosophy, *see* Descartes
Catherine of Siena, St., 213
Cedars of Lebanon, 12–13, 17
Celibacy of intellect, 6–7
Central America, nationalism in,
77–78
Ceylon, malaria control in, 46–47,
51
Cézanne, Paul, 19
Chantal, St. Jeanne, 214
Chapman, Abbot John, 202–203
Charcot, Jean Martin, 127
Chateaubriand, François René de,
13

Chaucer, Geoffrey, 68
China, Communist brain-washing in,
156
Chinese art: landscape painting, 39,
40, 194, 195; sacred figures,
150–151
Chinese philosophy, 36–37
Chinese writing, 193
Christ: representations of, 149–150;
in theology and dogma, 207–209
Christianity: atonement in, 207–209;
body and mind in, 133–134;
future in concepts of, 92–93; and
mysticism, 202–203; and original
sin, 59–62; and population control,
57, 58; progress condemned by
Church, 95; theology, 206–210;
unhappiness in, 155; watchfulness
of Church, 113
Chu Hsi, 37
Chuang Tzu, 36
Clairvoyance, 132
Coleridge, Samuel Taylor, 190–191
Communism, words in, 180
Computers, 106
Conditioned reflex, 156
Confucianism, 150–151
Conservation, 28–29; education in,
29–30; soil, 23–24
Constable, John, 40
Cortez, Hernando, 177–178
Cromwell, Oliver, 253
Curran, James, 243
Cyprus, goats in, 25–26

Daimon, 125
Dancing, psychological effects of,
126–127
Darwin, Charles, 32, 62, 94, 95, 110
Darwin, Sir Charles, grandson of
Charles, 97–98
Dase, calculating boy, 162
Degas, Hilaire Germain Edgar, 5
Delphic Oracle, 131, 158
Democritus, 187
Dermenghem, Emil, 201
Descartes, René, 123, 133, 137, 160,
165–166
Devils of Loudun, 126
Dewey, John, 137, 247–248
Diderot, Denis, 17–18

Dionysius the Areopagite, 202, 203
Draper, George, 67
Dreams, 162–163, 222
Dulles, John Foster, 88
Dumas, Alexandre, 222
Dupertuis, C. W., 67
Dysplasias, 143–144, 149

Eckhart, Meister, 210, 213
Eclipses, 176–177
Ecology, 34
Ectomorph, 68, 69, 143, 146–150
Edison, Thomas A., 160
Education: in conservation, 29–30;
    integrated, 1–11; and latent
    human potentialities, 242–243,
    248; and population increase,
    54–55; in Russia, 70
Ego, 135, 137–151, 166; Greek
    concept of, 129, 130
Egypt, population problems, 48
Electronic devices, 106–107
Emerson, Ralph Waldo, 106
Emmerich, Catherine, 164
Endomorph, 68, 69, 142, 145–147,
    150
Environment: dependence on,
    32–34; and heredity, 62–63,
    238–239; man's changes in, 12–27
Epimenides, 132
Erigena, Johannes Scotus, 202
Esdaile, James, 181
Eugenics, 105
Evolution, theory of, 95–96
Extrasensory perception, 165–166
Extrovert, 69, 154

Fantasy, 221
Flaubert, Gustave, *Madame Bovary*,
    72
Forests, destruction of, 17–20, 26–27
Foster parenthood, eugenic, 105
Fox, George, 205
Fox sisters, 128
France, unification of, 100
Francis de Sales, St., 214
Francis of Assisi, St., 205
Franklin, Benjamin, 127
French Revolution, 79, 115, 116
Freud, Sigmund, 65, 127, 152, 154,
    155, 159, 204

Freudian (neo-Freudian) psychology,
    147–148, 152, 163, 218
Fromm, Erich, 148
Fry, Elizabeth, 205
Fry, Roger, 214
Future, 91–107; hope for, 92–97;
    modern predictions of, 97–107

Galen, 141
Galileo Galilei, 187
Gaultier, Jules de, 72
Gauss, Karl Friedrich, 162
Genius, 160–161
Germany, nationalism and
    unification, 78–79, 100
Gestalt psychology, 187, 245–247
Glass, stained, 233–234
God: concept of, 208–210; union
    with, 210–212
Goethe, Johann Wolfgang von, 159,
    169, 187
Goncourt, Edmond, 244
Goodman, Paul, 245
Goya, Francisco de, 194
Greco, El, 194
Greek civilisation, 178; human
    nature in, 124–131
Grotius, Hugo, 209
Gynandromorphy, 144

Haeckel, Ernst, 34
Hartmann, Eduard von, 96
Hebb, D. O., 33, 225
Hebrew tradition, body and mind
    in, 129, 133–134
Hefferline, Ralph F., 245
Hegel, Georg Wilhelm Friedrich, 23
    n.
Helvétius, Claude Adrien, 62, 63, 71
Herbert, George, 192–193
Heredity: of acquired
    characteristics, 62, 96, 172; and
    environment, 62–63, 238–239; of
    physical characteristics, 63–65;
    and political doctrines, 69–70; and
    pre-destination, 60; of
    psychological traits, 66, 67
Hesiod, 164
Hinduism, 59, 60, 200, 211
Hippocrates, 141

History: indifference to, in literature, 115–116; and life of individual, 110–117
Hitler, Adolf, 82, 117, 170, 205
Hoffman, Albert, 226
Homeric poems (Homer), 158, 164; human nature in, 124–131, 133, 239
Hopkins, Gerard Manley, 179, 192
Housman, A. E., 134
Hubris, 31
Hugo, Victor, 94
Human body, *see* Body
Human nature, 123–136; in Homeric poems, 124–131, 133, 239; imitation in, 72; mind and body in, 133–136; variability of, 71–73
Human potentialities, latent, 236–253; education for, 242–243, 248; increase of perceptual awareness, 245–253; obstacles to self-knowledge, 243–245; pharmacological approach to, 241
Hume, David, 130–131, 135
Humours, temperaments related to, 141
Huntington, Ellsworth, 21
Huxley, Aldous, *Science, Liberty and Peace*, 86–87
Huxley, T. H., 1, 7–8
Hydrogen bomb, 89, 97
Hypnosis, 127, 221, 224; as anaesthesia, 180–181; complete recall in, 219

Imitation, 72; parrots imitating human voice, 139; smile of infants, 139
Incas, terraces, 23
India, 77, 201
Indian philosophy, 69, 91, 173, 247
Industrialization, 18, 19, 45
Inferiority feelings, 153
Inheritance, *see* Heredity
Inspiration, 158–161
Instincts, 238
Introvert, 69, 145, 147, 154
Ireneus, 207
Islam, 201

Italy: deforestation in, 24–25; unification of, 100

Jaensch, Erich, 195
James, William, 137, 167, 173, 175, 196
Japan, production control in, 50
Jefferson, Thomas, 24
Jews: Nazi persecution of, 179–180; *see also* Hebrew tradition
John of the Cross, St., 157, 203, 211–212, 228
Johnson, Samuel, 120–121
Joyce, James, 187
Jung, Carl Gustav, 65, 69, 163, 204, 218, 222

Kay-Shuttleworth, James, 46
Keller, Helen, 168–169, 173
Khrushchev, Nikita, 88, 146
Kierkegaard, Sören, 170
Kingsley, Charles, 7–8
Klüver, Heinrich, 227
Köhler, Wolfgang, 171
Korean War, 84
Kretschmer, Ernst, 142, 148–149
Kubie, Lawrence, 241

Lamarck, Chevalier de, 62, 172
Lamartine, Alphonse de, 159
Language, 168–181; vocabulary of science and philosophy, 4–6; words and symbols, 178–180
Laubach, Frank, 214
Laud, Archbishop William, 205
Law, William, 212
Lawrence, D. H., 187
Lebanon: cedars of, 12–13, 17; goats in, 25–26
Leibnitz, Gottfried Wilhelm von, 37
Life, individual, 108–122; and history, 110–117
Life, quality of, and population increase, 55–58
Life expectancy, 109
Lilly, John C., 33, 225
Literature: indifference to history in, 115–116; inspiration in, 159; metaphors in, 191–193; nature in, 37–40; science in, 3–4

Lloyd Morgan, Conway, 37
Locke, John, 170
London: Great Exhibition, 1851, 94–95; public health in, 46
Lorenz, Konrad, 75, 238
Love, 249–250
LSD, 226–227
Lucretius, 187, 206
Lysenko, Trofim D., 62, 70

Macumba dances, 126–127
Magdeburg, bombing of, 84–85
Maine de Biran, 115–116, 137
Malaria control, 46–47, 51
Mâle, Emile, 178
Mallarmé, Stéphane, 5, 237
Malleus Maleficorum, 205
Man: dependence on environment, 32–34; earth changed by, 12–27; latent potentialities, 236–253; and nature, 28–41; *see also* Body; Human nature; Life
Marmor, Milton J., 181
Marsh, George Perkins, 14
Marx, Karl, 79
Marxism, 69, 70
Maslow, A. H., 238
Mauritius, 47
Mazzini, Giuseppe, 79
Mead, Margaret, 144, 250
Memory, 157, 218–221; complete recall, 219–220
Mendel, Gregor, 62
Mental illness: Greek idea of, 125–126; and physical types, 148–149
Mescaline, 226, 227
Mesmerism, 127
Mesomorph, 68, 69, 142–147, 150
Metaphors, 191–193
Michelet, Jules, 94
Middle Ages, culture of, 178–179
Mills, Wright, 89
Mind-changing chemicals, 134–135
Mineral resources, 102–103
Mitchell, Weir, 229, 233
Mohammed, 228
Montaigne, Michel Eyquem de, 116
Morris, Charles, 73
Muller, Hermann, 105

Muses, 158, 164–165
Music, 187, 195–197
Musset, Alfred de, 159
Myers, F. W. H., 152–153
Mysticism, 201–203, 211–215
Myths, 199–200, 206

Napoleon, 70, 78, 79, 116
Napoleonic Wars, 115
Nation, definition of, 76–77
Nationalism: in Central America, 77–78; in Europe, 78–79; in former colonies, 80; and war, 74–90
Nature: balance of, 34–35, 48–49; in literature and art, 37–41; man's changes in environment, 12–27; man's relationship to, 28–41; and nurture, 238–239
Nazis, racial doctrine, 179–180
Needham, James, 37
Needs, human, 236–238
Neoplatonism, 202
Neurosis, 156–157, 243–244
Newton, Isaac, 187
Nietzsche, Friedrich Wilhelm, 91–92, 137
Nilsson, Martin P., 130
Nuclear warfare, 98–99
Nuclear weapons, 89, 97, 118

Olier, Jean Jacques, 203–204
Oracle, Delphian, 131, 158
Original sin, 59–73, 207, 208
Original virtue, 59
Orphism, 132
Otto, Rudolph, 178

Pageantry, 234–235
Parapsychology, 165–166
Parrots, imitation of human voice, 139
Paul, St., 158, 166, 170, 202, 227
Pavlov, Ivan Petrovich, 156
Pelagius, 60–62, 71
Penfield, Wilder, 220
Pepys, Samuel, 18–19
Perls, Frederick, 245
Peyote, 226, 227, 229, 233
Philosophy and art, 183, 186–187

Physiological intelligence, 138–140
Piero della Francesca, 150, 194
Pius IX, Pope, 95
Planck, Max, 10
Plants: destroyed by man, 17–18; developed by man, 14
Plato, 8, 9, 22, 125, 131, 133, 187, 228, 230; *Critias,* 21; *Phaedo,* 217–218
Plotinus, 227–228
Pollock, Jackson, 188
Population increase, 42–58; birth and death rates in, 45, 47, 51; and birth control, 51–53, 57–58; and education, 54–55; and food supply, 45, 47–50; political aspects of, 53–56; and production control, 49–51; and public health, 45–47; and quality of life, 55–58; rate of, 42–44
Possession, supernatural, 126–129, 153, 158
Predestination, 60–62
Prejudice, 251–252
Price, H. Haverley, 166
Prior, Matthew, 60
Progress: belief in, 92–96; experience of, 118–120
Psychology: body types and temperaments, 67–69, 141–151; constitutional, 67; Freudian, 147–148, 152, 163, 218; future of, 106; Gestalt, 187, 245–247; in Greek civilisation, 129–131; physiological factors in, 64–68
Pythagoreans, 132

Quakers, 200

Rank, Otto, 65
Read, Herbert, 248
Reincarnation, 132
Religion, 198–215; as belief, 201–202, 205; of experience, 199, 204–205; Freud's conception of, 204; spiritual exercises, 200–201; symbols in, 199, 210–211; *see also* Buddhism; Christianity; Hebrew tradition; Hinduism
Renan, Ernest, 244

Repression, 155–157
Rhine, J. B., 165
Richardson, Dorothy, 187
Richelieu, Cardinal de, 100
Riess, Stephen, 104
Rostan, Leon, 142
Rozanov, Vasili, 114
Rubens, Peter Paul, 150
Russell, Bertrand, 88, 98–100, 135–136
Russia, 82; education in, 70; individual life in, 117; nationalism, 79; Revolution, 118

Sardinia, 47
Satellites in space, 107
Schizophrenia, 148–149
Schopenhauer, Arthur, 137
Science: and art, 183, 186–187; ethical aspects of, 7–9; future of, 103–107; humility in, 9–10; in literature, 3–4
Sears, Paul, 33
Seeing, 242–243
Servetus, Michael, 205
Shakers, 201
Shakespeare, William: *Henry IV,* 5; *Julius Caesar,* 67–68, 184, 192; *Macbeth,* 112, 191; *The Merchant of Venice,* 58; *The Tempest,* 191, 193
Shamanism, 131–132
Sheldon, William H., 67–69, 142–144, 148–150, 253
Shelley, Percy Bysshe, 159
Sicily, 47
Skinner, B. F., 63, 148
Sleep, 112–113, 162
Smuts, Jan, 37
Socrates, 22, 125, 131, 217, 243
Soil: conservation, 23–24; erosion, 20–22; over-grazing, 24–26; terracing, 23
Sorokin, Pitirim, 81
Soul: Aristotelian concept of, 138; and body, 133–136; Greek idea of, 129–131
Soviet Union, *see* Russia
Spain, sheep grazing in, 24
Spencer, Herbert, 96

Spiritualism, 128, 131
Stevenson, Robert Louis, 222
Story-telling, 221–222
Subud, 201
Sukarno, Achmed, 88
Swedenborg, Emanuel, 164
Switzerland, 77
Symbols: in art, 182–183, 185–186, 188–190; in religion, 199, 210–211; selection of, 175–178; and words, 178–180
Szent-György, Albert, 103–105

Talleyrand-Périgord, Charles Maurice de, 169
Tantrism, 247
Taoism, 36–37, 59, 211
Temperaments: and physical types, 67–69, 141–151; and sociological pressure, 144–146, 153–154
Tennyson, Alfred, Lord, 93–94
Theresa, St., 203
Thought: and ego, 137; and unconscious, 160
Time, cycles of, 91–92
Tolstoy, Leo, 107; *War and Peace*, 82
Torquemada, Tomàs de, 205
Toynbee, Arnold J., 111, 117
Traherne, Thomas, 230–231
Turner, Joseph M. W., 40

Uexküll, Baron J. J. von, 174
Unconscious, 138, 152–167, 218; collective, 218, 222; inspiration in, 158–161, 222; negative, 152–157; positive, 158–167; repression in, 155–157
Ussher, James, 92

Varley, John, 163–164
Vigny, Alfred de, 94
Viola, G., 142
Visions, 163–164, 216–235; drugs inducing, 226–227; techniques of inducing, 224–226
Vittoz, Roger, 246–247
Voltaire, (François Marie Arouet), 160–161

Wall, Patrick D., 174
Wallace, Henry, 53
War, 74–90; conditioning for, 76; moral opposition to, 84–86; nuclear, 98–99; political aspects of, 86–89; preparation for, 81–82, 86; propaganda in, 180
Wasson, Gordon, 226
Watson, J. B., 9–10, 63, 71
Webb, Beatrice and Sidney, 52–53
Webster, Daniel, 114
Weir, John, 102
Wesleyan movement, 93
White, Father Victor, 204
Whitehead, Alfred North, 37, 190
Whitman, Walt, 39, 185, 194
Williams, Tennessee, 6
Willkie, Wendell, 100
Wolfe, Thomas, 219
Wordsworth, William, 3, 115, 230–232; philosophy of nature, 37–39
World government, 100–102
World War I, 85, 118
World War II, 82, 84–85, 118

Zen, 211, 247